Militarism

Militarism

Rule without Law

ERIC CARLTON

Routledge
Taylor & Francis Group
LONDON AND NEW YORK

First published 2001 by Ashgate Publishing

Reissued 2018 by Routledge
2 Park Square, Milton Park, Abingdon, Oxon OX14 4RN
711 Third Avenue, New York, NY 10017, USA

Routledge is an imprint of the Taylor & Francis Group, an informa business

Copyright © Eric Carlton, 2001

The author has asserted his moral right under the Copyright, Designs and Patents Act, 1988, to be identified as the author of this work.

All rights reserved. No part of this book may be reprinted or reproduced or utilised in any form or by any electronic, mechanical, or other means, now known or hereafter invented, including photocopying and recording, or in any information storage or retrieval system, without permission in writing from the publishers.

Notice:
Product or corporate names may be trademarks or registered trademarks, and are used only for identification and explanation without intent to infringe.

Publisher's Note
The publisher has gone to great lengths to ensure the quality of this reprint but points out that some imperfections in the original copies may be apparent.

Disclaimer
The publisher has made every effort to trace copyright holders and welcomes correspondence from those they have been unable to contact.

A Library of Congress record exists under LC control number: 2001022334

Typeset in Sabon by Manton Typesetters, Louth, Lincolnshire.

ISBN 13: 978-1-138-72533-1 (hbk)
ISBN 13: 978-1-138-72532-4 (pbk)
ISBN 13: 978-1-315-19193-5 (ebk)

Contents

Introduction: The Question of Social Control		1
1	War and the Professionals	7
2	Militarism and 'Human Nature': The Phenomenon of Massacre and Genocide	22
3	Militarism and Culture: Tribal Society	35
4	Militarism and Motivation	48
5	Militarism and Status: The Hundred Years War	62
6	Militarism and the Territorial Imperative	79
7	Militarism: The Economic Factor	94
8	Militarism: The Political Necessity Argument	107
9	Militarism and the Ethical Implications of Aggressive War	123
10	Militarism, Games and Ritual Compulsion	139
	Excursus: The Phenomenon of Blood-Sacrifice	150
11	Militarism as a Religious Imperative	153
12	Militarism as a 'Test of Manhood'	166
13	Militarism and the 'Warrior Death'	180
Summary		193
Bibliography		201
Index		209

'Don't speak to us of laws – we carry swords.'
Pompeius Magnus (Pompey)

Introduction:
The Question of Social Control

In all societies there are rules governing conduct both between social groups and between individuals who comprise those groups. These rules may or may not be codified; they are formally or informally formulated so as to ensure some measure of uniformity, regularity and predictability of conduct between members. Arbitrary behaviour only leads to social disruption and instability, and cannot therefore be institutionally condoned. There will, of course, be infringements, so all societies have sanctions which can be applied or ordered to deter and to punish deviant behaviour. Social control, then, denotes the processes which ensure that individuals conform to the norms of the group. Interests vary, so various control mechanisms operate to resolve conflicts of interest and, where possible, to promote an acceptable degree of social harmony. It follows that control implies regulation and social adjustment which may be brought about by different means. Therefore, any consideration of militarism must involve some discussion of both the persuasive and coercive forms of control.

Norms are observed either because they have been passively *internalized*, and may thus have become part and parcel of an individual's make-up, or they may be actively *inculcated*, say by educational institutions, so that they too become part of the individual's personality. They may be questioned from time to time, but by and large norms come to be seen as that which is done in any particular society. But we are also interested in the ways in which norms/rules can be enforced. So in order to analyse the nature of social control in a little more depth, we must distinguish between types of control, their functions, the means or agencies whereby they are transmitted, and – not least – the ways in which control is implemented.

For simplicity of analysis, we can say that in general terms control is mediated via the familiar socialization agencies, namely, the family, educational institutions, peer groups, and in developed societies the media which can have such a pervasive influence. This, in turn, is reinforced by politico-legal codes, custom, and – depending very much on the society in question – moral and religious precepts which try to anchor compliance to certain kinds of believed intrinsic good, or to interpretations of the will of the gods. All can be – and have been – effective in ensuring 'correct' types of social behaviour. To summarize, control can be *physical* in that it is brought about by repressive methods. Or it can be *material* in so far as it is utilitarian and economic in its operation. Or it can be *symbolic* and normative in that it is backed by ethico-religious imperatives which operate in different societies in different ways at different times.

Underlying the whole issue of control is the problem of *social order*. Why do societies cohere? Is society 'natural'? Why is there not social chaos? And how is this order achieved? To reiterate, social order requires mechanisms which ensure measures of unity and cooperation in order to resolve inevitable conflicts of interest. The military – for good or ill – is just one of these mechanisms. This raises the philosophical question of to what extent are the possibilities for unity and cooperation within the capacity of human beings to achieve? The optimistic view which has been transmitted through Rousseau and Marx (and, it may be added, much modern educational theory) is that 'goodness' is part of the human potential. It is society which is the corrupting agency, therefore the individual must free him/herself from the influence of society by changing society. On the other hand, there is the pessimistic (realistic?) view associated with such diverse sources as the Bible, Hobbes and Freud, that individuals are inherently egocentric, unsocialized animals who need society to force them into measures of conformity and cooperation. Hence the necessity of control mechanisms in various forms.

There is a view that control is necessarily a repressive thing, and that it comes about as part of a conspiracy to ensure that people do as they are told. Conspiracy theorists go so far as to suggest that various social institutions were contrived for this very purpose. Think, for example, of education. This is a ubiquitous social practice whether in simple exemplar forms or in the highly sophisticated forms which we find in developed societies. Does anyone *really* suppose that some time in the remote past some individuals planned education to be a means of keeping people in their places? True, at various times in various places education may have functioned like this, but this does not mean that it was contrived for this reason. Function and purpose are not the same thing.

However, this may not apply to the military which is surely designed to implement mechanisms of control. Ultimately everything depends upon this. But a number of factors condition the *mode* and the *intensity* of implementation.

1. *Dimensional factors.* Here we are concerned with the problems which arise in relation to the scale of the society in question. It almost goes without saying that a small-scale tribal society with

largely undifferentiated institutions and relatively simple social arrangements needs much less to maintain control than a highly differentiated centralized system which requires elaborate procedures. Where there are large barely manageable groups, as, for example, in pre-1935 Ethiopia (i.e. before the Italian invasion), control could only be achieved by the formation and utilization of state forces – and even then control was by no means assured.

2. *The degree and extent problem.* This arises from geographical rather than demographic factors. Where, say, the land is broken by hills and valleys which in earlier times made travel lengthy and sometimes hazardous, control could be something of a problem. In ancient Greece, for example, during the divisive Peloponnesian War (431–404 BC), it was not that easy for Athenian forces to control what was happening in some of her dependencies, although her control of the sea did enable her to intervene when members of her island empire were threatened. But all this took time. Similarly control has always been that much more difficult in extensive empires such as those of early China and Persia. Here the distances were so vast that there could be insurrections or nomadic incursions near the peripheries which would not be known to the central authorities for some time after they had occurred. And even then it might take weeks to prepare and dispatch the necessary forces to deal with them.

3. *Focus factors.* The direction of possible deviance will help to determine the nature and the forms of the control mechanisms required. It is not at all unusual to use inappropriate measures in dealing with particular situations. In militaristic societies where adequate forces are available there is a prevailing tendency towards overreaction, as can be found in the recent past in such societies as China, Chile and Indonesia. This problem is complementarily related to:

4. *Intensity factors.* Too much muscle, and the measures can be counterproductive, but too little and the effort becomes null and void. For instance, student or worker protests can usually be met with something less than armed force. The firm and disciplined use of police in the control of Kurdish political protests in London and elsewhere in 1999 was enough. Though where such protests become too vociferous and explode into violence as in, say, Israeli–Palestinian riot situations, water cannon, tear gas or even rubber bullets may have to be used. The question here is just who decides at which point a particular measure will be employed. In this sense, the *point of implementation*, is critical.

The operation of any effective mechanisms of control where they involve the police and the legal system, or in more extreme cases, the military, must depend on a traditional set of checks and balances which, in turn, subsume a prevailing system of *shared values*. These values will inform the behavioural patterns of society, although they will be expressed by different societies in different ways. It is important, however, to stress that these values may not be rationally chosen. As Max Weber was keen to point out, *ends* or *goals* may not be rationally derived, although the *means* may be rationally chosen. Military action may well be employed as a calculated means of achieving national status or of defending national pride, yet both are non-rational values, i.e. values that are only explicable *in terms of themselves*.

Max Weber (1964) has indicated that no system voluntarily limits itself to material, affectional or even ideal motives as a basis for guaranteeing its continuance. A belief in *legitimacy* is also essential. Control can only effectively be exercised – that is, willingly observed – when people accept the nature of its authority. Legitimation is seen as the 'grounding' for the normative order of society. It supplies the requisite self-evidence for the system. As the late Talcott Parsons emphasized, it implies an essential 'rightness' in the institutionalized order. It defines the reasons for members' rights and, by definition, the imposition of all necessary prohibitions. In this sense, it both justifies the system's expectation of members of a society and the constraints laid upon them. But this is hardly *self*-legitimating. In all societies norms are questioned, if only at the margins. Authority has therefore to be based on something substantial: tradition, national pride and – where necessary – military power. Yet the exercise of military power must itself be legitimized.

This can be largely the function of ideology which may be regarded as both a reinforcing and legitimating mechanism of control. Ideology is inextricably linked to the problem of *meaning* in society. Every society which has persisted for any length of time and has developed even a modest level of complexity, has also evolved some interpretation of its own way of life. There has to be an acceptable explanation of its particular system of institutional arrangements – its beliefs and ways of doing things – and these include its social disparities. In all societies there is a gulf between aspiration and achievement.

It can be seen, therefore, that ideological frameworks provide symbolic meaning-systems for those involved, and these are supported by sanctions which can be both this-worldly and other-worldly in nature (indeed, in many complex pre-industrial societies these might actually be seen as synonymous). Ideology then, may act as a motivational inducement. It has a special, perhaps convenient, role in legitimating social arrangements, not least military arrangements – the ultimate in control.

In one sense, military action may appear to be a non-rational – even lunatic – activity, a measure of last resort. But to many peoples historically it was a noble enterprise. Was it not the Greeks who referred to the battlefield as 'the dancing floor of Ares' (the god of war)? In certain circumstances, war may be inevitable. In Britain and France in September 1939, there was no other viable option even though neither state had been directly attacked (a point made much of by the Nazis). It is true, of course, that many wars are seen as 'defensive' or necessarily pre-emptive as in the 1967 Arab–Israeli conflict. But this can obscure various kinds of aggressive gangsterism. Yet, at times, military intervention would appear difficult to avoid, as in the Gulf War against Saddam Hussein's militaristic regime in Iraq, or against Milošović's Serbia.

Since the 1980s, there has been an average of about 40 armed conflicts taking place in any one year. These include wars of various kinds, though most are of a civil or revolutionary kind. Some disputes get resolved, yet others take their place. This year it might be Serbia, and next year ... who knows? One thing we can bank on is that it will be somewhere. Most of these will be separatist insurgencies of one sort or another, mostly in the developing world where it seems that everyone wants to get in on the act. Europe, however, has fared no better. Some 10 million people were killed in the First World War, and millions more died from what may have been war-related causes. The Second World War claimed some 50 million lives, less than half of whom were military personnel. It is probably true to say that humane people are genuinely affected by these spectacles, but is it equally true that reason can be thrown overboard, and that emotionalism is paramount, so that 'stupid sentimentalism ... [is] paraded at every blood letting' (McCrystal: 1993). This labels all military activity as though it is of equal worthlessness. Surely this cannot always be the case?

John Keegan (1998) in the Reith Lectures for the BBC argues that Europe has undergone a process of militarization during the last 100 years and – even more contentiously – that not only has this shaped society and its values, but that the military mindset is actually a relatively recent development. However, he suggests that because of modern nuclear technology and the fear of mutual destruction, possibly the worst wars are behind us. (Though if nuclear weapons really prevent war – as some argue – why not encourage every nation to have them?) Contra Keegan, however, it may be that as *direct* memories of war fade, today's generation is becoming more complacent. And if aggressiveness and territoriality are innate features of the human condition, can war ever cease? As John Keegan pointed out, it has been the development of the mass-produced assault rifle that has probably claimed more lives than anything else, 'its lightness and simplicity allow even untrained children ... to kill with a profligacy the veteran of the past could not achieve'. So small wars abound. This sounds like a counsel of despair, but history certainly does not leave us much room for optimism.

CHAPTER ONE

War and the Professionals

Most societies at some time or another have resorted to violent solutions to solve their politico-economic problems. Societies which have not been prepared to do so are rare, so rare, in fact, that it is *they* which are in need of some explanation. Why, then, do people go to war? Are people basically competitive and self-interested with war as an institutionalized outlet for their aggressive instincts, or is war not so much a biological necessity as a cultural invention? And is war inevitable, the natural extension – or perversion – of the political process? Are people so aware of the advantages as well as the disadvantages of aggression to attain their ends that they will always resort to violence, if all else fails, in order to further or protect their basic interests? These are some of the tortuous questions we must try to answer. As is so frustratingly usual with issues of this kind, there may be no really satisfactory solutions to such problems but hopefully a discussion of the issues may, at least, serve to clarify the problems.

At the very outset it is worth noting the distinction between the 'military way' and 'militarism' made by Alfred Vagts (1959) who maintains that war and military adventure can be differently defined. By and large, all societies engage in warfare – this is the 'military way'. They take the resigned and rational view that if war becomes a necessity, it should be prosecuted with care and the most efficient use of resources. By contrast, 'militarism' can be seen as a way of life. It involves a particular complex of values and traditions which, although not exactly singular and not always alike, are peculiar to a limited number of societies. We think of such distinctive cultures as those of the ancient Assyrians, the medieval Mongols, and the Zulus of the early nineteenth century. It is aggressive societies of this kind which will engage most of our attention.

With given qualifications, then, we can say that war is a cultural universal. As such, it must derive either from what we broadly regard as 'human nature', i.e. rooted in the human psyche, or it derives from the common situations in which people find themselves – if, indeed, these can be easily separated. Generally speaking, therefore, militarism and aggression must derive either from psychological or social causes, or some subtle combination of both. So are they due to personality factors – a kind of human infirmity, or certain structural variables which mark out particular societies?

First, however, we have to look at the views of some of the professionals, and for the sake of simplicity these may be divided into two groups: the professional military men, and the professional students of the military and its procedures. Having cited Alfred Vagts, let us look at a key issue on which his views and those of this text will clearly disagree or will, at least, have to be seriously qualified. Vagts says that 'An army so built that it serves military men, not war, is militaristic; so is everything in an army which is not preparation for fighting, but merely exists for diversion or to satisfy peacetime whims' (Vagts: 1959, Introduction). He further argues that militarism in the past has been the product of an aristocratic caste, the members of which were frequently uneducated and unemployable but nevertheless managed to persuade the masses that they were competent to protect their interests. He also castigates this elite's fancy uniforms, useless ceremonies, class distinctions, and strange, anachronistic, officer codes which are all part of the professional army. (Is Vagts too influenced by the bemedalled popinjays that adorn the military in small dictator states such as modern Chile, where personnel appear merely to be playing at soldiers rather than preparing for a defence of the realm?) Even more contentiously, he advances the thesis – surely based largely on the experience of the nineteenth and twentieth centuries – that democratic, unmilitaristic societies are better at waging war than autocratic militaristic ones.

Yet militarism is not all about display. And even when display is most evident, as among the Prussian military in the nineteenth century, it does not have to belie a supreme confidence in the act of war itself, as its performance in the Franco-Prussian War ably demonstrated. It is easy to overlook the psychological satisfactions that some derive from the wearing of uniforms, and the social bonding which can come from the right to sport certain insignia (note the continued esprit found especially among members of elite corps even when they do not know each other or meet as civilians after demobilization). And as for ceremonies, non-rational as they can appear to be, they can have the latent function of instilling respect and obedience without which no army can operate effectively in the field. The inculcation of instant compliance is essential in action. The word of command of a superior demands the appropriate response; one is reminded of the appeal – attributed to an American infantry non-commissioned officer (NCO) urging his men into battle – 'Come on in you sons of bitches, do you want to live forever?' Response does not have to be thoughtless, but hesitation, as for example when a paratrooper momentarily fails to jump, can endanger his companions if the plane has to take a second precarious run over the dropping zone. (This is regarded so seriously that if it happens in training it warrants instant dismissal, and after qualification it becomes a court-martial offence.)

It is at this point that Vagts becomes impaled on the horns of a dilemma. He argues (ibid., p. 15) that 'militarism flourishes more in peacetime than in war' where he contends that 'ends not identical with the winning of victory' are pursued. Again, we seem to be back with his needless display objections. But this does not quite accord with his statement (ibid., p. 17) that the military mentality involves bellicosity and 'the love of war'. Perhaps he means that militarism connotes the love of the *thought* of war, though without any actual battles, somewhat like those young people who like the idea of being a student as long as that does not involve any actual study.

Ostentatious display and readiness for war can obviously go together. The purpose of the display may not only be to make military personnel feel good about themselves, but also to intimidate any possible enemies. Before the Second World War, the principal European dictators, Hitler, Mussolini and Stalin, were extremely fond of exhibiting their military might to any who might be interested – or apprehensive. The impressive hardware and serried ranks worked wonders on their potential enemies – and actually on each other. March pasts, fly pasts and rallies of various sorts all did their work, and were duly – and often very ably – filmed for those who could not actually be present. It is all rather reminiscent of the ancient Spartans who openly and nonchalantly dressed their long hair before battle in order to 'psych' the enemy. The Spartans did well out of intimidation. Like so many other militaristic aggressors after them, it was not so much war they loved but power (Carlton: 1990).

The history of militarism is, needless to say, dominated by stereotypes. It has its all-too-identifiable heroes and villains, its brilliant tacticians and its incompetent blunderers. At worst, the record can be vitiated by Biggles-type escapades; at best it may consist of little more than a turgid – if scholarly – recital of war-game battles. More to the point, it may be consciously biased. Caesar, for instance, wrote of his campaigns in Gaul not so much for posterity as for the Roman senate/public to whom he wished to justify his actions and promote his own political ambitions. All too often modern writers of military history – and perhaps more particularly history generally – are telling us more about themselves and their own time than about those about whom they are writing. Frequently such accounts have a specific agenda and constitute a kind of polemic to further the interests of some particular cause such as Marxism, anti-racism, feminism or whatever. Indeed, some contemporary texts inveigh against the 'practice' of history itself. The postmodernist 'end-of-history' debate is still with us in various forms although it is not without its critics. We have already spoken of prejudice and bias in the writing of history, but to suggest, as postmodernists do, that there is no such thing as history, only narrative, is surely scepticism run wild. Documentary history may well be flawed in many ways, but even so it has its uses and, despite its uncertainties, is still all we have.

As there are no laws governing the nature of war, so there are no absolute laws governing the nature and causes of militarism. This has been endorsed by its practitioners. That eminent authority of yesteryear, General von Clausewitz (d. 1831) who has influenced much modern strategic thinking, suggested in his writings (1950) that theory must educate future leaders and guide them in their education but *not* accompany them to the battlefield. He made it clear that in his view the state was sovereign, and should recognize no authority above itself, and such states necessarily promote their own interests, sometimes at the expense of other states, therefore conflicts must inevitably occur. War may be 'normal', but, as things are – regardless of what many post-Clausewitzians recognize as the Geneva Convention – there exist no ultimate laws for warfare itself.

Clausewitz also believed that the study of war could be treated as a science. It was an instrument of policy, and like the philosopher Hegel, he maintained that it set the seal on the moral health of society – a kind of forge for the consolidation of national identity. Unlike Richard Cobden who berated the romanticism of war, he was not primarily interested in the moral issues, but was anxious that men counteracted the 'effeminacy of feeling' and the 'enjoyment of comfort' which, in his view, caused degeneracy. Friedrich Engels, Marx's alter ego, enjoyed Clausewitz but, having a cause to promote, reworked his idea of war as a science into war as the military counterpart of the destructive energy unleashed by capitalism. In this he rightly predicted that one day wars would be fought on a monumental scale.

In such writers it is not always strictly clear whether it is the *practice* they are speaking about, or the *study* of the practice of war. It is the romanticism of war which one detects in some of the writings that can lead to this confusion. Some have understandably seen war as a horrid trade in butchery which was being transformed into a magnificent and enlightened science. And John Ruskin argued that out of the humanly induced confusion of war could come 'creativity', and he criticized the mechanization of war because it destroyed war's 'higher meaning'. The Social Darwinists who flourished in the heyday of Victorian optimism saw war as a stage in human evolution that people would eventually outgrow. Though even at this time there were dissident voices which insisted that war was actually a form of evolutionary *regression* and not a stepping stone to a better and more enlightened age. Even Herbert Spencer, the one-time 'high priest' of Social Darwinism came to be increasingly disillusioned with the idea of progress and came to see militarism as a reversion to type.

We come back, therefore, to the basic question of what exactly is militarism and – more importantly – what makes a society militaristic? Patently, there must be a correspondence between the military ethos and modes of military organization, and the nature of the society itself. Further on in our discussion we will look at the relationship between the economy and the military structure, besides the critical issue of war and the role of ideas. Military institutions must take their cues from the dominant value systems of a society. Militarism is not only bound up with institutional organization, it is also characterized by a certain adulation of military virtues. Some authorities (for example Stanislav Andreski) argue that the term 'militarism' connotes a preponderance of the military in the state; it therefore implies some distinction between military administrators and civil administration. This being the case, it is contended that the term cannot be correctly applied to relatively undifferentiated tribal societies.

This argument seems rather strained, indeed artificial. Is the problem here one of semantics? It begs the question of just how much *organization* is the real determinant of what is and is not militarism. It means that notoriously aggressive societies such as the nineteenth-century Zulu and the Matabele, and such infamously expansionist societies as those of the Mongols and the Tartars, cannot strictly be categorized as militaristic. In these and many other societies there was no clear distinction between the civil and military spheres of jurisdiction. In certain complex pre-industrial societies such as the ancient Greek city states where there were ever-ready citizen armies, no such distinction was possible. Complementarily, the idea of a military–industrial complex, a term coined in a speech by the late President Eisenhower in the 1950s, could only apply to a modern highly differentiated society.

Another dichotomy worth mentioning is that between what Herbert Spencer called militant and industrial society. His evolutionary model of development maintained that *militant society* which was characterized by 'compulsory cooperation' would eventually give way to *industrial society* characterized by 'voluntary cooperation'. This was very much an idealized distinction, and Spencer realized that some modern societies, even in his own time, were reverting to more primitive militant forms.

Political organization too is key factor, especially the question of the relationship between militarism and political forms. Is it true, for instance, that authoritarian societies are more aggressive than non-authoritarian (e.g. democratic) societies? This is an assumption which is sometimes made, but, as we shall see, this is by no means always the case.

Militarism can therefore be said to connote the glorification of the ideals of strength and fitness, and the aggressive pursuit of war as something noble in itself. We can also say that, in general, the military forces in such societies will receive the endorsement of the people, and that political policies will be influenced by the society's capacity for intimidation and aggression. The ancient Assyrians, for instance, were past masters at the art, and in their time were feared throughout the Middle East. They were primarily interested in booty and the exaction of regular tribute from the conquered nations, and should those nations renege, the revenge taken by the Assyrians, who always returned, was fearful in the extreme. Those who rebelled against their subjection could expect the kind of unspeakable atrocities (impalings, flayings and the like) which made a quick death almost enviable.

In modern societies there is a fusion of political and military goals. But although the roles of the military and the civilian government can be fairly readily differentiated, there can still be appreciable intervention by the military into the affairs of government. In fact, the degree of intervention may well be another distinguishing feature of the militaristic society. Samuel Finer (1962) identifies four levels of intervention: influence, intimidation, displacement of civilian rules and the supplanting of a civilian regime by a military one. It is noteworthy that Finer sees these not as types but as *stages* in the takeover by a military junta, the sort of thing that has taken place periodically in a number of Latin American states, and in some of the post-colonial African states such as Nigeria. The usurpation of power is usually legitimized in terms of order and stability with the promise of free elections some time in the future. Although many military regimes are of short duration, it is not unknown for there to be an inordinate delay before such promises materialize. The military, which comprise an internally coherent group with clear administrative goals, are not always that willing to relinquish power once it has been established. Not uncommonly these are right-wing regimes such as the Peronistas which took power in Argentina immediately after the Second World War, but left-wing military regimes are by no means unknown.

A military ethos may actually develop by accident. A small-scale society which is forced to defend itself against hostile neighbours may soon find itself adopting a more aggressive stance especially against other belligerent neighbours. And where success produces even more success, a military ethos may be established. Many militaristic societies have started out this way. A classic example is early Rome which began by trying to find a place for itself among the hostile tribes in southern Italy from the late sixth century BC. Its eventual victories over the Etruscans established Rome as a power to be reckoned with, although it was not until its somewhat precarious success against the incursive Gauls (early fourth century BC) and its ability to tackle the maritime might of Carthage (third century BC) that her military aggression gave rise to imperialistic aspirations (Pallotino: 1991).

Once established, the military must not only develop an operating structure which, of course, in the modern world must reflect and adapt to the demands of new military technology, it must also learn how best to induct, train and indoctrinate new recruits and give them a special sense of military status. This professional socialization is calculated to give them an awareness of their place in this new order, and a feeling of pride *vis-à-vis* other members of the society. So, for instance, among traditional Bantu in South Africa, boys at puberty were initiated into the appropriate age sets, given spears as a sign of pre-warrior status and told that they had now reached manhood. The age sets marked youths out as warrior material and gave their members a certain social cohesion which was calculated to stand them in good stead under the stress of battle conditions (in a modern context, see Janowitz: 1960).

However, although an ethos of militarism may develop by accident, this is still some way from asserting that there are such things as accidental wars. It is certainly true that government ministers and even the military themselves have sometimes been surprised by the nature of the wars they have unleashed – as may well be the case with many of the statesmen not long after the beginning of the First World War. But, as Michael Howard has pointed out, this is not the same as saying that some wars are 'begun by mistake and continued with no political purpose' (Howard: 1983, p. 12). Yet, it might be argued, as by Leon Wolff (1958), that the First World War (1914–18) is actually a very good example of a conflict in which by the halfway mark the military – and certainly the common soldiers – had really lost track of what it was all for.

Although we are here considering the causes of militarism, it is not possible entirely to dissociate these from the causes of war itself. On this issue there is very general unanimity; the extension of one's territory, the defence of one's homeland, the desire for national independence, the propagation of a particular ideology – indeed, all *aggressive wars* might be broadly summarized as a means for the enhancement of power. This sounds rather reductionist, but is surely not that far from the truth.

What perhaps needs to be emphasized is that while in modern society war – though disturbingly common – tends to be regarded as a human aberration, in earlier society it was seen as an inevitable and necessary expedient. Whether in ancient Greece, medieval Europe or Renaissance Italy, war, either of the interstate or intrastate variety was considered the order of the day. Of course, alliances and hard political bargaining were well known. Negotiations might well be agreed by making small concessions, or unions between states cemented by judiciously contrived royal betrothals. Realpolitik is nothing new. Nevertheless, war was still seen as the obvious way of solving serious – and sometimes not so serious – conflicts, especially if these involved rival territorial claims or injured pride. It is surely the feeling that the need for war will always be there, that some states have made the rational calculation that if this is how it must be done, we are going to be better at it than the others.

Yet having said this, can we agree with Michael Howard (1983, p. 15) when he states that 'in general men have fought during the past two hundred years neither because they are aggressive nor because they are acquisitive animals, but because they are reasoning ones: because they discern, or believe they can discern dangers before they become immediate'? This assertion would seem to beg a number of pertinent questions. Is it too limiting to confine the argument to wars fought only in the last 200 years? Even within this short span – historically speaking – we might confidently assume that a gamut of motives was represented. This issue of limitation is important because it tends to rule out those small-scale conflicts which arguably come into another category (see Chapter 3). True, in particular circumstances war can be seen as rational, but it is also aggressive – and perhaps unjustifiably aggressive. (Is rational to be seen as the opposite of aggressive, or are we to interpret rational as anything which makes sense at the time? In this way, all aggressive acts can be justified.) If we take the Second World War as our example: what was rational about Germany's attack on Poland in September 1939? On the other hand, it could well be argued that the Allied declaration of war on Germany which followed was, in the circumstances, a pre-eminently rational act. More contentiously, Germany's attack on Russia in June 1941, and Japan's attack on the USA in December 1941 did have a kind of rationality if, as is sometimes argued, Germany expected an attack by the Soviets in the near future, and that Japan was intent on breaking American-imposed sanctions. What we are to make of Hitler's subsequent entirely gratuitous declaration of war on the USA under the fluid conditions of the Tripartite Pact is anybody's guess.

Howard argues (1983, p. 22) that in potential conflict situations, calculated decisions are made by *both* sides. Both think they can gain more by going to war than remaining at peace. But surely there are many incidences where one side is effectively forced into war. In which case the rationality of going to war may exist on one side only. For the other side it may not be a matter of calculation but sheer survival.

Perhaps the most important issue Michael Howard raises is that concerning the nature of aggression. Are humans innately aggressive or not? And is aggression justified because in certain circumstances it can be 'interpreted' as being rational? Is Howard's argument deficient because it lacks a moral edge? And is war a natural state of society or is it culturally contrived? Is it primarily about the balance of power or possession of territory? These are questions which impinge directly on the causes of militarism and which will be considered in the ensuing discussion.

It is probably more accurate to regard 'militarism' as a descriptive rather than an analytic term. As we have seen, it means somewhat different things to different people. In much current literature the study of militarism understandably concentrates on the situation as it is seen to exist in modern states. Inevitably, therefore, the emphasis is not so much on bellicosity and the propensity towards aggression as on military spending, arms industries and particularly on the maintenance of permanent armed forces. The causes of militarism are thus linked inextricably with the social and economic bases of these states and the international system within which they operate (Smith and Smith: 1983). In modern nation states we find that the world views and value assumptions of the leadership, once translated into rational decisions, help to determine the nature of military spending. This, in turn, decisively affects their preparedness for war and their calculations as to the possible outcomes of future hostilities. Should they take the risk? The uncertainty of embarking on a no-turning back venture is well exemplified by Saddam Hussein's miscalculation in attacking Iran in 1980. The Iranians were more prepared for such an attack than the Iraqi military had supposed. So instead of a quick and easy victory Iraq became embroiled in a long, gruelling war which cost upward of a million lives.

The existence of a large standing army is not an invariable feature of the militaristic state but it is a plausible indicator of militaristic intentions. It is always reasonable to assume that states which build up huge forces and which spend a high percentage of their gross national product (GNP) on weapons and weapon technology are not doing it just so that everybody can sleep better at night. In this respect one might compare the rather pathetic state of military readiness of Britain before the Second World War compared with that of Nazi Germany. The same applied to the USA *vis-à-vis* militaristic Japan. But, of course, the USA had enormous reserves of money, manpower and especially oil. This is why the Japanese who possessed none of these in such abundance, relied on a surprise attack and planned for a short war (Hoyt: 1987). Whether by these standards we should judge the former Soviet Union as militaristic is debatable, though in the 1939–41 period she certainly used her military muscle to intimidate smaller nations, most notably Finland and some of the Balkan States. Her defence would be that she was wary of the Western powers, especially Germany. This may have been a necessary explanation, but it certainly was not a sufficient one. Intimidation in our own time is very much the name of the game. Perhaps we still need to beware of the big battalions.

Perhaps the development of a military ethos in some states in recent history can be linked to the rise of colonialism. Imperialism was very much a feature of earlier societies – Rome and Persia spring readily to mind – but modern colonialism is somewhat different. In the scramble for territories from the sixteenth century onwards it has often been expansionism that wars and near wars have been all about. Until the radical reappraisals of colonialism – sometimes, though by no means always, justified – which we have seen in recent years, the story of colonial enterprise was largely characterized by derring-do and the perpetuation of heroic motifs. Not so much work has been done on the dynamic role played by the military in shaping the institutions and cultures of the societies which embarked upon these opportunistic ventures (Peers: 1997).

Expansionism was powered by impelling, largely economic, considerations and a kind of keeping-up-with-the European Joneses mentality. Not that territorial aggrandisement always paid off. Some colonial powers found that the benefits of acquisition were very marginal indeed. The Italians in North and East Africa in the 1920s and 1930 spent more on these territories than they ever received in return. European incursion was, of course, facilitated by the changes – and thus disparity – in weapons technology. The indigenous people of the invaded territories had nothing to compare with the cannon, the musket/rifle, and later the Maxim gun (a prototype of the modern machine gun). Well-armed and disciplined European troops could cut a swathe through hordes of often unruly, poorly led local levies. Even where the indigenes were brave and resourceful, as they were for example, during Clive's conquests in India, or the later Zulu wars, they were ultimately no match for the Europeans – this regardless of the minimizing counter-arguments of politically correct revisionist historians who wish to give native peoples more credibility.

Whether superior weaponry was devised to further colonial expansion, or whether expansion followed upon technological development, is an interesting question. Possibly both are true to a limited extent; patently each had a reciprocal effect on the other. There were undoubtedly many reasons behind colonization, and probably the most obvious ones still take precedence over the 'hidden' ones that some social historians are keen to find. It may well be that it was done, in some cases, for no better reason than that it *could be* done. Opportunism must have played a part. If the circumstances seemed to be right and there was every chance of success – why not? Instinctively, one feels that this was the prevailing sentiment of the aggressors. It was not that these societies were militaristic in the usually understood sense of the term, but we find that relatively small European states such as Holland, Belgium and Portugal became militaristic when the opportunities presented themselves.

Professor William McNeil, who has written what is regarded as 'one of the most comprehensive, incisive and stimulating histories of military power ever written', contends that the extension of warfare cannot be separated from the development of technology (McNeil: 1983). In a previous work (*Plagues and Peoples*), he argued that under certain changed environmental conditions microparasites interact with human populations in such a way as to constitute what we term a plague. These mutations then wreak their devastation on the world's peoples. By analogy, human parasites are those who 'by specializing in violence, are able to secure a living without themselves producing food and [the] other commodities they consume. Hence ... macroparasitism among human populations turns into a study of the organization of armed force with special attention to the kinds of equipment ... used' (McNeil: 1983, p. vii). His thesis, therefore, is that alterations in armaments resemble genetic mutations of micro-organisms in that from time to time they open up new geographical zones for exploitation.

It would be unwise to press this analogy too far for fear that at certain points it is bound to break down. Nevertheless, it is not difficult to grasp the essential thrust of the argument. There is, as we have seen – and will continue to appreciate as we take the discussion further – that there is a critical symbiosis between technology and the incidence of war, and even more so in modern war which not only excludes most of those elements of muscular heroism which gave earlier conflicts at least a tincture of nobility, but also involves – or can involve – mass destruction on an unimaginable scale. The industrialization of war has efficiently erased all those elements which once gave war a kind of qualified humaneness.

Yet another difficulty with McNeil's macroparasitism thesis is that its emphasis on the relationship between militarism and technology gives it a somewhat reductionist look. So many instances of military development cannot be neatly explained in these monocausal terms. If we take Ottoman militarism from the middle of the fifteenth century, for instance, we find that the wars against non-Muslims were not motivated by the fanatical religious fervour that characterized the earlier armies of Islam in the seventh and eighth centuries. Religion was a factor, but by no means the only factor. The campaign of Mehmed II in 1453 against the infidels of Constantinople (modern Istanbul), the last great bastion of western civilization in the East, was hardly a religious crusade, anymore than those later predatory campaigns of Suleiman the Magnificent (d. 1566). These were wars about power and territory, though religion could always be used as a post-facto justification for conquest (Barber: 1972). Marxist analysis in terms of access to the means of production is even less helpful, as is its corollary, the concept of class. An understanding of Ottoman motives and intentions is only possible by taking a broad sociocultural approach, and even this does not adequately take into account the psychology of individual rulers.

In another particularly influential text, John Stoessinger (1993) has argued that war results largely from misperception, perhaps in a leader's image of himself, or of his adversary, or of his adversary's intentions and his capacity to realize those intentions. It is probably true – as Stoessinger suggests – that most national leaders embark upon hostilities in the confident expectation that they will be victorious. Needless to say, this optimism is often unfounded. Indeed this has to be so in 50 per cent of the cases; somebody has to lose, unless there is a Pyrrhic victory for one side only, or – as can happen – there is some kind of stalemate or stand-off situation where nobody wins, in which case both sides retire to lick their wounds. There are too many instances where a nation will be forced into war with no certain expectation of success, yet its leaders really have no option, as with the Polish military in September 1939 when faced with the overwhelming superiority of the Wehrmacht (Bethell: 1976). It is either a choice of giving in straight away, or engaging in a noble but fruitless rearguard action.

Stoessinger's is an insightful but highly generalized analysis to which there are many exceptions. Furthermore, like many historians, he has a tendency to draw his examples from relatively modern wars between nation states. This is instructive, but it leaves out so many societies which can be considered overtly militaristic such as the Romans, the Turks and the Spanish conquistadores. In our own time the path of militarism is one which few dare take – there are just too many inhibiting sanctions to make it worthwhile – that is, unless a nation has overwhelming military force such as China (note how the British were prepared to go to war with Argentina over the Falklands, but had no apparent qualms over the surrender of Hong Kong – something that almost certainly would not have happened in the nineteenth century, regardless of any understandings with China), or is foolishly adventurous such as Iraq. Among the other matters raised by Stoessinger is the fundamental issue of natural aggressiveness. He takes a position which is similar to that of Michael Howard, but is less contradictory. This is so important that it merits a separate treatment (Chapter 2) when we will look at some of the biological implications of the debate.

In thinking about the importance of military hardware and of human agents in potential conflict situations, one is reminded of Napoleon's aphorism that 'morale is to the physical as three to one'. The arithmetic may be awry but the sentiment holds good. Given – and this is critical – that the sides are reasonably evenly balanced, morale may actually determine the outcome of a war. This point has been enthusiastically endorsed by Basil Liddell Hart, once one of Britain's most respected military historians, who maintained that in almost all decisive campaigns the dislocation of the enemy's psychological balance as well as his physical resources has been a critical factor (Liddell Hart: 1942). This is not, though, the opinion of Field Marshal Sir Michael Carver, who in his inordinately eulogistic appreciation of the German Commander, Field Marshal Erich von Manstein, lays great stress on clarity of objectives as the critical factor (Carver: 1990). The view here is that planning is probably more important than the actual execution. A notable contemporary of Field Marshal Carver, however, the late Field Marshal Bernard Montgomery, one-time Chief of the Imperial General Staff, and famous as the victor of Alamein in 1942, concurs with Liddell Hart. Naturally, he emphasizes the importance of good intelligence, and the right logistical preparation for war, and cannot speak highly enough of the superiority of an army's *matériel* (during the African campaign he was criticized for waiting too long before launching his great attack in the Western Desert, but he insisted that the build up was as vital as the actual execution of battle). But again, for him, it was the human factor that mattered; good leadership to ensure that the right decisions are made and carried out, which involves the ability to radiate confidence in the men. Most of all, though, he stressed high morale. As he put it, 'battles are won primarily in the hearts of men ... Armies are not merely a collection of individuals ... The real strength of an army is ... greater than the sum of its parts; the extra strength is provided by morale' (Montgomery: 1972, pp. 12–15).

In militaristic systems we find that this matter of morale, this 'fighting spirit' as Montgomery used to call it, is fostered not only by faith in the commander and – at the most pecuniary level – lust for booty, but often also by the ideology which motivates the troops. In earlier times, as in medieval England, when levies of peasants were raised who had no particular affiliation to anyone except their families and their local lord, let alone the king, ideology was hardly a pertinent factor. They were told that the 'cause' was the king's rightful claim to lands in Aquitaine, Anjou or wherever, territories which were of no special concern to them – if, indeed, they even knew where they were. Quite often, earlier armies were supplemented by mercenaries, paid troops who had been recruited elsewhere, sometimes from overseas. In some cases, they were highly skilled professional 'men at arms' who were prepared to sell their services to the highest bidder. Not infrequently though, mercenaries were drawn from the ranks of the unemployed or unenfranchised who took up soldiering as a means of livelihood. Rarely will any of these have had a 'cause'. They were in the game for the pay and for the loot which was regarded as a legitimate perquisite of the victorious army.

Such armies were quite different from those for whom the 'cause' was everything – or almost everything. One thinks of the not entirely aptly named Crusaders and of the Muslim armies who conquered much of the Middle East and parts of Southern Europe, and who have left a legacy of disputation and civil war in the Balkans even up to our own times. However, there have been expansionist movements of predatory peoples which do not fall into either of these categories. The Tartars and the Mongols who devastated vast tracts of Europe and the East in the Middle Ages, and left heaps of rotting skulls to mark their conquests, were certainly not motivated by any kind of religious ideology. Their only cause was plunder and pillage. If they had an ideology at all, it was that of hardy, ruthless warriors from the steppes who were superior to the effete urbanites of the rich cities. It was people such as these who first introduced the world to something approaching total war. It is roughly estimated that Genghis (Chingiz) Khan and his successors left some 18 million dead in China alone. It is now quite impossible to assess the destruction and death left by the Mongol and Tartar hordes, but it must equal that of modern despots such as Stalin and Hitler.

From the beginnings of recorded history, we find force was used in order to solve social and territorial problems. With time this application of force became more orderly, more organized, until we have what might be termed the professionalization of violence. This is typical of the militaristic society. As the late General Sir John Hackett says, the profession of arms has evolved into 'an occupation with a distinguishable corpus of specific technical knowledge and doctrine, a more or less exclusive group coherence, a complex of institutions peculiar to itself' (Hackett: 1983, p. 9). In the militaristic society armed force becomes not only a means to an end, but an end in itself. The classic example, as General Hackett (once Commander-in-Chief of the British Army of the Rhine) points out, were the Spartans, the militaristic society par excellence. The Spartan males, who were trained from childhood to harden their bodies by vigorous exercise and ascetic living, dominated their neighbouring states – indeed, much of ancient Greece, for the best part of 300 years – with the most powerful army the country had ever known. Everything about Spartan social practices from procreation onwards was subordinated to the end of military efficiency and Spartan dominance. It was said that the only thing a Spartan male feared was the law that governed his life, and that the only thing to be avoided was luxury. Sparta's was no citizen militia, as was the case in most other Greek city states (poleis), it was a totally professional army. Louis XIV is reputed to have said, 'L'etat, c'est moi' (the state, it's me); in the case of Sparta it would be no exaggeration to say the state was the army.

Having said what we have about the correlations between militarism, war and technology, it is still difficult to avoid the conclusion that there is a willingness – even enthusiasm – of soldiers to kill, and thus there is a tendency for war to become as destructive as the existing technology and resources will permit, as the proliferation of nuclear weaponry amply testifies. This has remained relatively constant throughout the course of human history. Indeed, it could be argued that war is the inevitable accompaniment of *any* human civilization. Why is this? Why does it seem to be that if humans have no missiles they resort to conventional weapons, and if they have no conventional weapons they make do with rocks and clubs. Is aggression simply a legacy of our primitive past? Are we evolving into more cooperative creatures? One writer, the author of a popular television series on war, has argued that war may be part of our history, but that it is not part of our *pre*-history. The implication is that killing (aggression) may have been present in the remote past, but that war (organized aggression) came about with the development of civilized communities about 10 000 years ago (Dyer: 1985). The view here is that war is a cultural invention; it is not in our genes, it is a learned activity, and that which has been learned can be unlearned. This seemingly intractable problem is something we must now consider in more detail.

CHAPTER TWO

Militarism and 'Human Nature': The Phenomenon of Massacre and Genocide

This section of our discussion leads seamlessly to our next topic (Chapter 3) in which we will consider psychological approaches to war and militarism, and the nature of human motivation. Here we are thinking more in terms of human biology and what can possibly be meant by the term 'human nature'. Underlying the biological approach are certain key assumptions:

1. That war is *not* simply a cultural invention, but is rooted in human aggressiveness which is part of our animal nature.
2. That human aggressiveness is inextricably related to the 'law of survival'. It is the consequence of the struggle to exist.
3. That war which is the institutionalization of aggressiveness derives largely from an innate sense of territoriality and 'possession'.

Just a glance at this list will indicate how much these points overlap. Indeed, they are all related to one another and can therefore be considered together. Ethologists have long contended that it is a basic premise of all forms of life that existence is only maintained by a struggle in which only the fittest survive. Dig up any square metre of earth in the average garden and – with a little patience – the process can be seen taking place; it is all a question of eat or be eaten. All creatures, ethologists argue, have genetically programmed predispositions. This is the position taken by such theorists as Konrad Lorenz (1966) and Desmond Morris (1971), and also Robert Ardrey (1967) who writes of 'instinctive traits' and a genetic make-up which is 'ineradicable'. As one writer has put it, 'War is an overt action resulting from man's innate aggressiveness. Like other social animals, groups of men defend ... definite boundaries and aggressively seek to own or control larger territories' (Alcock: 1972, p. 199). However, their critics insist that it is unwise to extrapolate from animals to human beings. Furthermore, they question the whole matter of 'instincts', and go on to point out that those primates that are genetically closest to humans do not always exhibit notably territorial behaviour, nor are they as lethal with their 'fellows' as their human counterparts.

The argument from animal behaviour is sometimes associated analogously with demographic factors. Here it is maintained that limited human adjustability has been outpaced by culturally determined changes in the environment (Tinberger: 1968, pp. 411–18). This is effectively saying that increases in the human population surpass that of human mortality, and this pressure of population increases the probability of wars. The implication, therefore, seems to be that perhaps wars are nature's way of keeping population density to viable limits. Ethologists further contend that recourse to violence is 'biological' in the sense that humans immediately (by implication, naturally) become defensive when they or their group/family/state are threatened (see MacDonald: 1975).

The argument here, then, centres on the question of whether aggression is natural or not. And if it is natural, to what extent is its expression something we can always control. The biological position is really quite straightforward. Evolution demanded that humans fought to survive. Our ancestors had an unending struggle against nature, in so far as this was possible, and consequently had to do battle against each other in the competition for limited resources. It can be further argued that such undesirable traits as egocentricity and the ready willingness to resort to violence comes from the natural order of things. Thus it is not society, as some theorists claim that is the villain of the piece, but nature itself. Civilization may have provided us with a veneer of moral rectitude but, underneath, the old instincts are still there. Humans are little more than intelligent animals, and when faced with crises, they often respond in animal-like ways. When the occasion arises we are no better than our early forebears.

Many theorists would endorse this general thesis. And curiously these range from religious unbelievers such as Freud to eminent theologians such as Reinhold Niebuhr and brilliant scientists such as Albert Einstein. It was Niebuhr's position that international relations were impossible without taking into account 'man's nature' and the 'potentiality of evil in all human acts' and, like Augustine and Spinoza before him, he insisted that progress did not move in a straight line but was affected by the distortions brought about by human failure. He readily admitted a capacity for good, but argued that we must be prepared to recognize that 'The seat of evil is the self ... Man is a finite being with infinite aspirations, a pygmy who thinks himself a giant' (quoted by Waltz: 1959, p. 21).

Einstein – who actually left Germany for Switzerland during the First World War to escape military service – like Freud, viewed the outbreak of war in 1914 with horror and despair. And in 1930 he was so disillusioned by war and the ever-present threat of war, that he denounced militarism as a 'shameful stain' on civilization which should be eradicated as soon as possible. Yet by 1933 he appears to have altered his position, possibly after reflecting on the rise of Nazism and its possible implications. This angered many pacifists, but he became more than ever convinced that people must stand up to Hitler and his rabid racist policies. So when he knew that German scientists were experimenting with forms of nuclear energy (ironically deriving from his own theoretical work) and were probably capable of producing an atomic bomb, he informed President Roosevelt who soon initiated America's own atomic programme (the Manhattan Project). His position had become totally ambivalent. He wanted an Allied victory, but he deeply deplored the bombing of Hiroshima and Nagasaki, and his later position on the possibility of nuclear warfare brought him opprobrium from the American Right. He began once again to despair of those whom he regarded as afraid to follow a morally right course and who were calling for his deportation.

The point at issue here is not whether he had serious misgivings about a nuclear strategy. The issue is to what extent he endorsed the natural aggressiveness view of human nature. The truth is that – like so many of us – he was quite inconsistent on the matter. He argued that humans were inherently aggressive, yet hoped that they might eventually renounce violence. Why, he said, does mankind attempt to abolish poverty, disease and starvation, yet fail to abolish war?

> Only one answer to the question is possible. It is that man has within him a lust for hatred and destruction. In normal times this passion is a latent state ... but it is a comparatively easy task to call these instincts into play and raise them to a power of collective psychosis ... Despite the counteracting influences of society ... in war they erupt among almost all men.
> (Quoted by Costigan: 1978, p. 233)

Freud's view was very similar. He felt that war in Europe perfectly illustrated the inability of human reason to control powerful emotions. War demonstrated that humans had primitive impulses such as hatred and aggression which were not uprooted by civilization, but which, for Freud, would be revealed by psychoanalysis. Whatever we feel about the therapy, we can appreciate his view that civilization is just a veneer, and that deep in the human psyche there lurk dark tendencies that not everyone wishes to recognize.

How accurate is this analysis of the human condition? Can we accept the basic evolutionary thesis that essentially life is all about survival, and that only those with the necessary strength, courage and cunning are likely to endure while the less adaptable perish? And, specifically, are we so constituted that we will ensure that others go under before we do, that we will survive even if this necessitates the destruction of fellow human beings?

There are many pertinent qualifications one can make of this thesis and they have been well rehearsed by others (e.g. Berkowitz: 1962) but it has many able supporters who argue that both history and experience tend to confirm its general conclusions.

Case studies

Strictly speaking, one should probably differentiate between massacre and genocide even though in everyday speech they tend to be used synonymously. The term 'massacre' is normally used about the gratuitous killing of defenceless people, whereas 'genocide', by definition, denotes the extermination or attempted extermination of an entire race or culture. It has been argued that in general terms massacres can fall into one of three categories (Carlton: 1994):

1. Accidental: as in the case, for example, of native peoples in Polynesia and elsewhere who were killed off by European diseases to which they had little or no immunity during the days of colonization.
2. Incidental: where indigenous peoples, particularly in Latin America under the Spanish were killed not only by disease but by work. Death was an unavoidable by-product of a form of enforced slavery. The high mortality in Japanese prisoner-of-war camps during the Second World War, would also fall into this category.
3. Intentional: premeditated killing of whole groups of 'undesirables' as in the case of the Nazi treatment of Jews, Slavs and others during the occupation of Eastern Europe during the Second World War.

In this discussion of atrocities, we are going to concentrate rather more on some of the *motivations* for massacre to see if it helps us to understand a little better the cogency or otherwise of the 'natural aggression' argument. Other than killing for the sake of killing – and in the history of massacre and genocide this certainly cannot be ruled out – the three most common reasons for the committing of atrocities are revenge, fear and expediency. We can look at these briefly in turn with examples taken from different periods of Roman history.

Revenge

In the heyday of their greatest expansion, roughly from the First Punic War against the North African city state of Carthage (264 BC) to the beginning of the Imperial period under Augustus (30 BC), Rome – unsurprisingly – made a lot of bad friends. Towards the last years of the second century BC there had been trouble in North Africa. The state of Numidia under its king, Jugurtha, once a client and friend of Rome, was involved in a war with its would-be patron which lasted for several years. Jugurtha's rebellion – if such it can be called – was finally put down by the Consul Marius (104 BC). The wretched former king was hauled off to Rome, together with a great deal of booty, to be publicly humiliated in a Roman Triumph, and then presumably killed – the usual fate of those who dared to defy the conqueror.

Not long afterwards there was a revolt of Rome's Italian allies in what is called the Italic or Social War (90 BC). Many of those who fought against Rome had also once fought *with* Rome and were battle-hardened veterans. But eventually, this too was put down by two of Rome's most successful generals, Sulla and Pompeius (Pompey). Nevertheless, the allies were at last granted the rights (especially the right of equality with Roman citizens) that had long been withheld from them. However, in their struggle against their overlords, the Italian confederacy had appealed to Mithridates, king of Pontus, a small but important state in Asia Minor, south of the Black Sea.

Mithridates was not really that nice to know. Of Persian extraction, but imbued with a great admiration for Greek art and culture (the official language of Pontus was Greek), in practice he was much like a stereotypical oriental despot. Said to be a larger than life figure of exceptional physical strength, he grew impatient with his somewhat Romanophile father who had reigned for almost 30 years, and ascended to the throne in 121 BC as Mithridates VI after imprisoning his mother and arranging the murder of his brother. He had just that kind of ruthlessness that would be a match for the Romans, and he was only too willing to take advantage of their preoccupation with the Social War. Yet he did not intervene directly. Instead, he aimed to take some of the pressure off the allies and also help himself to a little more neighbouring territory at Rome's expense. Posing as a champion of the Greek cities in the Crimea, he had already carved out a minor empire on the north coast of the Black Sea as well. He then moved eastwards into lands that afforded considerable wealth in produce and manpower. In time, therefore, he was able to build up an appreciable army and navy with which he intended to threaten other client states in Asia Minor and, eventually, the Romans themselves.

In 104 BC, he joined forces with the king of the adjacent state of Bithynia, and together they seized Galatia and Paphlagonia to the south. Next they turned against Cappadocia to the south-east, but then the two aggressors fell out, as 'partners' often do, over who was to be in control of these territories. By this time (96 BC), Rome had rather belatedly begun to take notice of what was happening, and decided to check Mithridates by making useful contacts with the rulers of states even further east (i.e. Armenia and Parthia) who were possibly in Mithridates' line of fire. Since 112 BC, Mithridates had made several moves to bring more lands under his control, but he had been effectively countered by Rome. Now the masters of the Mediterranean world were at it again, and this time Mithridates determined that it was not going to work. He was going to play Rome at their own game.

He first neutralized any threat from Armenia by arranging a marriage between his daughter and the Armenian king, Tigranes. Then together with his new son-in-law he seized both Bithynia and Cappadocia (90 BC). Rome, by means of its agent, Manius Aquilius, ordered the aggressors to withdraw their troops, which they did. He then asked them to supply him with troops, which they refused to do. Aquilius then ordered the restored king of Bithynia, Nicomedes, to attack Pontus, and this was the last straw for Mithridates who, until this time, had acted with uncharacteristic moderation. He decided that it was time to end his conciliatory pose, and challenge Rome directly. He again occupied Cappadocia (88 BC), defeated Aquilius, who had only one legion at his disposal, and then he had the captured Aquilius killed with all sorts of unnecessary refinements.

This success gave an enormous boost to Mithridates' ambitions. His army cut through the Roman province of Asia (effectively modern Western Turkey) and he promised liberation to the Greek cities some of which had been established centuries earlier in the first waves of Greek colonization. He was received with enthusiasm by many especially when he declared that he would cancel their taxes (normally collected at exorbitant rates by private 'tax-farmers' on behalf of the Roman state). Those cities and Aegean islands including Rhodes which resisted him he put under a siege, but by and large it would seem that any opposition he had was generated either because some cities feared Roman revenge, or because – perhaps rightly – that they might be exchanging one kind of despotism for another.

His problem was what to do about the thousands of Roman and Italian citizens who had settled in the lands that he had now overrun. Not only were they a social encumbrance, they were also a potential threat to Mithridates' 'new order' in Asia. But, as much as anything, they represented the enemy, the oppressor which he had sworn to eliminate. And eliminate he did. He ordered that on a specific day all Asian cities under his control were to turn on their Roman and Italian settlers regardless of sex or age. It is estimated that in the ensuing massacre some 80 000 men, women and children were murdered – an unspeakable act which must prompt the question, how is it that ordinary people can suddenly attack with such ferocity those who shared their communities? Of course it has happened many times since, in other places at other times (modern Yugoslavia is but one example). One can only presume that over the years the perpetrators had built up such a reservoir of distrust and hatred that extermination was not that difficult. We do not know just how many cities obeyed the call. The understanding is that most – if not all – willingly complied. One thing is sure, that in heeding Mithridates' command; those cities bound themselves to him by a blood-tie that would not go unnoticed by Rome. The arrival of the legions could only be a matter of time.

Inevitably, Mithridates became a figure to be reckoned with in the Aegean world, and he was soon invited to Athens to liberate its people from Rome too. (Athens had been spared the destruction meted out to some other Greek cities during the period of Roman conquest in the mid-second century.) But before Mithridates could act, Aristion, a member of the Athenian democratic party, had seized power and had murdered numerous members of the Athenian aristocracy. Nevertheless, Mithridates sent an army to Greece under one of his subordinates, Archelaus, who, en route, exterminated the Italian population on the island of Delos (an important centre of Roman commercial interests). Before it could meet with any appreciable success, it was met by the Roman general, Sulla, with five legions which joined the small occupying force already in Greece. But powerful as the Roman army was, it was in a precarious position. It was engaged against Mithridates' army in the Peiraeus (the port of Athens) and in Athens itself against the self-installed tyrant, Aristion, while another Pontic army was due to arrive from Macedonia in the north. Sulla therefore sent one of his captains to collect a fleet while he led his forces to Delphi and then to Olympia in western Greece where he plundered the rich sanctuaries for funds to sustain his campaign and possibly to finance his political ambitions in Rome where he finally became dictator. By 86 BC, he was ready to deal with his enemies in both the Peiraeus and Athens. Both were taken at considerable cost. Sulla, who could be as merciless as Mithridates, sacked Athens, but spared some of its most revered buildings. Nevertheless, the inhabitants endured the customary slaughter. Mithridates sent further troops, and although they probably outnumbered the Romans 3:1, they were decisively defeated on two separate occasions. He still retained control in Asia Minor but had alienated many of the cities he had 'liberated' because of his many exactions. Eventually, under pressure and intimidation from Rome, however, he came to a negotiated settlement whereby he had to pay a huge indemnity to Rome, give up his newly conquered territories, but retain his own kingdom of Pontus. Sulla also imposed a crushing burden of taxation on the province of Asia for which the cities had to borrow from Roman financiers. After this Sulla returned to Rome to combat his political opponents who had carried out a purge of his supporters. Sulla's response was immediate and completely pitiless. He was determined to eliminate all opposition, and in the bloodbath which followed perhaps as many as 3 000 people lost their lives (some estimates are much higher).

Fear

If the massacres by Mithridates and Sulla were largely motivated by a desire for revenge, those committed by Claudius early in Rome's Imperial period can be safely attributed to fear, particularly fear of opposition. The precedent had already been set by his predecessor who was also his nephew, the notorious Gaius Caligula who had reigned for a mere four years (AD 37–41). Caligula had exhausted the immense financial surplus left by *his* predecessor, Tiberius, and to secure funds he had imposed extra taxes, and resorted to judicial murders and confiscations to fill the treasury. These extortions led to his downfall. His arbitrary actions made all and sundry fear that they too might become victims of his capriciousness, and in January 41 he was mercifully assassinated by members of his own guard.

Claudius was by no means the genial gentlemen depicted by Robert Graves in *I, Claudius*. Neither was he the doddering old fool that some have come to imagine from the television series. True, he was over 50 when he became Emperor, and had certain physical deficiencies, but he was also something of a scholar who possessed a half-concealed native cunning. Technically, Rome had no monarchy, but since the days of Augustus (d. AD 14) the Princeps – theoretically, the first among equals – was a monarch in everything but name. Claudius came to power almost by accident. After Caligula's death and the murders of his immediate family (the plotters were taking no chances with vengeful offspring), Claudius, fearing for his life, was found hiding behind a curtain and had 'greatness thrust upon him'. It seems fairly obvious that the Praetorians who brought him to power believed that his apparent *naïveté* could be exploited to their advantage. This was almost certainly also the view of the Roman Senate who reluctantly endorsed his appointment. But they were all to prove mistaken.

Generally speaking, Claudius was a conservative – though not so conservative and pedantic that he could not be unduly influenced by others, especially by his wives and his freedmen. He made no attempt to introduce new, radical policies. He has been criticized for showing his gratitude to the Praetorians by rewarding them generously, not only for bringing him to power, but also keeping him in power despite the various plots that were made against him. He came into conflict with the Senate on a number of issues, particularly those concerned with the administration of the treasury and on the question of extending Roman citizenship to non-Romans in the Empire.

Like all of us, Claudius had his virtues and his vices. He is said to have overindulged his appetites, but this was nothing new among the Roman aristocracy. On the plus side, he was a keen student of Roman history, and had written a number of books on Julius Caesar and on Augustus whom he much admired. And in addition to a treatise on the famous lawyer Cicero, he wrote books on both the Etruscans who had been *the* power in Italy before the Romans had really come to prominence, and on Republican Rome's old enemies, the Carthaginians. Yet though an enlightened scholar, Claudius had his dark side. But then we have long known that education is no proof against cruelty.

Claudius displayed undoubted administrative skills, and he showed republican tendencies in his willingness to depart from the extreme autocratic style of Caligula. But he did establish a highly centralized bureaucratic system, and much as we are told that he wanted to remain on good terms with the Senate and the highly placed Equestrian Order (Scullard: 1963, pp. 301–9), we know from what eventually transpired that he could sometimes exhibit character traits not that much different from those of his infamous nephew. His interests not only extended to legislation; he was also concerned with the judicial system, and it is suggested by his main biographers (Suetonius and Tacitus) that he occasionally interfered with the actual working of the courts by trying certain cases himself, perhaps as a means of getting rid of personal enemies.

In favouring the traditional religion of Rome, he inevitably clashed with those of other belief systems, though in some cases perhaps more from political than religious reasons. Thus he banished astrologers from Rome, and decreed the suppression of Druidism after the partial conquest of Britain (AD 43) which was one of the five provinces that Claudius added to the Empire during his reign. Normally Rome was reasonably tolerant about other peoples' religions, but on a number of occasions Claudius came into conflict with the Jews who, it is thought, were eventually expelled from Rome, possibly because they could be so vociferous and determined in relation to their faith. In AD 6 Judea had become a Roman province and it was Claudius who later installed his friend Herod Agrippa as its ruler. It is often said to Claudius' credit that he was particularly generous in the granting of citizenship, a privilege which carried with it certain obligations not only to recognize the authority of Rome but also to respect – if not revere – its gods.

It is from Tacitus and especially Suetonius (who liked to dwell on the more unsavoury goings-on of the Julio-Claudian dynasty) that we know something of the court history and its scandals. But in Claudius' case, they often have a direct bearing on what we might broadly call political events. Claudius had a cruel streak anyway (it is said that at the Games, he liked a defeated gladiator's visor to be lifted so that he could see the expression on his face when his throat was cut), and his dealings with some of his officials confirms this. He was quite ruthless in punishing any hint of treason or conspiracy – although in some cases this may have been suggested to him by his wives or other confidants for quite ulterior reasons of their own. He can certainly be understood if not excused for the execution of his extraordinarily licentious wife, Messalina, who flaunted her infidelities to the point of going through a form of marriage with her last lover, a consul-designate, possibly with a view to doing away with Claudius and setting herself up as head of state (AD 48). It was quite another thing, however, to carry out a wholesale slaughter of senatorial officials and members of the Equestrian Order. In all, Claudius is said to have executed about 35 senators during his reign. This did little to increase his popularity with those who, ideally, he really wanted to please, but also wanted to keep under control. Suspicion was even more rife among the Equestrian Order (equites or knights). Conspiracies arose in their ranks, and it is reported that Claudius may have had as many as 300 of them put to death (Suetonius as reported by Momigliano: 1961).

These killings on the grand scale can only be attributed to Claudius' obsessive fear of usurpation and possible assassination. The precedents for senatorial suppression and control of the aristocracy had already been established by his predecessors, especially Tiberius who had ordered the deaths of a number of Rome's leading men (a few actually opened their veins in front of the Senate) and Caligula who made senators kiss his feet and wait upon him at table. According to one authority, 'Each emperor in turn in a different way by dramatic exercise of arbitrary power created terror and destruction, havoc and faction in the elite' (Hopkins: 1985, p. 122).

Expediency

By the early years of the second century AD, things did not look quite so rosy for the Empire. Certainly by the reign of Trajan (AD 98–117) almost all of its extensive conquests had already been made; having won these territories it was now a question of how to keep them.

Trajan, the son of a distinguished soldier who had risen to become consul, was the first emperor to have come from the provinces (Spain). Almost his first act on coming to power was to apprehend those Praetorians who had compelled the execution of the murderers of Domitian, one of his predecessors. Domitian, not the most engaging of Rome's emperors, had become increasingly unhinged and vengeful towards the end of his life and had conducted a series of executions of those whom he suspected of failure and treachery. Actually, his only real affection led to his undoing. Emperors tended to have their own way in their courts, and Domitian took his wife from her former husband. There was little love lost on her part, and she began an affair with an actor, whereupon Domitian divorced her, but then took her back again. When he started to threaten members of his own family, she conspired with some of the guards to kill him (AD 96) – an occupational hazard for unpopular despots. We need shed few tears over this; by all accounts, if anyone deserved his fate it was Domitian. So perhaps Trajan was justified in dealing with those who had killed the 'regicides'.

Domitian had been immediately succeeded by Marcus Nerva, an elderly yet distinguished Roman lawyer, who invited the state's foremost general, Trajan, to share in the work of governing the Empire. So when Nerva died in 98 after a very short reign, Trajan (Marcius Trajanus) took over automatically as Emperor with the approval of both the Senate and the Praetorians. In Roman politics one just did not argue with the person who had the complete support of the army.

Trajan had written to the Senate promising that he would never execute a senator, and prior to his accession he had modestly entered the city on foot, presumably as a symbol of his sincerity and humility. At first, the masses reserved judgement, but when all Trajan's early efforts seemed directed towards conciliation, his position was assured and he was unofficially called 'Optimus Princeps' (the best) which began to appear on his coins in AD 105. He was obviously an able administrator and a respected military leader, and it is during his reign that the last significant additions were made to the Empire. The ostensible reason for further conquest was to reaffirm Rome's authority over the tribes of the Danube, something that had been seriously neglected by Domitian who, although very authoritarian, lacked what

Romans would have seen as the martial spirit. However, there is no reason seriously to doubt that among Trajan's mixed motives was the desire for military glory and the intention to enhance the status of the Empire.

The specific focus of Trajan's campaign was Dacia (roughly modern Romania). The Romans seemed always to be having trouble on the Danubian frontier, and the disturbances caused by the Dacian king, Decibalus were proving to be more than just irritating. Trajan and the Roman military were convinced that the Dacians had to be taught a lesson. There had been no important conquests since the time of Augustus some 90 years before and Trajan was as aware as any ruler that when there were murmurings among the populace, there was no better distraction than a foreign enemy that was said to be a potential threat to the state. Furthermore, it was feared that the tribes on the outer periphery of the Empire might interpret Rome's defensive stance as a sign of weakness. So now was the time to show them where the real power lay. The only problem was that by enlarging the frontiers Rome extended its boundaries and thus increased the number of foreign tribes with which she had to contend. There was always yet one more enemy to conquer. Roman rulers were beginning to discover that militarism can involve ever diminishing returns.

Trajan's rationale for the Dacian campaign was not, therefore, very compelling. There were hints that the Dacian tribes were about to launch a campaign of their own. How much this was really believed is disputable. What was much more attractive to the Senate was the prospect of plunder, especially of Dacian gold, silver and captives. The imperial treasury always had room for a little more cash.

Preparations for the campaign went ahead almost from the time of Trajan's accession. A very large army was assembled possibly comprising ten legions together with auxiliaries. It was anticipated that the drive into the Carpathian mountains would be both arduous and hazardous as it gave a determined enemy plenty of opportunity for guerrilla warfare. The Roman army set off in AD 101, and Trajan divided his forces which then took two different routes into enemy territory. One force won its initial encounter, yet the Dacians were not defeated but simply melted into the mountains. After this the Romans wintered on their own side of the Danube, and with the two forces united resumed their advance in the spring of AD 102. This time Trajan was able to compel Decibalus to capitulate and submit to Roman authority. Dacia was not annexed but Roman garrisons were set up in part of Dacian territory. It counted as a victory, and when Trajan returned home he was accorded the customary Triumph.

But the war was not over. Once the main legions had left, the Dacians decided that they were going to take the initiative themselves. By early AD 105 they had regrouped and rearmed, and were ready to go on the offensive. Trajan soon learned what was happening especially the annihilation of the Roman garrison that had been left in Dacia. With exemplary haste he quickly mustered his legions, now 13 in all, for an all-out assault on those who had dared to raise their hands against Rome.

It then becomes interesting that this man who pursued a policy of benevolent paternalism in Italy, and extended low interest loans to poor landholders and organized a system of financial relief for needy boys and girls, could also set about slaughtering the Dacians simply because they wanted to preserve their independence. With the tenacity and skill that were recognized features of the Roman armies, the Dacians were completely defeated, their capital taken and the land denuded of much of its population. Those who did not surrender or refused to abandon their lands were hunted down and mercilessly exterminated. Dacia became a Roman province, peopled by foreign settlers, and its gold mines were avariciously exploited.

Trajan celebrated his victory by erecting a stone column in Rome over 100 feet high. It still exists, and depicts his conquest of the Dacians in a graphic series of sculptured reliefs. This martial success seems to have received greater acclaim than his further victories over the Nabataean Arabs and his wars in Armenia and Parthia. What is not so well known is that his Dacian campaigns were celebrated with yet further massacres – this time for entertainment in the Roman arena. Trajan's predecessors, Titus and Domitian had completed the Colosseum built from stone transported by Jewish prisoners. It was left to Trajan in AD 107 to put on gladiatorial displays lasting four months involving 10 000 men, many of whom were unskilled prisoners who were cut down for amusement. And Trajan was considered one of the more enlightened and humane of the emperors. Yet he knew that expediency paid. The writer Fronto praised Trajan for his expansiveness and attention to detail, but admitted that he was simply giving the people what they wanted, 'all in all, [they] are less avid for money than for spectacles ... [which are] needed to satisfy the people as a whole' (quoted by Auguet: 1972, p. 187). This appetite for blood may initially seem incomprehensible to us, yet the public still revels in violence, albeit at several removes. The media still regard it as staple fare. So are we really so different?

CHAPTER THREE

Militarism and Culture: Tribal Society

Social anthropology (together with its close cousin, sociology) is particularly concerned with the social conditions which facilitate or encourage war and militarism. One of the basic assumptions is that war is a product of cultural evolution, simply a stage in human development. This idea, however, can take one of three main forms. For some theorists (e.g. Freud) it is characteristic of an early, primitive stage which humans will eventually outgrow. For others (e.g. Margaret Mead) war is a cultural invention which was *not* a feature of early, less well-developed societies. It is primarily this latter view which we are going to examine at this stage of our discussion. There is another view, associated with Quincy Wright, that war results from rapid social transformations. Actually, this is a variant of war as a cultural invention because its advocates are really saying that war results from the difficult situations brought about by *accelerated* social evolution. A quite different theory is that put forward by Malinowski (whom we shall be looking at in more detail) that wars, though culturally determined, are waged by tribal groups/states for political ends.

Additionally, we must ask whether there is any correlation between the frequency of war and cultural development. If we conclude that there is, this is not the same as saying that war *promotes* cultural development. Furthermore we should not confuse this issue with that of development and the *magnitude* of war which is primarily a demographic question. Perhaps most people would agree with Arnold Toynbee (1957) that only devastation and decline have followed in the wake of war, although there are those more reactionary thinkers (e.g. Andreski: 1968) who have insisted that war can, and has, made a positive contribution to cultural development by eliminating the weak and the effete from society and making way for human progress (Lider: 1977).

Early – and not so early – anthropologists have often assumed that a study of society in its most primitive forms was likely to yield insights into human interaction that could not be found elsewhere. The approach was largely functional in orientation. The thinking behind such studies was that if one could get down to basics and examine the ways in which a society's institutions and practices functioned to create a coherent whole, then one would have discerned the essentials that make a society tick. All social practices are therefore assumed to express a value. Nothing is without purpose. Even the most seemingly meaningless acts are held to have some kind of social significance. If only we knew enough, everything would apparently make sense. The politically correct would go along with this because it gives more credibility to those of other cultures no matter how primitive (i.e. without technology or written language) and unsophisticated they happen to be. (One eminent theorist, the late Ernest Gellner, aroused the ire – and incomprehension – of some of his colleagues by daring to suggest that many tribespeople indulged in totally irrational acts which on any analysis, Western or otherwise, made no sense at all.)

It must also be admitted that there has been a tendency among some professional anthropologists and other writers on tribal societies, to see – or *want* to see – the very best in their subjects. Consequently, some of the more distasteful aspects of those societies such as war and atrocity have been overlooked if not ignored altogether. The 'Roots' phenomenon which afflicted the USA some years ago is a case in point. To listen to its proponents one could be excused for thinking that West Africa was peacefully idyllic until the arrival of the Europeans. Such, of course, was not the case, as even superficial studies of, say, Dahomean or Ashanti societies would show. (I recall mentioning the Mfecane, the untold death and devastation caused by Shaka's Zulu impis in the Transvaal early in the nineteenth century, and discovering that there were those at the lecture who just refused to accept it. The facts went against everything they believed – or wanted to believe – about the nature of black Africa.) It is interesting, too, that in some modern popular literature variants of the same phenomenon seem to obtain. In books by both McLynn (1992) and Hibbert (1982) there are no index entries under war and militarism. Yet, typically for the resolutely correct, there are 28 entries under 'women' in every possible context and position. In McLynn there are eight, and in Hibbert – whom one might suspect as being rather too old for such ultra-modern niceties – there are 20. Alas for the days of scholarly balance in ethnographic studies.

Social anthropologists (or cultural anthropologists as they are sometimes termed in the USA) are especially interested in 'The conditions under which wars arose in the course of group life' (Bramson and Goethals: 1968, p. 197). The implication being that war – as a collective act – is a phenomenon of *society*, and may not necessarily be attributed primarily to individual tendencies or proclivities. But then this argument as to whether warlike acts have their origins in the human psyche or whether they are all part of the corrupting influences of society is still unresolved. In one form it runs alongside related arguments between the Social Darwinists and those schools of social theorists (most notably Emile Durkheim) which emphasized the humanizing and cohesive influences of society.

This all raises yet again the whole question of the rationality of war and militarism, especially in terms of their consequences. It is worth noting here that the *motives* from which people act – and they are many and various in relation to war – may have little or nothing to do with the *consequences* of their actions. Leaders in particular may determine on what they believe is a wholly rational course of action which will then bring forth the intended results. In practice, of course, things often do not work out this way. But this is all quite different from saying that people are essentially *irrational*, and that they only act from immediate and interested motives, and that such actions – especially the practice of war – have all sorts of unpremeditated and unanticipated consequences. This is sometimes the case, but it is not so much a matter of rationality versus recklessness, as the results of incalculable or conflicting rationalities.

Rationality is often closely linked with the idea of competition, and the function of competition, as the late Charles Cooley once intimated, was to assign each individual his place in the social system. Here, one must naturally distinguish between competition and competitiveness. Not all competition is the result of conscious action. From earliest years, individuals – possibly without any hostile intention – are forming judgements and fashioning careers based on implicit notions of competition. But competitiveness may be defined as the *conscious* attempt to outdo others, to trounce the opposition, even to the point of trying to bring about their destruction by conflict and war. Thus militarism may be seen as a kind of institutionalized competitiveness; the means whereby one group always remains dominant. Realistically, this often does not mean the complete elimination of the opposition, but rather their subjection. In the modern world in particular, destruction is often not the object of the exercise (Hitler's totally ruthless policy in Poland and Russia, regardless of the extensive atrocities, was not so much the eradication of the Slav peoples as their enslavement). This would not be practically possible in most cases anyway. Rather it is to ensure their subservience, and to compel them to work for the interests of the dominant power, as was the practice of the Spartans with the indigenous peoples of the Peloponnese over whom they exercised a hegemony for several hundred years. Gaetano Mosca expressed it succinctly many years ago when he wrote that 'In a struggle between two human societies, the victorious society as a rule fails to annihilate the vanquished society, but subjects it, assimilates it, [and] imposes its own type of civilization upon it' (Mosca: 1939, p. 29).

Competition can, of course, be an individuating process. It rarely does much to bring people together. Complementarily, conflict can be an integrating process, particularly where – as in early Hebrew vow-making procedures – 'your enemy will become my enemy'. Groups can form on the basis of common interest *vis-à-vis* the 'others', or competition can itself facilitate the union of those with a group-forming potential. Either way, the result is much the same.

Paradoxically, it is those systems which are based upon close integration such as the family, the community and the tribe that are most likely to generate those norms and values which can so easily lead to conflict and war. The closer the ties of identity of the 'in-group', the more likely it is that they will see themselves as essentially different from the 'out-group'. So different, in fact, that they may come to feel that there is no place for such a group. Their moral solidarity may actually involve the conviction that other group(s) cannot be allowed to exist. In a much milder form, these attitudes existed in some early Greek city states (poleis). Here local polis feeling was often so strong, especially where their forms of polity were diametrically opposed (such as Athens and Sparta), that conflict was inevitable.

Perhaps the most renowned anthropologist of the twentieth century was the Polish-born Bronislau Malinowski who turned from the physical sciences to the social sciences, and carried out fieldwork in the Trobriand Islands during the First World War, after which he eventually became the first Professor of Anthropology at the University of London (LSE). For Malinowski, war was an undesirable cultural survival – a little odd for a theorist who tended to see all social practices, no matter how bizarre or outdated, as having some implicit functionality. He felt that anthropology as the 'science of human beginnings and human evolution' should have some views on the place of war in primitive society. He was intrigued by 'the question of whether war, like family, marriage, law and education, can be found in all human cultures at every stage of development, and more specifically whether it played an indispensable part of the earliest beginnings of mankind' (*A Scientific Theory of Culture* quoted by Bidney: 1967, p. 231). He goes on to state that war is neither primeval nor biologically founded, and suggests that it appeared rather late on the scene of human history.

For Malinowski, war was an affront to civilized behaviour, and just prior to the Second World War he took up an appointment in the relative safety of the USA, and remained there until his death in 1942. To the end he maintained that war really had no place in the modern world; it was simply a destructive residue of earlier times. Functionality implies rationality, but as we know – and as Malinowski must have realized at the time – people are so rarely completely rational, especially about certain contentious issues.

The corollary of the question, 'is war a primeval residue?' is the related issue of whether primitive societies are ever militaristic. Given that we are defining militarism in terms of aggressive and aggrandizing expansionism, we have to admit that forms of militarism were common features of some primitive societies. Needless to say, we have almost no documentary evidence for *early* non-literate societies, but there is much disquieting evidence from relatively modern tribal societies, especially that relating to the warlike activities of African societies such as the nineteenth-century Zulu and Matabele. These have been ably recounted by modern writers (for example Becker: 1979; Morris: 1967; Roberts: 1977). It may therefore be more diverting to look at some less familiar material, always remembering that these accounts are very much about things *as they were* in the very early days of colonization.

Case studies

The Jivaro (or Shuara, as they call themselves) are a relatively small tribal group who live in the tropical rain forest in that rather ill-defined area of the Amazonian basin which borders Ecuador and Peru. The area known as the montana supports a number of tribes who until the twentieth century were not that well known to Europeans. The Jivaro (Spanish for uncivilized) excited the attention of the civilized world because of their practice of collecting trophy heads which were then shrunk as mementoes – a custom, incidentally, which was not peculiar to the Jivaro, but which was known in many tribes in the north-western parts of South America. Living conditions were quite harsh, and existence was conditioned not only by availability of plant life and game, but also by the perpetual menace of ants, bees, hornets, snakes and scorpions which infest the forests. Life was all about competition; an ongoing competition with natural hostile forces.

Alliances with other kindred groups (jivaria) often existed as military expedients – if that is not too grand a term to use about such small-scale warfare. These groups were often related either by blood or by affinal ties (exogamy was the normal practice between the 'villages'), and the expeditions were usually mounted against non-related groups, possibly because of some long-standing feud. Jivaro men aspired to be great warriors, and warrior status was largely determined by the number of heads that were taken. Feuding apparently merited prior warning to the target village. But when the Jivaro considered the enemy as 'outsiders' (for example, early white intruders), then they were in a state of war when no warning or mercy was given. In intergroup hostilities, only the heads of men were taken; women and children were taken as captives and assimilated into the life of the victorious village. The whole affair was marked by celebrations with dancing round the shrunken heads (tsantas), but – unlike some other forest tribes – there was no practice of torture, sacrifice or cannibalism (Service: 1978, p. 209).

Although Jivaro raids had no territorial dimension, they did have an economic function in so far as women were taken as wives. Neither was there any ideological motive; religion does not appear to have played any part in the bloodletting, although it is believed that the dead conveyed certain 'spiritual qualities' to the victors. The ostensible reason for the hostilities really does seem to have been the taking of heads, rather like the North American Indian practice of taking scalps. Head-taking can be seen in widely divergent primitive societies, and does confer enhanced warrior status on the victors. But it does beg the question of why certain societies historically chose *this* way to denote prestige, when other societies have chosen less lethal – in modern times, more humane – methods of showing the same thing.

In contrast, the Trobriand Islanders of Melanesia, according to Malinowski (1922), were nowhere near as warlike. He found that these people, comprising at least three ethnic groups, lived on this group of very tiny, scenically unimpressive, islands and were divided into a rather elaborate series of kinship groups. There was a clear ranking system among the four clans, and special honour was duly accorded to chiefs and their families who were seen as quite distinct from 'commoners'. Warfare does not appear to have been about conquest, and hostilities were brief and 'controlled'. Trobrianders, unlike some Melanesians, did not practise headhunting, but defeat in war was, nevertheless, a series business because it could mean the destruction of the losers' villages. Again, ideology played little part in affairs, although one sanction available to offended people was the invocation of evil spirits which were, so we are told, greatly feared by the people (Malinowski: 1926).

The Trobrianders may be reasonably compared with those living on more remote Pacific islands. A considerable amount of research has been conducted into the social life of the Polynesians who have fascinated people in the West ever since Captain Cook's intrepid voyages of exploration late in the eighteenth century. The Tahitians in particular intrigued Europeans because of their seemingly happy, uncivilized existence – and, not least, their carefree sexual habits. Sailors were understandably reluctant to leave these superficially paradisal islands where feasting was frequent, and sex could be had for a few nails. But things were not quite as they seemed. In Tahiti, for instance, there was a god of war in whose honour various ceremonies were held. And there was also human sacrifice, and fierce tribal warfare. This was sometimes quite large scale, and might involve all the island groups. On some islands, it was war captives that were reserved for sacrifice or simply kept as slaves. Cannibalism was common, and slain enemies were often disposed of in this way. Subjugation of one island group by another may account for the surprisingly high degree of stratification found among many Polynesians.

This is unusual. There is a general anthropological rule of thumb that the smaller and simpler the society the less stratified and differentiated it will be. But there are a number of exceptions. Very generally speaking, we can say that all societies have ranking of some kind or another. They may not all have class, but all societies have basic forms of differentiation even if it is only to make social distinctions between males and females, or between the old and the young. But did these or other distinctions necessarily lead to hostilities?

It is certainly true to say that there are – or were – some very simple tribal societies where war and militarism, at least as we understand them, were apparently unknown. But this state of affairs is so rare, that one feels that it is *these* societies that are really in need of explanation. The Arapesh of New Guinea and the Bushmen of the Kalahari would come into this category as would also the Lepchas of Sikkim who, according to Geoffrey Gorer (1938) did not understand the meaning of 'war'. Such societies are so remarkable that they are often held up as exemplars; their very existence is a challenge to Western assumptions about 'human nature'. Their uncharacteristic singularity is sometimes cited as examples of a shaming moral simplicity which calls our so-called sophistication into question. But they are *very* unusual. Perhaps they represent a lost ideal, or perhaps their very existence demonstrates the exceptions that prove the rule (Carlton: 1990).

A much more common situation is that once found, for example, among the Yahgan (Yamana) Indians of Tierra del Fuego. They were one of those rather rare people who had little sense of unity, yet whose language had no affinities with any other. They lived mainly by hunting game, and fishing in the abundant but not always friendly waters of the South Pacific. They were extremely primitive, having virtually no simple technology such as nets or traps, and often caught fish by hand. Other than rough sealskins, they had almost no protection against the harsh weather except the grease that they smeared on their bodies. Indeed, their lifestyle approximated to that which we associate with Stone Age people. It was not until 1880 when they were first introduced to steel tools that they were able to make dugout canoes in which they spent much of their time. But the Yahgan did have warfare – of a kind. There were no organized battles, but there were hostilities between groups usually as the outworking of a blood-feud. Murder was not that uncommon for which vengeance had to be exacted, though cannibalism does not seem to have been practised (there is some debate about this) and – surprisingly – suicide was apparently unknown.

Anthropologists looking at them through Western eyes, have sometimes queried why the Yahgan remained quite so complacent and uninventive. The answer – if there is any clear answer – is that their remoteness, the force of their traditions and so forth, kept them in a kind of time warp. But things have changed – though not for the Yahgan. They have become extinct. The decline began soon after contact. In those early days there were about 3 000 Yahgan, but European diseases took their toll and by 1933 there were only 40 left (Service: 1978, p. 48). Some primitive societies have fared better. For good or ill, Western culture has made rapid incursions into their domains. Look at any modern film about the indigenes, and you will invariably find a liberal sprinkling of T-shirts and the odd Coke can. That is progress.

As far as warfare is concerned, primitive peoples who live on the edge of subsistence tell us something about the focus and nature of aggression, but almost nothing about militarism. This is necessarily the case. Militarism requires scale. It is all about power and aggrandizement, and where there are few to dominate and nothing to take, militarism, which implies organized force, cannot exist. On the other hand, centralized tribal societies are another matter. In a number of African kingdoms tribal wars were not only common but often took place on an intratribal basis as conflicts over succession. When members of a royal lineage knew that they were likely to be eliminated by their sibling(s) on the death of the chief/king, wars to secure dominance were not unusual. This was common among the Baganda of Uganda into the late nineteenth century. Conquest for whatever reason brought tribute, booty and slaves. And, if anything, war increased with the introduction of European trade. In many West African states the exchange of goods was the prerogative of the royal family. They were especially involved in the slave trade, raiding and conquering tribes in the interior in order to bring victims to the Europeans who shipped them abroad. The whole process was a vicious syndrome as the native kings often took in exchange more European weapons with which to make further conquests (Lloyd: 1972, pp. 96–7).

In considering certain societies 'as they were', it is interesting to look at the accounts of early travellers in various parts of Africa. In the late sixteenth century, Andrew Battell arrived in Portuguese Angola as a prisoner, and later spent many years in the African interior. For 16 months he lived with the Jaga people (who may have originally come from Sierra Leone), a particularly warlike branch of the Juba tribe who lived around the headwaters of the Congo. Battell attributed their extreme ferocity to an evil presence among the people, and reported that of their 12 war captains the leader 'took the devil's counsel in all his exploits'. This leader, he says, is 'always making sacrifices to the devil' and in so doing believed that he would only die in war (quoted by Oliver and Oliver: 1965, p. 114). Before battle there were elaborate ceremonies including human and animal sacrifice, as a form of 'doctoring' the warriors. Like certain other militaristic groups, they did not harvest or keep livestock themselves, but simply took from those whom they defeated in battle, and then set up forts in their country. After the battle and as a sign of status, warriors extracted some of their front teeth if they were deemed to have been brave. Apparently having a full set of teeth was the Jaga equivalent of having a white feather among Victorians, and any warrior who retreated in the face of the enemy was killed as a coward and his body was eaten. Defeated enemy adults were also killed and eaten, but their children were taken and adopted into the Jaga community.

Somewhat earlier in the sixteenth century we have an account of a Portuguese, Duarte Barbosa, who had visited various trading stations on the East African coast and had gathered information about the inland empire of Monomotapa. He testified to the attire, weaponry and warlike attitudes of the warriors, although it is obvious that they enjoyed good trading relations with the 'Meors' (Muslims). The army, which included several thousand women, made regular expeditions to surrounding territories in order to subdue yet more tiny states which had either risen against the power of Monomotapa or who had not as yet been conquered. Those who duly submitted were treated mercifully, but it was quite otherwise for those who resisted.

Well before this, Islam had made considerable inroads upon the African interior. Besides establishing trading stations in East Africa, Muslims had founded kingdoms in many areas of West Africa for which there are eyewitness accounts from as early as the tenth century. Ghana, Mali, Songhai and the Hausa states are particularly notable examples. The accounts suggest that these Islam-influenced kingdoms supported larger native armies (eleventh-century Ghana is reported to have had an army of 200 000 men) with which they sought to enlarge their territories and exact tribute. Ibn Battuta, himself a Berber, travelled extensively in this area in the fourteenth century on an extended 24-year pilgrimage to Mecca, and recorded the grandiose nature of the royal courts and the elaborate rituals of their functionaries and their hundreds of slaves. He distinguished between those whose religion was 'pure Islam', and those who practised a syncretistic amalgam of Muslim monotheism and native animism, and refers to the 'Nupe ... whose ruler is one of the most considerable of the Negro rulers but who cannot be visited by any white man because they would kill him before he got there' (Battuta: 1927, pp. 317–31).

In these accounts the expansionist and militaristic nature of such systems can be clearly inferred, and is in keeping with both Islamic ideals and recognized native practice. With all that can rightly be levelled at the later incursive Europeans, it is quite evident that these West African states were exploitative, slave-owning societies from very early days. Indeed, it can be convincingly argued that the infamous European slaving operations of later years could not have been carried out without the active cooperation and connivance of the native rulers. As late as the mid-nineteenth century explorers found in the Bornu-Kanem area around Lake Chad native rulers with harems of up to 400 slave girls, one ruler even displaying 'ethnological' as well as a 'sexual interest ... in certain rare specimens'. Apparently if he lacked a particular type for his collection 'he would instruct his servants to catch him one, as a rich lepidopterist might order a valuable butterfly' (Hibbert: 1982, p. 182). Some explorers were even invited by the rulers to accompany them on slaving expeditions which they afterwards regretted. In one such venture, the ruler of Kukawa (a territory west of Lake Chad) decided to combine the resubjugation of a recalcitrant neighbouring state with the chance to replenish his coffers by capturing and selling its people as slaves. His army took some 3 000 slaves, and left many hundreds more with their limbs severed so that they bled to death.

In West Africa, the situation among the tribes of the south-west, especially the Yoruba, was quite different from that of the Hausa-Fulani Emirates in the north. These tribes lived in highly forested areas where communications were difficult, agriculture was not that simple and disease was rife. Indeed, it would seem unlikely that organized communities, let alone states, would arise in such unfavourable conditions in what is now Nigeria. When the Portuguese arrived in the fifteenth century, the Yoruba had already evolved a number of separate states whose unity was reflected in the broadly common language (though with numerous dialects) and a common cycle of myths. Yoruba society was hierarchically organized with a sacred priest (oni) and a paramount chief (alafin) at the head of a federation of semi-autonomous states. These were governed by hereditary sub-chiefs and their councils. Below these was the mass of the people organized in a system of patrilineal descent groups, and – of course – the slaves.

A sub-chief did not possess full control of the military in his state. His war leaders made the key decisions, but only he could actually authorize a campaign. Yet since he had his own bodyguard and attendant slaves, he was in a position to exert a certain amount of pressure within his own area of jurisdiction. It would appear, however, that his war leaders/officials had the final whip hand in that they could, *in extremis*, either depose him or compel him to commit suicide. The evidence – such as we have – would indicate that war campaigns were so frequent as to be normal. The alafin, who lived in some style with his wives, ministers and eunuchs, did not normally go to war himself. The logistics and the implementation of a campaign generally were in the hands of the war leaders and their captains. These men together with their subordinates, including bodyguards and slaves, formed the nucleus of the army, but this was implemented as and when emergencies arose. All able-bodied free men were liable for military service, and could be mobilized by their respective chiefs for a campaign. So each area had a military force of some kind, although the main army – one might almost say, the standing army – was that of the capital. With full mobilization for a large-scale engagement the army could number many thousands (estimates differ), and one authority suggests that the Yoruba army was probably as big as any in Africa (Smith: 1969, p. 122).

Most of our evidence for the Yoruba army comes from the early to middle nineteenth century. Its equipment conforms to the usual patterns of spears, swords and the like, that is until the introduction of European firearms. This came about from the seventeenth century onwards, although they were not used extensively until the early nineteenth century. For the most part, towns – certainly those of any size – were surrounded by walls (sometimes double walls) although these were rarely of brick or stone. These mounds of hardened mud hardly presented a formidable obstacle to the enemy, and were subject to rapid deterioration during the rains even when they were reinforced with wood and thatch. Often the actual fighting took place around these walls or around the campsites which were constructed with similar defence works. In the intrasocietal conflicts, casualties were often low, but – as is to be expected – these numbers could rise dramatically in full-scale engagements such as those against the particularly fierce warriors of Dahomey. The fate of the captives could vary. Some were gratuitously butchered on the battlefield, some were ransomed, but the majority were usually sold into slavery.

Some of the most serious conflicts arose over the slave trade and just how it was to be controlled. Those tribal groups that were prepared to supply slaves to the Europeans received in exchange much prized goods such as swords, iron, salt, cloth, mirrors and, later on, muskets. The apogee of Yoruba power was probably in the middle of the eighteenth century during the personal rule of Gaha, an *éminence noir*, of whom we read that 'He lived to a good old age, and wielded his power ruthlessly. He was noted for having raised five kings to the throne, of whom he murdered four, and was himself murdered by the fifth' – possibly by having his body dismembered and the parts distributed throughout the empire (Smith: 1969, p. 47). At this time the Yoruba, who had recently defeated a powerful Ashanti army, were described as warlike and powerful. Yet militaristic as the Yoruba proved to be, the later years of the eighteenth century saw the apotheosis of the empire, and their eventual decline was inevitably marked by defeats by many of their enemies.

In southern Africa the story was not very different, although here there was very little influence from the Islamic world. In the early nineteenth century there were several large kingdoms whose native rulers were often extremely aggressive and predatory. These were mainly Bantu peoples who had moved south during the European late Middle Ages, and had subjugated the indigenous peoples of South Africa who were of Bushman/Bergdama stock (Schapera: 1956). Most notably there were the Swazi under Sobhuza, the Matabele under Mzilikazi, the Tsonga (in what was then Portuguese East Africa) under Soshangana, and – most notoriously – the Zulu under Shaka, who is known to have subjugated well over a hundred tribes, absorbing their warriors for his impis and killing villagers. Warfare led to the flight of many tribespeople such was the oppressive treatment they could expect from the conquerors. Some of those who fled became ruthless conquerors in turn, such as Mzilikazi in what became Rhodesia (modern Zimbabwe). Others, such as Moshesh who founded what became known as the Basuto nation, did so partly by absorbing those who were refugees from the depredations of others. There is no evidence that those thus taken into the dominant tribe were treated as inferiors; in fact, their leaders often became well-regarded sub-chiefs or indunas (advisers).

As we have seen, scale is undoubtedly a critical factor in warfare, and certainly one can hardly speak of militarism in societies that are so small that their conflicts can be little more than skirmishes. Yet small-scale relations do not preclude serious animosities, as some theorists have been keen to point out. However, it was – and perhaps still is – an abiding dream of many social scientists (and here I have in mind social anthropologists in particular) that in time aggression might be harnessed by culture; that what we fondly regard as 'civilization' or 'progress' will make all the difference. Perhaps the ensuing discussion will compel some change, or at least modification, of that rather idealistic point of view.

CHAPTER FOUR

Militarism and Motivation

Psychological approaches to the study of war and militarism subsume some of those ideas we have already discussed, especially aggression (Chapter 2) which is so central to our theme that it deserves some elaboration.

When psychologists speak of aggression, they tend to distinguish four different, though not entirely distinct theories (Lider: 1977, pp. 7–9).

1. *Aggression as an evolved trait* which is really just another form of the natural instinct theory. War therefore becomes institutionalized (i.e. collective) combat. As the fittest survive and aggression is seen to pay off, so some communities/societies adopt a militaristic stance in relation to others in order to improve their living conditions.
2. *Aggression as transformation* is associated with the psychological school and again argues that aggressiveness is rooted in the human psyche. But given that we all have to live together in groups/communities, these instincts must be suppressed – sometimes with indifferent success – for the sake of social harmony.
3. *Aggression and frustration* is something of a favourite with many theorists. It has its own kind of immediate plausibility. If people cannot obtain their goals, it is known that they can be more than just irritated. Indeed, at more extreme levels, especially if people are not inhibited by fears of punishment, they may well be tempted to act aggressively. It is not difficult to see how collective frustrations, say, over property, resources or whatever, could lead to group and even social conflict. No one is suggesting that this is an invariable rule, but from an experiental point of view, it does carry some conviction.
4. *Aggression as learned behaviour* is another well-established – one might almost say revered – theory of aggression. The Behaviourist school in Psychology is particularly fond of the idea which we have already examined in some detail (Chapter 2) that human beings are not by nature aggressive but that they 'acquire' such tendencies by exposure and example. Some humanist critics modify this by insisting that people do not act mechanistically (e.g. from instincts or frustrations) but in accordance with adopted and well-tried principles.

Not one of these theories is adequate by itself. Even together they are not able to explain the causes of aggression or the development and incidence of war. Nor are they sufficient to account for the ways in which hostile views and emotions become transformed into the kind of collective behaviour that we term militaristic. Yet, despite this, theorists insist that one or the other has more cogency than the rest, and at least goes some way towards explaining the phenomena in question. Very generally, social scientists do not seem to want to think the worst of people, thus learning theory possibly continues to lead the field, but whether it has any greater explanatory power than the rest is very much open to debate. Some eminent theorists seem fully to endorse the learning theory view; Anthony Giddens, somewhat contradictorily, writes,

> War has little to do with the expression of aggressive impulses, although the battlefield may provide some people with the chance to express murderous feelings they would otherwise keep concealed. Aggression is a feature of many aspects of human activity but it leads to very few of us to murder anyone. The vast majority of those who have killed others have done so in wartime ... All armies involve drill training and the learning of discipline ... [this] helps to alter people's usual attitudes towards indiscriminately shedding blood.
> (Giddens: 1990, p. 345).

Similarly Gwynne Dyer who was responsible for preparing a series of programmes on war for television: 'The business of armies ... is killing, and so a crucial part of training people to be soldiers is teaching them to ignore the limits they normally place on the actual use of violence ... For the vast majority of people killing has to be taught' (Dyer: 1985, pp. 117–18). But Dyer is willing to concede that there are those who have no objection to killing if they feel they have to because it occurs within a justificatory moral framework such as war. He seems to think that such people are mainly found within the ranks of what are normally called 'special forces', and that 'ordinary men' have to be persuaded to kill. One wonders how much Dyer has studied the accounts of armies that have gratuitously sacked towns and who could not be restrained from indulging in an orgy of looting, rapine and murder – sometimes leaving absolutely nothing alive when they left (Carlton: 1994).

It has to be disputable to argue (as Giddens: 1990, p. 346) that war only exists in large-scale societies. It is natural to assume that war, as we have come to understand it, is mainly to be associated with extensive conflicts between nation states. And certainly, as we have already observed, *militarism* is almost by definition, a function of such states. But surely it is highly questionable that 'the fighting of war, then, does not derive directly from human aggression'. It is only possible to say that among hunting and gathering societies war did not exist in any recognizable sense if war is only to be seen in terms of scale. Similarly, it is positively incorrect to insist that among such peoples the armed conflicts they staged were 'exciting and dangerous rituals (and) more like sport than war' (ibid.). We have already seen how mass killing, even if it did not entail many lives in an absolute sense, was still *relatively* extensive. It is this kind of argument which betrays something of the 'noble savage' mentality, and suggests that aggressive traits have only fully developed in centralized, especially modern advanced societies. Is one to suppose, then, that tribal peoples would not have indulged their aggressive tendencies if they had had the means at their disposal? It is interesting to note that when such peoples were first introduced to firearms they coveted them more than just about anything else the Europeans had to offer. And we know that in a number of 'Third World' countries, a disproportionate amount of their GNP is still spent on armaments.

There are those among the social science fraternity who think that recourse to psychological explanations of aggression simply confuses the issue. This is because the term tends to be used differently by those concerned with the political and legal implications of aggression. Obviously no state has a psyche which is capable of any kind of objective examination. Neither, of course, is the idea of aggressive *intention* susceptible to any really satisfactory definition. Even social psychologists, in their effort to be as precise and 'scientific' as possible, feel that we should abjure the thorny and ultimately unverifiable question of aggressive*ness* and instead concentrate on the reality of observable aggressive *acts*. What is being suggested here is that there has to be some correlation, no matter how inconclusive, between those acts considered aggressive and an innate propensity to act aggressively.

What particularly concerns us here, however, is another matter about which psychologists have quite a lot to say, and which is certainly relevant to the issue of militarism, namely *motivation*. What makes societies, and especially their leaders militarily aggressive? Are there any key psychological factors involved? Strictly speaking, the term can only be precisely used about individuals; the notion of 'group motivation' (i.e. an aggregation of motives) is vague and uncertain and is really only derived by analogy. Motivation has to be related to *goals*. It is not some kind of latent facet of personality, rather it is a *propensity* we all possess. We are presumably all capable of being motivated. Human behaviour is directed towards some specific object or state of affairs. Hence we think of motivation as being *selective* in nature. And this, in turn, may well be influenced by incentives. Behaviourists would no doubt insist that motivation is therefore a kind of conditioned response to particular sets of circumstances. In this sense we can say that motivation may have an intrinsic dimension such as when a person plays a musical instrument for enjoyment. But evidence suggests that motivation is largely extrinsic in that it depends largely on external reinforcements. So people may take up jogging to keep fit, not because they enjoy running; being in trim is the motivation – jogging is simply the means to an end.

Motives are notoriously difficult to study because:

- they cannot be observed; only their outcomes are examinable
- specific behaviour does not necessarily reflect a particular motive
- much depends not only on the appropriate incentives and the long- and short-term goals, but also on the capacity to realize those goals – often a matter of misjudgement with militarists and sundry would-be aggressors.

We must now bring our two themes together and ask about the possible motives for aggression. First we should summarize the three main 'explanations':

1. The biological explanation stresses the innate nature of the aggressive instinct, and may imply a sociobiological variant which argues that aggression is nature's way of ensuring that we achieve some clear biological advantage by obtaining more resources or increased recognition. This is something we will examine in more detail when we look at economic and territorial factors involved in militarism.
2. The learning theory explanation which maintains that aggression is culturally acquired either by example or some other form of inculcation. The instilling of nationalistic/militaristic ideologies would come into this category.
3. Some amalgam of the two which concedes that we all have the capacity for aggression, but that it requires certain sets of social circumstances for it to find expression. It is possibly this compromise, common-sense position which finds most general acceptance within society at large.

Also, before we try to exemplify these themes we should take a closer look at motivation from the psychologists' point of view. We have already seen that motivation implies *selectivity* of response which, in turn, determines *directionality* of behaviour and *adjustment* of that behaviour to specific goals. Also implied is the capacity to adduce reasons for this selection of the means – aggressive/coercive or otherwise – for achieving particular ends. It could be argued that the cause of any sentiment/urge or whatever may already exist in some half-recognized or unarticulated way, yet it does not become a motive until it is acknowledged and becomes the basis for future actions. But motives are not always clearly identified, or – more commonly – they are rationalized to suit the occasion (Carlton: 1995, pp. 54–60).

Motives are not usually that much of a problem in militaristic societies. The reasons for aggression are fairly unambiguous. In order to appreciate some of the theoretical points more clearly it may help to look at two militaristic cultures of the past which had modest origins. The first came to rule most of India for about 140 years, and the motives were transparently clear. The second which came to prominence in Greece about the same time eventually had far-reaching repercussions, but the motives of the leader in question are still not entirely clear.

Case studies

Alexander's invasion of India was neither particularly successful nor especially enlightening. His army did not penetrate beyond the Punjab, and his encounters with native princelings in the north-west have only come down to us in Greek accounts – perhaps a somewhat biased source. So we know rather little about affairs in the heart of the country except that it seems to have been divided into numerous petty states with a hegemony exercised by the largely unknown kingdom of Magadha in the lower Ganges valley. With Alexander's successors in Asia, the Selucid dynasty, we know rather more. About 300 BC, a Greek traveller-cum-ambassador, Megasthenes, reported some highly embroidered 'facts' about this fabled land which are difficult or impossible to believe. But he did record that at the city of Patna there was a great ruler, Chandragupta, of whom we know something from other sources, notably Plutarch. He may have been the youth referred to as 'Sandrocotos' who met Alexander, and from whom he took his example as a renowned conqueror.

Such evidence as we have, suggests that Chandragupta ousted the ruler of Patna about 324 BC and became the founder of the Mauryan dynasty, India's first imperial family. He is said to have been variously the son of a menial herdsman *and* the son of a lady of the harem (both could possibly be true – but it is hardly likely). It is reported that he had a magnificent palace surrounded by a timber wall with 570 towers, and a moat 900 feet wide and 30 feet deep. The city was administered by six boards of five men each (it was normal for towns and villages to be governed by five-man boards of elders). It was a very sophisticated system which according to Megasthenes, dealt with everything from tax collection to the upkeep and repair of the marketplaces and the temples. Chandragupta must have been a ruler of some reputation if it is true that Seleucus himself sent one of his daughters to Chandragupta's court, perhaps to become one of the Yavani, Greek women guards of his sleeping quarters.

At the height of Mauryan power, the army, including an espionage network and the administrative bureaucracy besides the military proper, may have comprised upwards of a million men. This was an enormous force for those times, and comparable to the muster of troops in the almost contemporary Persian empire. The whole edifice was sustained by a swingeing tax system which claimed between 25 and 50 per cent of the value of all crops grown, beside further taxes on trade and other forms of wealth. Megasthenes observed seven classes in Mauryan society ranging from royal councillors (interestingly set above the Brahmins) to spies (often people who posed as travelling merchants) who were obviously not regarded as practising in a particularly prestigious profession.

The empire was divided into districts roughly coterminous with the earlier tribal boundaries. These were under the control of the king's closest relatives and friends, presumably on the supposition – or hope? – that this would increase his control and reduce the possibility of insurrection. Tax remissions were granted for the clearing of forests which was actually done by the slave-like peasants (shudras) who, except for those technically deemed to be outcastes, were at the bottom of the traditional caste hierarchy. All land was regarded as state land, which effectively meant that it all belonged to the king. By extension this included all those enterprises which – in a rudimentary way – functioned as mines and industries. These included everything from spinning and weaving to the production of armaments. Weights and measures were all state controlled, as were wage categories which show that there were marked disparities between the aristocracy, say the royal counsellors, and the peasants who – as often as not – barely existed on subsistence wages (Wolpert: 1989).

The army, of course, was the Mauryan key to success. Besides the regular forces, there was also a kind of territorial militia based on craft-guild (shreni) organization. These were men who could be mobilized as and when required by the central authority. In some ways, this para-military set-up overlapped with those of the sub-caste (jati) which were also mainly village based, but which were also largely organized according to occupational criteria.

Chandragupta abdicated his throne in 301 BC, and according to tradition became a somewhat reclusive monk of the Jain order which adhered to an extreme form of asceticism. During the reign of his grandson, Ashoka (269–232 BC), Mauryan power reached its zenith. Ashoka left extensive records of his reign, many of them imperishably carved into rocks and in sandstone pillars. So it is probably true to say that we know more about him than any other king in ancient India. Although considered one of the most enlightened of India's rulers, he spent the first years of his reign ruthlessly consolidating his position. Once internal matters were settled, he turned his attention elsewhere. It was part of Brahmin received wisdom that 'any power superior in might to another should launch into war' (quoted by Wolpert: 1989, p. 62). Consequently, he initiated an attack on the neighbouring state of Kalinga (modern Orissa) and devastated the land killing and destroying and taking captives, presumably as slaves. Ashoka recorded on pillars an account of this campaign – rather like the self-laudatory inscriptions of earlier Egyptian pharaohs – but unlike them, he also recorded his decision to turn away from violence to further his purposes. But then it might well be argued that he who was called 'Beloved of the gods' could afford officially to do so now that he had got what he wanted. His 'conversion' to non-violence may well have been due to the influence of Buddhist teaching – but of this we are not sure. He certainly sent emissaries abroad to preach the new doctrine. But this new policy of reconciliation may all have been part of a new state expedient. Subjects were reminded that the king, though compassionate, still wielded considerable power and could invoke any sanctions he wished.

When Ashoka came to the throne most of India was already subject to Mauryan rule. During his reign, India was regarded as a power to be reckoned with, and enjoyed equality of esteem with states such as Syria and Ptolemaic Egypt. Although entirely different from his near contemporary, the Emperor of unified China, the entirely ruthless Ch'in Huang-Ti, they were alike in that towards the end of their reigns they retreated from public life and became almost inordinately preoccupied with their relationship with the gods and the hope of immortality – a very vague concept both in Hinduism and its offshoot, Buddhism.

Mauryan rule began its inevitable decline after Ashoka, and various contenders vied with each other in an unseemly – and hardly non-violent – manner to secure power for themselves. The empire which had been created by military might began to disintegrate – as all empires must. As Arnold Toynbee, who had a penchant for cyclical theories of history, might well have said, 'Nothing fails like success'.

The motive behind Mauryan aggression would seem to have been unashamed expansionism. There are, of course, other motives for militarism, though one is never quite sure whether the militarists themselves were altogether clear about what they were. And what of their 'victims' – how important was motivation to them? Did a militarist's motives condition *their* response?

To illustrate the ambiguity – even the confusion – of motives for taking the military option, we could do worse than look at the rationale of Philip II of Macedonia, father of Alexander the Great, who lived just about a hundred years before Ashoka.

Although not on a par with, say, the Assyrians or the Mongols, the Macedonians were a warlike people. The tradition was that any man that had not killed a wild boar should not be allowed to eat sitting down, and that a man who had not killed an enemy should suffer the humiliation of wearing a halter. The evidence suggests that the Macedonians were a hardy pastoral people who had little of the sophistication or refinement of their city-living Greek contemporaries. Their reputation was such that the Greeks were reluctant to recognize that Macedonians could even be regarded as Greeks and, for their part, the Macedonians regarded the Greeks with some ambivalence, envying them yet also seeing them as somewhat effete – a charge that was hardly warranted, especially when one considers the Greeks' military record.

One key difference between most Greeks, who lived in relatively small autonomous city states (poleis), and the Macedonians who did not, was the institution of kingship. Most Greek communities were administered by citizen-based assemblies or ruled by appointed or hereditary oligarchies (the most notable exception being that of Sparta). Indeed, in the majority of city states there was an actual distrust of monarchy, although many of them, at one time or another, had been ruled by tyrants (Greek = tyrannos), that is to say men who had seized power unconstitutionally and who had usually – though not always – ruled despotically. For most Greeks of the Classical age one-man rule was a negation of liberty, and those who were elected to office (or in extreme cases chosen by ballot as in Athens) were there for a limited time only, and as with the later Roman consuls could be impeached for any supposed or actual misdemeanors committed while in office. Macedonians, on the other hand, were content with a hereditary system of kingship with the important proviso that the candidate in question had to meet with the approval of the people.

The king was regarded as the living representative between the people and the gods – a notion that was anathema to most Greeks. Even some

Macedonians had their doubts. When Alexander declared his own divinity to some of this Companions (a special category of friends-cum-advisers) they just could not take it seriously – much to his annoyance. It is important therefore to stress the term *representative* of the gods; no Macedonian king could be regarded by other Macedonians as a *living* god, even if – as with Alexander – some of his Asian subjects chose to do so.

The military was the central institution of Macedonian society, and as supreme commander of the forces, it was the king who led the army into battle. There was no question of sitting on a transportable throne and watching the action from a vantage point as was the practice of some oriental monarchs. In fact, a Macedonian king had to set an example to the troops and be the first man into the fray. His troops swore a solemn oath to follow him, and any who broke their vows were liable to the most dire punishments, flogging or even execution in extreme cases (in the case of a man found guilty of treason, not only he but also his family might be put to death). When a king won land 'by the spear', it was considered to be *his* land. So too was all property and all taxes payable by residents and farmers. However, with these riches he was expected to be generous in rewarding his officials. When he died or was killed in battle, it was the army that effectively conducted the obsequies including army games and combats between selected warriors as a form of honour to the deceased.

Macedonian society was militaristic in that it was on a permanent wartime footing. There was no clear distinction between civil and military posts. War, or the possibility of war, was what Macedonian society was all about. Its aristocracy – if such it can be called – comprised those who were suitably honoured by the king, particularly the Companions and the Royal Pages (youths who were being trained as future potential Companions). Such a system had no heritable permanency. It naturally had inbuilt weaknesses, not least that of favouritism – always a problem in a patron–client culture. In this there was an acknowledged homosexual element that sometimes involved petty jealousies which on occasions led to accusations of treason and suspicions of homicide (Hammond: 1991, pp. 40–41).

It would appear that not all males within the Macedonian state had the franchise. This was also true of both the democracies and the oligarchies in Greece. It was common to distinguish between 'citizens' and others who might be resident aliens or indigenes of one kind or another. It was usually only the citizens who were allowed to hold office and vote at the assemblies. In Macedonia it was significant that the citizens – the Macedonians – were those under arms and those who had been soldiers but who could no longer serve the state in a full-time capacity. When mobilization took place they and others who were in what today we would call reserved occupations comprised a militia to augment where necessary the regular forces. It was the Macedonians who alone had the right to choose/approve who was king – the person who would also lead them into battle. And it was the king and his immediate staff who made the critical decisions. The kingdom was always under threat from predatory neighbours, thus the army was always in readiness for attacks either from land or from the sea – a situation that was quite common in other Greek states where fratricidal war was a national pastime. But as like as not, it was the Macedonians who were the aggressors. The army had to be kept finely tuned for action against other states. It was all an exciting game – and any resultant loot was always welcome.

The real architect of Macedonian military success was Philip II. More than any other royal leader he fashioned a military machine that eventually subdued most of Greece and provided the foundation for Alexander's victories in the East. As a youngster, he had spent three years as a hostage in Thebes and had carefully studied the tactics and equipment of the crack Theban army. By the time he was 18 he had been put in command of his own military area. He became king in his early twenties and after he had experienced the shameful defeat of the Macedonians by the then ascendant Illyrians he immediately set about rearranging and re-equipping the Macedonian army. He also astutely bought off – albeit temporarily – some of his potential enemies and came to terms with the powerful Athenians. He also expediently arranged for the convenient demise of those who threatened his position as king, thereby setting an example to his son who eliminated his opponents some years later.

The two particular innovations Philip initiated were the introduction of the 16-ft counter-weighted pike (sarissa) used in the phalanx formation, and a realignment of the phalanx itself into wedge-shaped 'human tanks'. Greek battle tactics were crude at best, with opposing lines of heavily armed troops (hoplites) pushing against each other until one line broke, when it was every man for himself. He also ensured the physical fitness of his troops by insisting on forced marches with full equipment, after which the men had to be prepared to go straight into battle.

Once he decided the army was ready he attacked and defeated the Illyrians. He then enlarged his army by recruiting men from adjoining territories which were either unaffiliated or which had previously given their allegiance elsewhere. Philip built a number of new towns and fortifications. He even went to the extent of transplanting whole populations, partly in the interests of integration, and partly – perhaps mainly – with the intention of enlarging his military state. With his forces now augmented and his borders adequately defended, he was all set to make a few valuable acquisitions elsewhere.

Philip added to his domain by a judicious combination of bribery, diplomatic horse-trading, and – when all else failed – unabashed intimidation and the use of military force. The fratricidal warfare between a number of the poleis played into his hands. The more the cities were divided, the more he was able to exploit their enmities and general acquisitiveness to his own advantage. Much of his activity was directed against Athens, regardless of the fact that he was supposed to have come to terms with what was still one of the most powerful states in Greece. This was done indirectly by picking off Athenian allies. He was still not quite ready to take on a coalition of states under Athenian leadership. But this was to come – as Philip knew it must.

His minor conquests in Eastern Greece brought him considerable booty, including gold and silver mines which provided him with the revenue he needed to finance further military expansion. As his strength grew through accretion and acquisition, he felt the time was ripe to tackle some of the large city states. He now had quite a large army under his command, including mercenaries who were sometimes used for garrison duties, and the siege specialists who were professional engineers. He embarked on a campaign against the more formidable cities of Pydna and Methone where he actually lost an eye in battle (354 BC). In some cases, he allowed his conquered cities to continue much as before, but if there was notable resistance, he sometimes had the populations sold into slavery. He might – as in the case of Olynthus – have the city razed to the ground *and* the population sold into slavery. Cruel and unfeeling as this was, it was nothing unusual. It was a common treatment for conquered cities. Indeed, it could sometimes be worse; at Sestus in 353/2 BC, the Athenians massacred all the adult males (i.e. those capable of bearing arms) and sold the rest of the people into slavery. When this sort of thing happened it was a known practice to repeople the city and its environs with those the conqueror wished to benefit – in Philip's case, with more Macedonians. In other instances, he is known to have displaced and relocated whole populations (e.g. 20 000 from Scythia alone) because this would give the right 'balance' to his burgeoning empire.

Once the army had successfully flexed its military muscles, it was time to initiate a more serious programme of conquest in the Balkans. Philip attacked the tribal groups in Thrace and Illyria in the 340s BC, and then encroached on Scythian territory (a state that even the Persians had found a problem in the past) where he defeated the king and took his daughter as a wife. Thracians made a practice of enslaving whole populations, and Illyrians – like the Spartans – kept huge numbers of serfs. Their 'liberation', therefore by the Macedonians *may* have meant that their treatment and their status underwent a modest improvement.,

Philip had already become involved in Greek affairs, especially in the Sacred War (356–46 BC) over the control of the sanctuary of Apollo at Delphi. As the name suggests this was ostensibly a war about a sacred Oracle when in fact it was more about the appropriation of the Temple's gold and silver treasures. It was a pretty ruthless affair, with one side executing their prisoners as violators of sacred property (the fate of temple robbers was to be drowned in the sea) and the other side responding by killing their prisoners in return. Having fought themselves to a standstill the various protagonists, including Phocia, Boeotia and Athens, came to an understanding in a deal brokered by Philip himself. The Phocians – the guilty party – lost and were suitably punished (some delegates at the arbitrating Council actually proposed their extinction, but this was rejected). Philip was then elected President of the Pythian (Delphic) Games which further enhanced his prestige.

By the 340s BC, Philip felt himself powerful enough to intervene in Greek politics, per se. His horizons had now enlarged, and he wanted to become the controller of Greek destiny. He had already made a number of prudent alliances, and some of these were cemented by marriage – though even Philip must have realized that there is a limit to the number of wives one can usually manage. He came to feel that only he could unite the warring Greek states, by force if necessary, the object being to lead them against the might of the Persian Empire. At least, this was the theory. This was the *declared motive* for his series of manoeuvres and campaigns in mainland Greece.

The takeover proceeded swiftly – but it was not without its hitches. Philip's allies, the Thessalonians, elected him President (archon) for life of their league, and the prominent Athenian, Isocrates, wrote to congratulate him for what he was doing for the Greek cities (344 BC) regardless of the fact that he had destroyed quite a number of them. But this was not lost on an equally famous Greek orator, Demosthenes, who warned that if something was not done about Philip soon, he would subjugate the whole of Greece, Athens included. And he was right. Demosthenes in a number of rousing speeches convinced the Athenian Assembly (ecclesia) to begin making alliances with other city states, particularly Thebes and those in the Eastern Aegean which were also apprehensive about Philip's conquests. Money even came from the Great King himself to help the anti-Macedonian cause; Persia, too, was becoming wary about Philip's intentions – as well they might be.

By 340 BC, the situation looked so threatening that the Athenians and their allies (including the powerful cities of Megara and Corinth) decided to take the initiative. There was nothing for it but to resist Philip by force. But Philip, possibly through his network of informers, was always a jump ahead. Athens depended critically on corn supplies from the area of the Black Sea in order to feed its citizens. But Philip's ships seized a convoy of grain vessels from the Bosphorus bound for Athens which exacerbated an already desperate situation. Philip's army was poised to attack the allies, but then withdrew only to return the following year with his equally aggressive colleagues, the Thessalonians. He also tried to involve the Thebans, but they chose an alliance with Athens (this may have been *one* reason why much later Alexander determined to crush Thebes out of existence). From strength, Philip then made overtures to Athens which may or may not have been genuine. Whatever, there was so much distrust that the Athenians, led by Demosthenes, rejected them and voted to continue with hostilities. They were hoping that the Persians, their former enemies, would join them in force, but the Greek King was content to give them money – and, of course, moral support.

The situation had now reached a climax. Philip, using the stratagem of a feigned withdrawal, successfully dealt with many of the allies' mercenaries. Still he offered peace, though one wonders for how long? This too was rejected – it would have smacked too much of appeasement. The battle was eventually joined with the forces of the coalition at Chaironia in August 338 BC, and despite being outnumbered, the Macedonians defeated the allies and took hundreds of prisoners. The Theban 'Sacred Band', an elite unit (thought by some to consist largely of homosexuals and bisexuals) died to a man and were accorded an honourable burial. Other Theban captives were either ransomed or sold as slaves and their leaders executed because it was felt that they had reneged on an understanding with their former allies. By contrast, Athenian prisoners were returned unransomed, and the ashes of the cremated sent home – an uncharacteristic gesture.

Philip was now master of Greece. Other states fell into line. There was no further resistance (this was to come later when Alexander took over from his father); this may have been out of fear, and because they were at least half-convinced – contrary to Demosthenes' rhetoric – that Philip was intent on a policy of reconciliation. Philip's blueprint for a federation of Greek states was adopted by all the mainland poleis except Sparta whose leaders kept themselves aloof from mainstream affairs. This was intended to end intrapoleis rivalries as well as interstate conflict. Each state was free to have its own political arrangements, but it also meant that no one should contest the will or intentions of the hegemon – the first among unequals. To all intents and purposes, the task of a united Greece was to liberate the Greek states of Asia Minor (within the jurisdiction of the Great King) and to exact retribution from Persia for the profanation of the Greek temples by Persian warriors some 150 or so years before. This seems to be accepted rather uncritically by some scholars (e.g. Hammond: 1991), but as a *casus belli*, it strikes the modern reader as a little thin. The riches of Persia and the glory of conquest would seem to be more persuasive as motives for the campaign which Philip began and Alexander set out to complete (Burn: 1973; Green: 1982). The Persian state was notoriously weak at this time (its Great King, Ochus, had recently been assassinated together with many of his family). Alexander's task was formidable but by no means impossible. It was all over in record time, but it did not and could not last (Green: 1991). Eventually the Macedonian Empire crumbled and became divided among the dead Alexander's subordinates.

CHAPTER FIVE

Militarism and Status: The Hundred Years War

When we look at militarism in terms of particular disciplines, in this case the social sciences, we have to consider again the whole question of interpretation. So much turns on how the phenomenon under discussion is defined. All the many ways in which militarism can be 'seen' are of particular interest to sociologists who tend to derive their theories from an analysis of the structure of society. This perspective – and it is only one perspective amidst a number of complementary perspectives – sees wars arising from the formation of groups who pursued their own conflicting interests.

The term 'militarism' can be used in several senses, and generally connotes the adulation of military virtues, but this can be further refined as follows.

1. *Aggressiveness*, especially in foreign policy, and a readiness to resort to war and expansionism. Thomas Hobbes came close when he wrote, 'the nature of war (and by implication, militarism) consisteth not in actual fighting but in a known disposition thereto during all the time there is no assurance to the contrary' (Oakeshott: 1957, p. 82). It is in this sense of belligerency and combativeness that it is used in this text. However, it can also mean:
2. *The dominance or preponderance of the militarism within the state.* This brings us back to the differentiation or otherwise between the civil and military spheres – something which is not always possible in both simple and complex pre-industrial societies. The notion of military preponderance also connotes the privileged nature of the military within society, and all the perquisites that go with military status, as has been the case in certain petty dictatorships. Interestingly, however, the dominance of the military may not go with *overt* aggressiveness, but in an effective show of force.
3. *The subordination of most aspects of social life to the needs of the military* as happens in time of war or preparation for war. This harnessing of social activity, especially economic activity, to the requirements of the state can be usefully designated as militarization.
4. *Display* (NB, Chapter 1), that is the drills and ceremonies, and the

preoccupation with – sometimes supererogatory – military rituals and procedures.
5. *The ideology* which often, in some form, accompanies this complex of attitudes and practices.

As we have already noted, it may seem inappropriate to apply the term 'militaristic' to small-scale societies, although there were quite a number of aggressive tribal groups, especially in the larger more centralized societies such as the Iroquois on the eastern seaboard of the USA. But, generally speaking, we reserve the term for those more complex societies which we may correctly regard as states. It would apply particularly to systems where there were extensive arsenals from which large armies were supplied with the accoutrements of war. In eleventh-century China, for instance, we find evidence that 'factories' were producing 32 000 suits of armour every year, besides other weapons such as spears, bows and so forth (Needham: 1975). States have grown and coalesced over time, especially in Europe, partly as the result of unification, but also because of war and conquest. In 1500 it is estimated that there were some 500 or so European states, most of which were so small as to be hardly worthy of such an appelation. Today, there are a bare 25 (Tilly: 1975).

This emergence of large nation states together with the enormous increase in population have greatly heightened not so much the frequency of war as the often gigantic *scale* of war. For example, in the battle of the Somme which began in July 1916 and ended after intermittent attacks on the German lines in the following November, about a million men died – roughly equivalent numbers on both sides, with no clear result. No other offensive in military history has claimed so many lives – certainly not on a single battlefield (Wilson: 1986). Today, even after the colossal carnage of the Second World War, the Somme episode is seen as a kind of tragic and unnecessary lunacy.

If a more synoptic view is taken of war in the eighteenth–twentieth centuries, the picture is even more disquieting. The following is a comparative general estimate of the figures:

Numbers of wars		*Numbers of deaths (in millions)*
Eighteenth century	68	4.4
Nineteenth century	205	8.3
Twentieth century	237	98.8

It is obvious from these figures that there has been a quantum leap in violence during the twentieth century. With wars taking place somewhere on the globe at any one time, it is little wonder that the statistics are so staggering, and these take no account of the ever greater numbers of those who were wounded, disfigured and maimed for the rest of their lives. Can this all be put down to the developments in technology? Are the reasons primarily economic or political? How important, too, are demographic factors? Are there just too many people in the world? And are more societies prepared to resort to violence to solve their problems? The really intriguing aspect of all this is that the limited – one might almost say, rational – use of force has given way to an ethos of almost unrestrained violence. And this at a time when society, in so many ways, is becoming more and more humane. Slavery is largely a thing of the past; in the developed world, at least, there is better and more universal education; people are better medicated and more hygienically housed on the whole; it is a better world both actually and potentially, yet war and militarism are still with us, and the overall death toll continues to increase. Are we becoming *more* aggressive? And why this puzzling contradiction? Why do more fervent attempts to secure peace go along with the greater incidence of violence and aggression? It is probably true to say that most people are aware of the futility of war, yet it still goes on and is likely to continue, and – what is worse – nobody seems to know quite how to stop it.

Another factor which has contributed to the magnitude of war has been universal conscription. This is not really new, and could be found in the citizen militias in the ancient world. But when, as in Rome, it was decided to rely instead on a trained, professional army, conscription was not normally required. With the industrialization of war, however, from the early nineteenth century onwards massive forces became the order of the day. Only universal conscription could help keep pace with the huge losses involved. To give some idea of the differences in the scale of war, Alexander set out to invade Persia (334 BC) with probably no more than 40 000 men; Hitler invaded Russia in 1941 with an army of some 3 million men. It is interesting to ask just how states have been able to recruit men and women in such numbers. Why was there no resistance? How is it that people are so compliant? Was it simply – or not so simply – a matter of coercion, or did conviction (ideology) play a part?

Related to these questions is the further problem of how societies come to be ruled by the military. According to some theorists (by implication, Wittfogel: 1957) it is because they have no really developed competing institutions. It is certainly true that in modern democracies – especially what are termed liberal democracies – with their industrialized technologies and their highly diffuse administrations, there is less scope for domination by the military. Furthermore, in democracies where civilian government has become politically acceptable, the military often lacks legitimacy, the popularly accepted right to rule. Neither do the military have the necessary expertise to administer such complex systems (Giddens: 1990, p. 357). Nevertheless, we find that in earlier non-industrialized societies such as ancient Egypt, China, Persia, Byzantium and the like, where there were extensive, very powerful bureaucracies, the military still played a dominant role. And even in modern democracies, the military are hardly devoid of influence, and it is they and their oversees links who generate work in the lucrative armaments industries. The USA, for example, besides the untold billions of dollars in military expenditure for its own defence, is estimated to have provided some $90 million in military assistance elsewhere since 1945.

So why does war appear to be one of the ineradicable constants of world history? Rousseau made a break with the view that people are necessarily animal-like in nature, and therefore subject to uncontrollable passions. He argued that all humans were born in a 'natural condition' which was neither good or bad. It was society that shaped human life. Society influenced human development for both good and ill. It could be both a degrading and a moralizing agency. People are what society makes them. Like Plato, he believed that good polity makes men good, and that bad polity makes them bad. Not that people are totally malleable and incapable of resisting the influences of society but, in general, Rousseau takes up the position of many social theorists, that it is socialization that really counts.

People live in communities, therefore political organization becomes a critical factor. Rousseau thus found the main causes of war not in the nature of people, but in the nature of the state system itself (Rousseau: 1950). But whether such states go to war or not – and one might add, whether they become militaristic or not – depends very much on their relationship with other states. This very obvious point was made clearly by Thucydides in his brilliant analysis of the war between the militaristic states of Athens and Sparta (431–404 BC) which eventually drew in most of Greece.

If, therefore, war is made by states, and it is people that constitute states, what of the people? Are they – either directly or indirectly – the final arbiters of war and peace? The nineteenth-century writer and pacificist, Richard Cobden, maintained that the constant interest of the people is peace. And the late Dwight Eisenhower who was not only US President but also formerly Commander-in-Chief of the Allied Forces in the Second World War, expressed the same sentiment. Yet one has to set against this the mass demonstrations that have taken place in favour of war from the days of the ill-fated Athenian expedition to conquer Syracuse in 415 BC (Thucydides: 1972) to the voluble crowds in Berlin at the outset of the First World War in 1914. War has usually excited the interests of the people when there was something tangible to the gained.

A reiterative theme in much sociology has been the relationship between militarism, war and capitalism. Inevitably this involves some consideration of the Marxist thesis that the development of capitalism has caused the masses to become increasingly impoverished. This breeds tensions in the struggle for scarce resources, and thus we have one of the causes of war. This, however, must be reconciled with the additional thesis – also favoured by some Marxists – that war results from the competitive machinations of unscrupulous capitalists. Not that many capitalists are not unscrupulous, as are also many politicians – Marxist and democrat alike – but whether we can lay *all* the blame at their doors, is another question. Fundamentally, therefore, war is about two things: economics (*who* gets what) and power (*how* it is got and retained). This is something we will have to discuss further (Chapter 6) as it again implies that war and militarism arise due to extrinsic circumstances rather than intrinsic attitudes.

Race, too, is an issue which is much in the news with sociologists. This is something we have already considered (Chapter 2), but it is as well to emphasize at this point that there is no known correlation between militarism and ethnicity. Westerners were once prone to such expressions as the 'yellow peril', and the Nazis made much of the anticipated dangers of the 'Russian hordes'. Given the medieval experience, there may have been some basis for apprehension. But no doubt those in the East harboured similar fears about the depredations of Westerners, especially colonizers. Both 'cultures' at different times have exhibited warlike tendencies, but any causal connection between militarism and race would be impossible to prove.

Militarism will undoubtedly be seen by some as something that is antithetical to rationality. This issue has become particularly pertinent since we have entered the nuclear age. The 'bomb' with all its frightening implications has raised the fundamental question, can being prepared to launch a nuclear war possibly be a rational decision? Can even being willing to retaliate with such weapons in the event of a nuclear attack be a rational decision? In fact, is there any sense in which a nuclear strike is a viable option? (These are the types of matters raised by some social historians – see for example, Thompson and Smith: 1980.) Yet although this is a perfectly valid point, it can be argued that under certain conditions war can be seen as an apparently rational option, and a peace settlement as both unwise and dishonourable. If we take the Czech crisis in September 1938; the pressure by the Nazis could almost certainly have been resisted if the French (who had treaty obligations with the Czechs) and the British had resolved to present a united front to the Germans instead of capitulating so abjectly in the way they did at the Munich conference. Not only can war – especially defensive war – be rational, but a case could also be made for the rationality of militarism as well, particularly (as, for example, with early Rome) where one state either has to strive for hegemony *vis-à-vis* other states, or go under.

Case study: The Hundred Years War

What we loosely term the Middle Ages in Europe was characterized principally by the feudal system, a politico-social order founded on the tenure of feuds (or fiefs) given as compensation for military services. It was a contractual arrangement for services rendered by a hierarchy of subordinates and vassals from the king down to the most humble serfs who were rewarded with strips of land which they cultivated as rent and for their own livelihood. This estate system of stratification (in practice somewhere between a class and a caste system) allowed for minimal social mobility. The system was based upon economic rights which were 'frozen' (notably in France) in the sense that a lord could not prevent a vassal from passing a fief to an heir, but he could not pass it to anyone else. However, what was termed a benefice – most usually associated with the clergy rather than secular vassals – was not always hereditary. A lord could revoke a benefice or, if he chose, promote the benefice-holder, in much the same way that the king could appoint or depose members of the higher clergy. At the upper echelons of the system, therefore, the arrangement was that the nobility had an obligation – in theory, at least – to supply knights and foot soldiers when required in exchange for a generous benefice (involving income) or fief (involving status honour). Certainly this is how the system was supposed to work, but – as we shall see – this was an ideal which was often overlooked in practice. Oaths of fealty were not always binding. A powerful baron, for whatever reason, might actually refuse to support the Crown or even rebel if the occasion was deemed serious enough.

Medieval society was also characterized by marked decentralization and, in general terms, a weak monarchy. Much of the judicial and administrative authority was vested in a largely autonomous nobility which, in many cases, was bound by marriage ties – though, again, not always effectively. Kings, particularly, 'conquered' by encroachment. What they could not get by marriages of convenience which brought dowries and land titles, they sometimes appropriated by confiscation (say, of lands of an attainted vassal) or by building castles on open plain territories where there were indeterminate geographical boundaries. In this general absence of strong central government 'every man who had anything worth having, including his life, had to worry about whether he had strength enough to keep it, [thus] the powerless submitted to the powerful for Protection' (Johnson: 1965, p. 233). It also encouraged an increase in the power of the nobility whose ambitions were such that eventually the system degenerated into a fratricidal series of power struggles culminating in the Wars of the Roses. These were punctuated – indeed, aggravated – by the prolonged conflict between England and France which we call the Hundred Years War (1337–1453).

The causes of the war are not really in dispute although they can hardly be attributed to the break up of the marriage of Eleanor and Louis, king of France in the twelfth century, and her subsequent marriage to Henry II of England, as some writers have suggested (Harvey: 1972, p. 49). Put somewhat simplistically, there was status rivalry between England and France, or – more specifically – between their respective monarchs. This rivalry or hostility had its roots in the feudal system. The treaty of Paris in 1259 had left the English king in an ambiguous position. English territory in France – perhaps an anomaly in itself – was confined to a small area around the Channel port of Calais, from whence trade was carried on with Flanders, and, much more importantly, the extensive duchy of Aquitaine on the southwestern seaboard. The problem was that technically the English king was therefore a vassal of the king of France and had to do the necessary homage to his liege-lord. And this was not all. As time went on, the French, who understandably resented the English presence on what they felt to be their mainland, gradually nibbled away at their continental possessions until the English were left with little more than a coastal strip.

This was the position in 1307 when Edward II succeeded his father, the aggressive Edward I who had successfully asserted his claims in both Scotland and Wales. Wars are expensive, and Edward I left his son massive debts. Worst still, the new king was faced with the alternative of either trying to live up to his father's reputation and pursue a warlike policy which the monarchy could hardly afford and would only increase the power of his barons, or lose face and give the nobility an impression of weakness by taking a more conciliatory line. Temperamentally, he was no warrior. He did what he could to foster peace, but this merely gave rise to factious opposition from and among his nobles. His artistic pursuits, homosexual tendencies and apparent lack of interest in the day-to-day discipline of running the country soon alienated his nobles. Disenchanted by Edward's indifference, they began to apply considerable pressure for reforms to which the king agreed in principle (1310), but his ongoing infatuation with his favourite, Piers Gaveston, continued to unite the opposition led by his own cousin the Earl of Lancaster. The king's constitutional impotence was such that when the Earl of Warwick and others seized Gaveston and had him executed, Edward was not able to do anything about it.

Lancaster had five earldoms, and was probably the most powerful of the nobles. His support for the king was critical, so when he failed to rally to Edward's aid when the king set out to check Robert Bruce, who now ruled most of Scotland, the result was decisive. Robert Bruce was in the process of devastating England's northern counties, and when he defeated Edward's inadequate army at the battle of Bannockburn (1314), it further depleted the king's stock as far as his subjects were concerned. The Scots were now able to ravage the countryside almost at will, yet when the king was forced to give the command to protect the borders to Lancaster, the Earl proved that he too was not up to the task (1315). Later as chief councillor, he also proved a failure, and was eventually deprived of his authority.

Problems with the Scots continued when they invaded Ireland and further reduced English possessions there. But this was not all. Edward tried to build up a royalist faction, but some of the marcher lords to whom Edward I had given considerable power and licence on the Welsh borders also raised objections and joined the reinvigorated Lancaster and his supporters. The king mobilized what barons he could, and his army defeated the Lancaster forces in the battle of Boroughbridge in 1322. It did not pay to be on the wrong side in trials of strength of this kind. Lancaster and a number of the chief conspirators were executed, and others were imprisoned. Edward was thus able to dispense with some of the most dissident elements in the country, assert his authority and annul a number of the Ordinances to which he had previously been forced to give his assent. But, on the whole, the lords remained opposed to Edward's increasingly oppressive government, and – as yet – the merchant and artisan classes were not powerful enough to exert any appreciable influence on affairs.

At this time France was the refuge for a number of English exiles, and – coincidentally – it was to Paris that Queen Isabella, Edward's wife went on government business in 1325. She was sure of a welcome as the king, Charles IV, was her brother. A little later she sent for her son, the infant Edward of Windsor, ostensibly so that both could help to bring about the restoration of Gascony. But soon she met and became the mistress of Roger Mortimer, one of the marcher lords who had been imprisoned after the battle of Boroughbridge but had escaped two years later and made his way to France. Meanwhile, Edward suspected nothing, not even when a betrothal was arranged for his young son from which Isabella would receive a rich dowry which she and Mortimer then used to equip an army to dethrone her husband. Their forces arrived in England in 1326 whereupon the unpopular Edward was deserted by most of his lords. Members of his entourage were hunted down and killed, and he was forced to abdicate four months later (January 1327). His son was proclaimed king as Edward III with Isabella and Mortimer acting as unofficial regents. Effectively, they were the powers behind the throne. The former king was imprisoned and, because he was considered too dangerous to remain alive, he was murdered in Berkeley Castle (September 1327).

The regents had barely enjoyed a political honeymoon before Mortimer – regardless of baronial opinion – began to take full advantage of his position. He appropriated lands in Wales and Ireland where English authority was all but lost. The royal coffers were seriously depleted, so he was in no position to wage war in either Scotland or France, which actually added to his unpopularity. He even alienated those among the nobility who might well have become his allies, and in 1330 his rule was ended by the Lancasters in league with the young king whom – we are told – was disgusted by his mother's behaviour but who, more likely, was growing tired of his own subservience. The victorious faction wanted to wipe the slate clean, so Mortimer was executed, and Isabella was placed in the kind of captivity appropriate to her station. The 18-year-old Edward did not intend to commence his reign with a disquieting matricide.

The new king was an altogether different proposition from his predecessors. Indeed, he was quite unlike his own father, being popular with his barons – as far as one can assess – and acceptable with the people as a whole. One particular reason for his popularity was his intention to pursue a warlike policy with England's traditional enemies. Despite his limited resources, he was determined to deal with France especially. But neighbours came first, so his initial ventures were against the Scots who had remained unmolested for several years. He linked up with a number of disaffected Scottish nobles and won notable victories in 1332 and 1333, but experienced a series of setbacks and abandoned his Scottish campaign once he had decided that there was more to be gained in France. Thus began the Hundred Years War, the *casus belli* being the dispute over the English possessions in France. Not unjustly, the French did not take too kindly to English claims on what they felt was their territory regardless of the legacy of former monarchs. But it was unthinkable to the English that they should renounce these claims. And Edward III certainly had no intention of doing so.

War in the Middle Ages was very much a part of life. Indeed, the satirist may well have said that it was what taxation was all about. It was not the plague which civilized society now wishes to eradicate, but rather an accepted part of human existence. Not that everyone relished the prospect. It could be quite terrible for the vulnerable and defenceless. There is evidence, for instance, that Northumberland, Cumberland and Westmoreland were seriously wasted by the Scottish incursions in the reign of Edward II, and the ravages of the English soldiery in France in the reign of Edward III were a byword for horror. Where death did not come by the sword and the lance, it might well come indirectly from starvation. Plunder could leave people poverty-stricken for life, and mutilation was a fearful prospect where adequate medication was virtually unknown.

For the nobility and the knights it was another matter. For them, war was not so much normal as essential. It was a mark of manliness; it was a matter of honour, what the Greeks called 'arete' (often translated as virtue, but excellence would be nearer the mark). The chronicler Froissart in the fourteenth century said that 'prowess is so noble a virtue and of so great a recommendation that one must never pass over it too briefly ... the noble man cannot [bring] ... glory to the world without prowess' (quoted by Holmes: 1974, p. 72). War was combat, a knightly art – the applied version of the tournament. And all this was in addition to the wealth that could accrue from confiscation and the ransoms for prosperous captives. It was said of Edward III's son, the Black Prince, that he was 'never weary nor full satisfied of war'.

Knights, however, were only a small proportion of the fighting force. The core of the army was the infantry, especially Welsh bowmen who won a high reputation in the Hundred Years Was (the 6-ft longbow was a formidable weapon; it took considerable strength and skill to handle, but its range was its great virtue – its arrows could pierce chain mail in excess of a hundred yards). Medieval armies also sported mounted archers, a feature of some Middle Eastern armies where the similarly effective composite bow was used. During the Hundred Years War, Edward III made more use of professional mercenaries than any of his predecessors, and this made his expeditions enormously costly. Taxation was thus considerably increased, though it was always hoped that any losses would be recouped by plunder. Taxation was supposed to be 'by consent', especially those taxes raised from the Church. But unlike some earlier monarchs, Edward could hardly claim that his monies were needed for a Crusade, although he did try to give his wars an ideological gloss, and portrayed his campaigns more as missions than expeditions.

A further cause of the wars that ensued was English dependence on the wool trade. Officials and entrepreneurs in Flanders appealed to Edward to ease the pressure being applied to them by the king of France. It was not, therefore, difficult for him to build up a series of alliances there and in the Rhineland. The French king retaliated by supporting the Scots and by encouraging Norman crews to carry out what amounted to piratical raids on some of the English coastal towns. From this it was but a short step to open warfare, especially when the French confiscated the duchy of Aquitaine in 1337.

In the initial stages, the war was fought mainly in Flanders and Picardy, and Edward felt confident enough in 1339 to proclaim himself the rightful king of France. But although doing well at sea, Edward was not doing so well nearer home. The Scots were still a menace, and Edward attributed his lack of success in Flanders, where he led the army himself, to dissension in his own camp. However, once he had sorted matters out with his own barons, his fortunes began to pick up. A truce was called in 1340, but under what Edward felt to be provocation over rival claims to Brittany, he renounced the truce in 1345. The following year, the English won one of the great set battles of the war at Crecy against a much larger French army. It was one of the first battles in Europe in which cannon were used, and it was also the battle which established Edward's prestige as a general. The siege of Calais followed which took nearly a year; the inhabitants were expelled – a characteristically heartless act of so much warfare – and the town was repopulated by the English. Meanwhile, Edward's nobles (notably from the great Neville and Percy families of the North) had achieved important victories against the Scots, so Edward no longer had to fight a war on two fronts.

In 1348 came invasion from the Continent – not from the French but from black rats. These creatures carried what was almost certainly a highly infectious form of bubonic plague which had already killed huge numbers of people in Asia and in Europe. So, to add to England's troubles, the Black Death had arrived. The effects were devastating, especially in the urban areas. The epidemic did not abate until late 1349, but there were further outbreaks in the 1360s. The mortality figures are hard to assess, but there is a consensus among scholars that it probably killed about 30 per cent of the population. Yet regardless of the untold ravages and repercussions of the disease, the war carried on – admittedly in a more desultory way. But the lull could not last. In 1355, Edward again commenced hostilities from his bases in Normandy and on the west coast of France. This time, he was aided by the king of Navarre whose unenviable sobriquet, Charles the Bad, tells us something about current opinion at the time. Charles was the son-in-law of the king of France, but his unpopularity did not deter Edward who needed all the friends he could get.

It was during this renewal of the war that the English achieved some of their most resounding victories. Edward, the Black Prince, led an expedition from Bordeaux to France's Mediterranean coast, and this *chevauchée* was an outstanding success. The Black Prince 'won his spurs' at the battle of Crécy when only 16 years of age, but his fame – and notoriety – were enhanced by his subsequent campaigns when he cut a swathe of destruction through France. At the Battle of Poitiers in 1356, with a force of perhaps 12 000 men he defeated a French army three times larger than his own. The French king was captured (Edward wanted 3 million gold francs for his return), and he was able to get a small fortune from the sale of some of his other more affluent prisoners.

The Black Prince is an interesting study in himself. Some would see him as the archetypal militarist. The treaties which followed Poitiers recognized England's claims to Calais and Aquitaine (1360), and three years later the Black Prince became Prince of Aquitaine. He settled in his new domains as a feudal lord, but his rule was something of a disaster. He took the attitude that as conqueror, he had every right to exploit the situation. He maintained an extravagent lifestyle which could only be subsidized by heavy taxes. His lavishness and arrogance bred increasing dissent among his vassals which led inevitably to revolt. While he was away campaigning in Spain supporting the claims of the deposed ruler of Castile, Pedro the Cruel, his subjects took the opportunity to rebel. He had again been successfully campaigning in a very doubtful cause, and had won an impressive victory at Najera (1367) even though considerably outnumbered by the enemy. The losses in his army, composed of both French and English, were extremely low compared with those of his opponents, and this was considered one of his most outstanding feats of generalship. However, the revolt in Aquitaine was aided by the French king who was only too willing to take advantage of any disaffection with the English.

By this time, Edward had alienated so many people in his province that by 1369 hundreds of towns and castles declared against him. His mercenary army dwindled as his treasury diminished, and in his desperation he resorted to the tactics of the worst kind of militarist. His assaults became increasingly savage, culminating in the cruel sack of Limoges in 1370, the responsibility for which some writers would wish to absolve him (Harvey: 1972). The following year, he returned to England a sick and ruined man, and died five years later of 'dropsy' (which indicates severe heart disease). He is said to have been a literate and – in his own way – pious man, a lover of the arts and what we usually term the finer things of life. He apparently had considerable physical presence and, like so many of his kind, could be cruel and generous by turns (Windrow and Mason: 1997). This kind of dramatic inconsistency is one of the almost invariable marks of the despot (Carlton: 1995).

By the treaty of 1360, Edward III, in gaining Aquitaine and Calais, had renounced his claim to the French throne. In doing so, he should also have renounced any further hostilities. In theory, this ought to have been an end to the war. But the rejoicings were short-lived – the king was unable to retain what he had won. His mercenaries were unwilling to be demobilized, and when not enough was forthcoming from the ceded territories to pay them, they resorted to a form of quasi-official brigandage and brought further misery to those they were supposed to 'police'. The Castilian expedition, too, in 1367 made heavy financial demands on the people of Aquitaine who were subjected to additional taxation. All in all, it had been a hollow victory for the king. The discontentment in the province was such that the peace could not be maintained. In 1369, King Edward once again advanced his claim to be king of France, and the war started all over again.

The English recommenced their raids on French towns which were costly for both sides and largely futile for the aggressors. Neither side, it would appear, had either the stomach or resources for large-scale pitched battles. The French retaliated, especially after the destruction of Limoges, and by the time Edward III died in 1377, the English had little more than a foothold on a few coastal areas.

Now that both the king and his son were dead, disputation among a number of the English barons came to a head, and it was decided to make the Black Prince's 10-year-old son, Richard, the king of England. During the young king's minority, the government of the country was in the hands of a small council which represented the varying interests of the nobility. But it did not work very well because the factions found it impossible to reconcile their interests. In the meantime, the war with France dragged on. English coastal towns were ravaged, expeditions failed and the treasury was nearly exhausted. All in all it was hardly an exciting inheritance for the new king. Indeed, the only thing that really saved English interests in France was the fact that France also had a new boy king, Charles VI, and there, too, the barons fell out among themselves.

In England more taxes were imposed, and these fell so heavily upon the poor that by 1381 the peasants were in revolt. History tells us how the young Richard met their leaders and promised to look into their grievances, but not much is said about how he and his officials reneged on those promises, revoked their charters, and had the peasant leaders arrested and executed. Richard is reported to have said 'Villeins [serfs] you are and villeins you shall remain' (Myers: 1969, p. 30) and then to have justified his actions by saying in an inexplicably worldly wise way that promises exacted under duress counted for nothing. One suspects that the 14-year-old boy either had some particularly cynical advisers, or that he was beginning to display some of those indisputable traits that were to make him so unpopular later on.

The country became increasingly unwilling to finance a war that could not be won. The arguments were violently acrimonious and this dissension brought England to what was virtually civil war in 1387 when Richard's uncle, the Duke of Gloucester and others, raised an army which defeated the king's forces. A new Parliament was formed whose members rewarded themselves with various honours and appointments while many of Richard's chief supporters were either imprisoned, executed or fled abroad. The king himself was untouched, and soon he was back, wheeling and dealing, and generally confirming his authority with the new Parliament. He abandoned any continental ambitions and made a truce with France, much to the disapproval of some of his magnates. As a token of goodwill in 1396 he sealed the new arrangements by marrying Charles VI's daughter, Isabella, who was a mere 7-year-old child. Moreover, he gained the support of the Pope – or, at least, one of them (it was the time of the Great Schism in the Church) – despite the increasing anti-papal feeling in England. His 'pacifism', however, did not extend to the British Isles. He turned his attention to Ireland, then with a battle-hardened army he returned to England and dealt with his opponents among the aristocracy. This meant the current Parliament, and some of its closest supporters who were peremptorily executed or imprisoned.

Richard's calculated capriciousness won him few friends, and soon a number of his most powerful barons, notably the Duke of Lancaster and the Earl of Northumberland, conspired to seize the throne. His forces were defeated, and he was captured and imprisoned in the Tower of London, then later transferred to Pontefract Castle in Yorkshire. He still had supporters who tried to effect his release, but their efforts came to nothing. Yet again, a king who was considered too dangerous to be kept alive was quietly murdered (1400). His wife was packed off back to France – minus her dowry – and the new king, Henry IV (grandson of Edward III) could now safely resume the war with France.

Hostilities recommenced in a half-hearted fashion. Technically there was still a truce, nevertheless there were raids on towns on both sides of the Channel where piracy was rife. The Welsh under Owain Glyn Dwr were causing trouble, and the Scots aided by the French continued to be a source of aggravation. In France itself, hostilities were largely confined to the north. Henry did not seem to have any burning ambition to secure the French crown, and Aquitaine as a province was virtually neglected. But by 1411, the internal situation in France was such that the country was bordering on a state of civil war. This was an opportunity which was too good to miss. The English, in league with the Burgundians and the dukes of Bourbon and Orléans, decided to step up the pace a little, but in 1412 their forces led by Henry's son Clarence were surprisingly met by a united opposition. Clarence was bought off, and returned through Bordeaux with his army plundering as they went. By the time Henry died in 1413, power was already slipping from his hands.

The war with France entered an altogether different phase with the accession of Henry V. No sooner had he been crowned than he was making quite outrageous demands of the French. He wanted not only Aquitaine, but also Normandy, Maine, Anjou, Touraine and the extra concession made when Henry IV had been in alliance with the Burgundians and the recalcitrant French princes. For the new king, the icing on the cake was to be the hand of Catherine, the daughter of the French king and the sister of Isabella who had been ignominiously returned to her father years before. The French understandably baulked at this, and Henry V reduced his territorial demands and even said that he would be prepared to settle for a smaller dowry. But when the French again refused his conditions, Henry decided that the issue could only be decided by war.

In August 1415, an English army landed in Normandy and immediately set about besieging the town of Harfleur on the Seine which was regarded as impregnable. After six weeks' heavy bombardment by English cannon, the town capitulated and its officials appeared before the king appropriately clad in penitential shirts with ropes about their necks. Henry received the keys of the town and magnanimously spared it the customary medieval sacking. Encouraged by this, but against the advice of his commanders, he then decided to lead his army, already decimated by disease contracted in the salt marshes during the siege, on to Calais which was a week's march away. Almost outmanoeuvred by the French army which had been trailing him, he then turned the situation by winning one of the classic battles of late medieval history – Agincourt.

By 1415, knights had largely replaced their chain mail with plate armour. This meant that those who could afford the best – and the best came from Italy – were virtually impervious to serious injury (that is unless they were unhorsed). There was, too, the danger of suffocation or the forcing open of the visor and a dagger in the eye (Earle: 1975, p. 63). Knights on both sides were pretty evenly matched, but it was in the archery department that the English were markedly superior. And it was with this well-trained but depleted force weakened by famine and disease that Henry faced what is still described as 'the flower of French chivalry', though without its king or the Dauphin. He was greatly outnumbered and he sought terms, even offering to hand back Harfleur, but the French were not going to be denied the chance of smashing the interlopers. So he determined to fight – indeed, given the situation, he had very little choice. Against all the odds, it was an English victory against the overconfident French, and was largely due to superior tactics and staying power. In fact, it was all over in about half an hour, and what was once a cornfield became a killing ground. Those who survived were taken prisoner, but except for the French nobility who were to be ransomed, these men were slaughtered on Henry's orders by a special squad of 200 archers, ostensibly because the king thought that his men might still be in danger from a further attack. (Even the nobility did not fare well if they could not raise the ransoms; the Duke of Orléans spent 25 years in captivity for this very reason.) The massacre was a totally ruthless and, almost certainly, an unnecessary act, typical of a certain type of militarist, and often unmentioned by historians. Perhaps it has tended to be overlooked (as it was in Laurence Olivier's *Henry V*) because of the all-condoning image of a 'glorious victory'. Henry went on to further military success including the conquest – or reconquest – of Normandy. But 'In the meanwhile, England and her king were to live for many years on the reputation won on that autumn day' (Allmand: 1988, p. 28).

When Henry died in 1422, his son succeeded him as Henry VI. As the king of France, Charles VI, had also died, for a while an English king ruled both in Paris and in London. But not all France was in English hands, so the war continued especially in the southern half of the country. At first things went well, particularly under the aggressive leadership of the Duke of Bedford between 1422 and 1428. But after the fatal siege of Orléans when Joan of Arc rallied the French to increased resistance in 1429, English fortunes changed and from then onwards never really recovered. Joan was only 16, but she was able to give the French and the Dauphin new heart, and before her capture by the Burgundians the following year she did much to lead to the expulsion of the English. She was sold to the English who disregarded her youth and dismissed her 'voices' as evil delusions and burned her on the charge of heresy, an outrage which is still not forgotten.

From this time onwards, English prospects went from bad to worse. A treaty of sorts was made at Arras in 1435 under the auspices of the Pope at which the English delegates initially walked out. The French took advantage and their new king, Charles VII, was crowned in Paris in 1437 when the English moved out. Still the fighting went on, and by now allegiances had changed and the English were at war with the Burgundians as well as the French. Various expeditions were mounted by different English barons, especially the Earl of Warwick, but the French gradually encroached on lands which had previously been the special preserve of the English. It was time, therefore, for another attempt at a rapprochement, and a diplomatic marriage was arranged between Henry VI and Margaret of Anjou, the niece of Charles VII (1445). The truce lasted four years, and was broken by English mercenaries who gave the French an excuse to begin large-scale hostilities all over again. Despite the efforts of their war leaders, the English were now in disarray. Normandy was retaken, then Gascony and Bordeaux, and by 1453 the English had nothing except the town of Calais. Their defeat was probably as much to do with poor, uncoordinated leadership at home as with inefficient command on the battlefield. It is interesting to ask why the English militarists/nobility persisted in their often vain and fruitless attempts to secure that to which they had only very tenuous rights. Tracing their claims to the earlier Angevins was doubtful indeed – some might say, spurious – after all, almost anything can be justified by the judicious use of historical precedent.

Sociological theories obviously subsume such factors as economic and territorial considerations which we are going to discuss under separate headings together with different – and appropriate – case studies. What we have done in the present discussion is to concentrate on status issues, and try to show how these overlap with territorial and personality factors which are integral to any historical appreciation of militarism.

CHAPTER SIX

Militarism and the Territorial Imperative

The term 'territorial imperative' was coined by the American playwright and journalist, Robert Ardrey (1967) to denote the priority given by individuals and communities to the critical importance of territoriality as a determinant of human and animal behaviour. In this he may have anticipated some of the later writings of sociobiologists. He has been criticized by some social scientists who concede that such ideas may be relevant to ethologists in their studies of animal behaviour, but that it is highly speculative – even unwise – to extrapolate from these to the behaviour of humans. Again, we may be dealing with opposing schools who wish to see humans in a particular kind of way – *their* kind of way. Such is the proclivity of academics.

Territory itself may be generally defined as a geographical area under the formal jurisdiction or control of a recognized political authority. Though here it is important to distinguish between modern nation states where borders are strictly demarcated and highly administered, and the much more loosely defined and frequently contested frontiers of many pre-industrial empires. Anthony Giddens sees this as an exemplification of the much greater control of time and space possessed by modern governments. He proceeds – with perhaps unnecessary elaboration – to spell out how the spatial and temporal location of societies profoundly affects the outcomes of action in these societies. To this one can only add, 'of course'. It is just another way of saying that circumstances affect outcomes, and nowhere does this better apply than in the matter of militarism.

The idea that militarism and therefore war are functions of land hunger is extremely persuasive. The notion of economic expediency is something we will discuss in more detail (Chapter 7), but one interesting variant of the argument has been put forward by the sociologist, Stanislav Andreski, who maintains that war is all about 'ophelimites', i.e. desired things. This is well exemplified by the actions of notoriously predatory societies such as the Mongols, Tartars, etc., who appeared to make war for no better reason than what they could get. Andreski repudiates certain forms of the 'hidden variables' argument. He is particularly impatient with psychological explanations, and insists that the causes of conflict are reducible to struggles for land, food, women and power; in short, to demographic-economic imperatives (Andreski: 1968). His 'common-sense' contention is that struggle is omnipresent because resources are perennially scarce. Therefore, war has a functional importance in ensuring the necessary balance of wealth over population.

It is probably true to say that most military conquests involve at least an element of land hunger. It has long been a practice for conquerors to take possession of lands that are not their own and use them for their own purposes. This may be compared with the more 'liberal' and thus undemanding variant practised by the Romans and the British in their days of colonization, of allowing the subjugated people to retain possession of their lands providing they made the necessary contributions to the controlling power, usually in the form of tribute, taxes or favourable trading concessions.

Land hunger may be said to arise from a number of economic or other circumstances. It is therefore assumed that many of the great mass migrations which we know took place in pre-modern times, and which were sometimes accompanied by military conquest, were occasioned by such crises as drought and famine. Though it must be stressed that there is little hard evidence for this assumption. Indeed, it has been argued by some (e.g. LaPiere: 1954), that the land-hunger theory of war is a myth. It is further argued that demographic explanations are, at best, unprovable, and that conceptions of underpopulation and overpopulation are simply social evaluations and are therefore relative to particular situations. As exemplification of this counter-thesis it is pointed out that history is replete with examples of societies that have lived for ages at near subsistence level without resorting to war with their neighbours. Furthermore, there are other instances of peoples, especially European peoples, who have sought out and confiscated others' territories even though there was no pressing need to do so. There is ample evidence that in extreme cases when a technologically superior people subjugates a technologically inferior people, as happened with the European colonization of the Americas, the result is sometimes extermination. But this is not 'ultimately inevitable' (LaPiere: 1954, p. 451) as may be witnessed by, say, the British in India.

Schism and fragmentation as the result of internal conflicts can also be a reason for some groups within a society to break with the parent body and seek lands of their own. This can often happen where there is a strong, centralized – and repressive – administration. This is not confined to advanced societies, as can be seen in the early nineteenth-century Transvaal when the Matabele under Mzilikazi broke away from their fellow Zulus ruled by the tyrannical Shaka. The irony was that they then became as bloodthirsty and predatory in what is now Zimbabwe as the Zulus were further south (Becker: 1979). Perhaps the tendency towards dissolution and rebellion are endemic in societies of this kind, given their histories of violence and disorder (Parsons: 1966).

Robert Ardrey has argued that it is a 'law of nature that territorial animals – whether individual or social – live in eternal hostility with their territorial neighbours' (Ardrey: 1963, p. 171). He further maintains that the only real difference between creatures and 'civilized man' is that wrought by the demands of living in civilized society and cannot be attributed to his inherently genial nature. This is what Ardrey terms the 'romantic fallacy'. In short, society demands an exercise of quid pro quo; whether they like it or not people must make compromises in order to live with each other. This may prove difficult and irksome, but in both personal and social relations it is the only way to achieve some kind of harmony.

It almost goes without saying that the territorial instinct – if such it can be called – applies to defensive as well as offensive warfare. Perhaps even more so. When the determined proprietor of a particular territory is challenged by the predatory ambitions of an aggressor, the defensive instinct becomes paramount. What has been called the 'lonely, irrational heroism' of Britain in 1940, generated a will and tenacity that superseded what some observers felt to be down-to-earth common sense. If anything, defenders can be more highly motivated than aggressors. But aggressors – if resisted – can prove to be more ruthless in their revenge if and when they eventually overcome that resistance. There is often no special respect for the stubborn heroism of the defenders. In past campaigns, when the city fell, this was almost inevitably followed by carnage and destruction; witness, for example, the devastation wrought by Alexander the Great at Tyre and Gaza for delaying his Persian campaign.

People are bound to territories for all manner of reasons apart from crude economic interest. Territoriality becomes coterminus with the community, and members find attachment to places in terms of a variety of often intangible sentiments, not least religion which involved the custodianship of sacred places. (We have already seen how the Greek cults were associated with Delphi, Eleusis and so forth.) Historically, the distinctive nature of a society found expression in religion, and ritual symbolized and legitimated the collective identity of a society. So leaders – particularly military leaders – made appeals to their tutelary deities before campaigns in order that they might prove victorious. Ostensibly, this was also to show their enemies the superiority of their gods. Consequently, if successful, they might allow the inferior gods into their probably already overcrowded pantheon (the Romans, for example, were usually very liberal about this). But if they failed, it was not uncommon to think that their gods had deserted them both personally and territorially.

The importance of the territorial factor can perhaps best be demonstrated by looking at two pre-modern societies. The first of these was a byword in Classical times for its migratory movements, and the dangerous pressure it applied to both Greece and Rome. The threat posed by the great waves of Gauls (Celts) from Northern Europe were probably as feared as the Viking invasions of Britain, Ireland and elsewhere in later years. They were seemingly irrepressible, and had either to be bought off or countered by considerable military force.

Case study 1

The Romans divided Gaul into two regions: Transalpine Gaul, the area bounded by the Alps, Pyrenees and the Rhine, which was settled by Celtic tribes about 1500 BC; and Cisalpine Gaul, effectively Northern Italy, which was not settled until about 500 BC. It was from these areas that these tribes began to present a danger to both Greece and Rome. The warriors themselves are only known to us through the writings of their enemies who depicted them as savage and illiterate. They did have a distinctive culture of their own, but near contemporary accounts portray them as being overawed by the riches and achievements of Graeco-Roman civilization. They were admired for their courage in battle, but this was seen as being no match for the skill and discipline of trained soldiers. The famous Roman marble sculpture known as *The Dying Gaul* which now resides in the Capitoline Museum in Rome, says it all. This is almost certainly a copy of one of a group of figures originally commissioned by Attalus of Pergamum (Asia Minor) after his defeat of the Gauls in 290 BC. Here we see a powerful barbarian warrior in his dying throes, accurately symbolizing an inferior people overwhelmed by a higher civilization.

The Celtic people, of whom the Gauls were one branch, were the first of what might be termed the prehistoric peoples north of the Alps who were known to the Classical Mediterranean societies. Their tribal institutions which were pretty much held in common, gave the Celts a certain semblance of unity, and this together with the fact that they occupied reasonably well-defined territories gave them a kind of national character. True they were seen by the Greeks and Romans as barbarians, but nevertheless it was recognized that they possessed considerable military strength. They were apparently noted for their cleanliness and physique and 'terrifying aspect'. The Romans referred to the Gauls as 'lofty of stature, fair and of ruddy complexion ... very quarrelsome, and of great pride and insolence' – and of their women as being equally impressive (Ammianus Marcellinus quoted by Chadwick: 1970, p. 50). They were particularly feared as headhunters (though this was practised by a number of early peoples). The human head figured prominently in the Gauls' art and religion; their sanctuaries were often decorated with severed heads – a nicety which struck their southern enemies as both ghoulish and uncivilized. Posidonius, who had encountered the practice, is reported by the geographer/historian Strabo as having written of 'that custom, barbarous and exotic which attends most of the northern tribes ... when they depart from battle they hang the heads of their enemies from the necks of their horses, and when they have brought them home, nail the spectacle to the entrance of their houses' (ibid., p. 49).

The Celtic tribes were certainly on the move in Europe by the seventh century BC, and by c. 450 BC were in Gaul and in Spain. It is not clear whether their motive was land hunger or simply plunder, and in this they were not always on good terms among themselves. Whatever, they occupied much of central Europe, and by the early fourth century BC they were ready to take on the peoples south of the Alps. Other groups, the Teutones (possibly of Celtic extraction) took much of what we now know as Germany, and the Helvetii were forced to leave their lands adjacent to the Rhine, and eventually settled – somewhat uneasily – in Switzerland.

The territory known to the Romans as Gaul was actually occupied predominantly by three different tribal groups, the Galli (Gauls) themselves, the Aquitani to the south and the Belgae to the north, although they were often referred to collectively as Gauls. These tribes had obviously assimilated over time with the earlier indigenes, and there were also admixtures of other ethnic groups such as the Iberians and Ligurians who, in their own way, were equally as fearsome as the Gauls. Classical writers, especially Julius Caesar, suggest that the Gauls were structured around the civitas, a political entity which seems to have been roughly analogous to a Greek city state (polis) and included not only the 'city' proper but also the territory surrounding it. These larger groupings had their own name (e.g. modern Paris was once the capital of the Parisi). Often, too, they had their own fortified centres and originally their own kings (later to be largely replaced by magistrates). It was the factional strife which existed among these different groupings which eventually led to their conquest by Caesar in the first century BC.

Had it not been for this ongoing disunity, the Gallic resistance might well have been more successful.

Gallic society was organized into five principal divisions (the term 'classes' here might be slightly misleading), the king and the royal family, and what Caesar called the druides, equites and the plebs, and – characteristically – the slaves. The equites included the warrior aristocracy and what we might call the intelligentsia, i.e. those broadly involved in the cultivation of the arts including the bards who were highly esteemed for their eloquence and entertainment value. It also included those accorded the status of artisans, designers and craftsmen. The plebs were the commoners – freemen who comprised the largest mass of the population. And then there were the slaves of whom little is known but who one supposes were either war captives or debtors. The druids (druides) are largely associated in the popular mind with Celtic religion, but they were more than priests in the usual sense of that term. They were also the educators in Celtic society, though admittedly of the upper strata. The religious aspect of their teaching still remains somewhat obscure because it was part of the druidic stock-in-trade to retain a strong esoteric element of which only they had knowledge. One feature which Caesar brought to light was their firm belief in the survival of the soul – a doctrine which is thought to have helped their warriors to overcome the fear of death. Hence, it is supposed, their practice of charging their enemies en masse regardless of the consequences – sometimes, as Polybius suggests, wearing nothing but their neck ornaments, perhaps because they believed that they brought supernatural protection.

Popular religion seems to have centred around various nature deities, and was celebrated largely in open-air sanctuaries. These were often secluded groves, and according to Roman sources, it was there that Gauls practised 'savage rites' involving 'hideous offerings', presumably connected with the cult of the human head – something which figures prominently on many of their extant artefacts and monuments. Religion and warfare obviously went together. Like the much later Aztecs of medieval Mexico, one of the important functions of warfare was to secure captives to sacrifice to their gods. Some modern authorities try to play down the violent nature of Gallic society (e.g. Chadwick: 1970), but there is little doubt that warfare and all its possible advantages were important to the nation's aristocracy. Indeed, Strabo suggested that the whole nation was 'war mad' and always ready for battle. The exploits – fictionalized or otherwise – of such characters as Boudicca and Cartimandua in England, and Maeve in Ireland, together with stories of women warriors in Gaul, suggest that women may also have enjoyed military status along with their male counterparts. However, as in many other early societies, there is a certain ambivalence about the fair sex. Evil women, especially witches, are commonly found as agents of misfortune in some of the Celtic sagas.

We first hear of the Gauls in relation to classical society when they made incursions into Italy *c.* 400 BC. At this time Rome was one of the many states vying for ascendancy in the seemingly continuous wars between the Italic and Latin tribes who were seeking hegemony now that the once powerful Etruscans to the north were no loner capable of exerting the influence they had a century before. The Romans further humiliated the Etruscans when they blockaded and took their important city of Veii which they then destroyed in addition to enslaving the population. The Romans really did believe in starting as they meant to continue.

These wars were almost certainly precipitated by a combination of conflicting commercial interests and the land hunger of the hill tribes who were seeking the better agricultural land of their neighbours. But the Gallic invasions were something else. The Gauls from central Europe emerged over the Brenner Pass and into the Italian valleys, probably pressed by Germanic tribes from further north. En route, the Gauls first made short work of the now somewhat enfeebled Etruscans and occupied the area later known as Cisalpine Gaul. As we have seen, they were a formidable foe. Bigger and physically stronger than the Romans, their tribes (possibly eight in all at this time) were often at enmity with one another, and this was not uncommonly occasioned by quarrels between their respective chieftans. Ancient writers (especially Livy) speak of their vices as drunkenness and a love of strife, and their virtues as exquisite metal working and a gift for oratory – often a characteristic of non-literate peoples.

To some extent, the Romans were prepared for them. They had developed a system of payment for troops which meant that they were able to keep their citizen soldiers in arms throughout the year, if necessary. By contrast, the Gauls were hardly professional. They carried long two-sided slashing swords made of soft iron which easily blunted and sometimes actually bent. For defence, they only had small wicker shields and normally wore no helmets. In offence they tended to charge as undisciplined mobs, greedy for plunder and anxious to get it all over with as soon as possible. Yet although the Romans had honed their skills as regular soldiers, the sheer recklessness and ferocity of the Gauls either on foot or in their two-wheeled chariots were enough to inspire fear even in veterans of proven quality.

There is a tendency on the part of some writers to romanticize – even idealize – Celtic life and values. The women were blessed with 'long, golden tresses', and the men were 'tall, blond and blue-eyed' fearless and noble in battle (Ross: 1970). One suspects a read-back method here. This kind of adulation hints at an atavistic tendency to see people as you wish to see them, carefree girls and clean heroic warriors living in a never-never land. It hardly ties up with the bloodthirsty, headhunting marauders who appeared over the Apennines and besieged towns in northern Italy. Roman ambassadors arrived to persuade – even implore – them to leave and return to their homelands, but this incensed the invaders even more and they marched on Rome itself. The two armies met near the Allia, a small tributary of the Tiber. We have little idea of the size or composition of the respective forces, but we do know that the Romans, quite unused to the screaming masses of Gauls, were unnerved and overwhelmed. The rout left large numbers of Romans dead, and the survivors fled to some of the already ruined cities for refuge. The Gauls entered Rome (390 BC) which had only a small garrison and no effective city wall, and sacked it but were unable to take the Capitol (they tried, but legend has it that the people were alerted by the honking geese of Juno). Fortunately, the citizens had already evacuated the city and fled to neighbouring towns, otherwise the carnage would have been far worse. The invaders stayed for seven months, but obviously had no intention of settling there. When they heard that their own settlements were being overrun by rival tribes and that a new Roman army was being formed to oust them, they decided to accept a bribe of 1 000 pounds of gold and returned home. Rome was rebuilt and within 12 years a new wall was erected, and this time it was provided with increased – though still inadequate – fortifications (Boak and Sinnigen: 1965).

Some writers maintain that the sacking of Rome changed nothing. This is not to minimize the destruction of the city, but there is some evidence for its 'fundamental irrelevance' because it had a negligible effect on the expansion of Roman power (Crawford: 1978, p. 39). Nevertheless, this did not prevent further Gallic incursions 30 years later when they penetrated as far south as the Alban Hills. But this time the Romans, fearing another humiliation, stayed safely within their walls. The third invasion in 349 BC saw the Romans much better prepared. They and their allies took the initiative and successfully blocked the onslaught of the Gauls who then retreated, being uncharacteristically unwilling to risk a battle. Perhaps this time they were outnumbered. Rome was now seen as the champion of the Italian peoples, and eventually (331 BC) came to an understanding with some of the Gallic tribes and concluded a peace which lasted for the remainder of the fourth century BC.

In the late third century BC, the Romans learned that the Gauls were massing for a further invasion, and had invited some more northern tribes to join them. But their army of some 70 000 men was completely overwhelmed by Roman forces many times that number – if true, a huge army for those times. We are told that the Romans annihilated the Gauls, killing 40 000 and taking 10 000 prisoners. This was quite an achievement considering that Rome was also engaged in a war with Carthage. There were further Gallic wars between 210 and 191 BC in which the Gauls were again eventually defeated. Rome really had to be thankful that they did not join the Carthaginians as their leader, Hannibal, had wanted.

We next hear of Rome's military exploits against the Gauls when Julius Caesar and his legions – hardly suffering the pangs of land hunger – invaded their territories in the first century BC. This campaign which lasted several years (58–51 BC) was marked by considerable heroism and brutality on both sides. In his account, Caesar (1951) may well have exaggerated the death and devastation his legions wrought, mainly to impress the Roman Senate at home. But if the figures are at all accurate, the cost was horrific (Caesar says in his Commentaries that on one occasion he turned his legions on masses of refugees and killed 430 000 of them). Caesar's invasion was not entirely gratuitous. As we have seen, the migratory tribes on Rome's borders were always a potential menace. But personal ambition and aggrandizement seem never to have been far from Caesar's mind, as indeed was his sheer love of campaigning. The Gauls and the Germans fought with a kind of uncoordinated desperation, but even their famed cavalry could not match the practised skill of the legions. Thousands of tribespeople who were not killed either died of wounds or starvation, or were sold into slavery (350 000 among the Belgian tribe of the Aduataci alone). The resistance of the Gauls was finally broken in 52 BC with the failed revolt of the Aveni tribe and the capture of their leader, Vercingetorix who was imprisoned for six years, then paraded in Caesar's Triumph with other captives, and then executed. It does leave posterity wondering who exactly were the barbarians.

Case study 2

The Gauls (Latin, Galli) or Celts (Gk, keltai) had been known to the Greeks from at least the fifth century BC when some of them were employed as mercenaries in various armies, especially those of Dionysios of Syracuse. He sent Celtic cavalry to aid the Spartans in a war against

Thebes, and the soldier/writer, Xenophon, was extremely impressed by their performance both there and in the later Greek wars in the 360s BC. But the most significant episode concerning the Gauls/Celts and the Greeks started with a raiding expedition in 279 BC which developed into a full-scale war. The tribes poured out of their homelands in the north and pillaged Thrace and Macedonia. Their numbers grew with success until under their chieftan, Brennus, they embarked on a large-scale invasion of Greece itself.

The Greek states, rarely known for their national spirit, decided that the threat was too great to ignore. If they could not achieve some kind of temporary unity, the invaders would pick them off one by one. Their combined armies met the Gauls at the pass of Thermopylae (famous for the stand of the Spartans and their allies against the Persians almost exactly 200 years before). They had already heard of Gallic atrocities as their hordes swept through Thessaly, so they knew that they had a real fight on their hands. They tried a delaying action by destroying certain strategic bridges to hinder the Gallic advance, but Brennus forced local inhabitants to rebuild them and, in gratitude, plundered their lands. The Athenian contingent tried a flanking movement, but with only limited success. There was then a lull in the fighting during which time Brennus – so we are told – suborned some Greek peasants who led the invaders over a mountain pass to surprise and cut off the Greeks – much as had happened all those years ago. Most Greeks managed to extricate themselves from the situation and retreated to the south, but this inevitably opened the way for the Gauls to enter the Greek heartland. From now on the Gauls moved quickly. The prizes Brennus had particularly in mind were the riches at the sanctuary at Delphi, one of the most sacred of Greek religious centres. Normally the Gauls were hesitant about violating temples; they had a superstitious awe about ravaging certain holy places. But the treasures of Delphi were too much to ignore. Yet even with the sanctuary lying helpless before them, they paused. Pausanius, writing in the second century AD, says that there was a minor earthquake and consequent rockfalls, as well as a storm. It seemed as though the Greek gods – and especially Apollo, the god of the sanctuary – had acted to defend the holy place. Not only that, but the very real physical presence of the Greek army appeared and launched a devastating night attack on the Gauls which caused them to retreat, after which Brennus took his own life.

There are some discrepancies in the accounts of what actually took place (Newark: 1986). It may be that in 279 BC (an agreed date) the Gauls as part of a general migration did approach Delphi and were defeated by the Aetolian army, but only after the Gauls had butchered the inhabitants of an Aetolian village (Walbank: 1981, p. 59). On the other hand, perhaps it was an attack in force by Galatians (as the Greeks called the eastern Celts) who 'had set out originally in quest of new lands for settlement – for which purpose they brought their families with them – [but] during their wanderings they developed habits of plunder and blackmail' (Cary: 1972, p. 59). It may be, too, that the invaders actually did enter the sanctuary (though there is no mention of harm to the priests or the Pythia herself) but were prevented from plundering it systematically.

Concurrently with Brennus' invasion of Greece, another migration was taking place through Thrace (278 BC) which divided its forces into a colonizing group and another which pushed on across the Dardanelles and the Bosphorus into Asia Minor. Here they continued their marauding expeditions, although from time to time they were hired by one or another of the petty kings as mercenaries in their local wars. The coastal Greek city states, still – by and large – unwilling to sink their differences, were ideal targets for the Galatians who also had their revenge for the Delphi debacle by looting the temple of Apollo at Didyma near Miletus. Then they were halted by another of those Greeks who traced his line back to Alexander's warring successors. Antiochus forced the Galatians to retreat to Phrygia where some groups eventually decided to settle. But others of them were still restless, and it was not until they were defeated by the rising power of Pergamum in Asia Minor that one could say that their great days were finally over.

It may well be that this assessment of Gallic/Celtic expansion is something like correct. Perhaps the initial impetus was to seek new lands because they, in turn, were being pressed by other – perhaps more powerful – tribes from the north. We know that they were not only having trouble between themselves which may have caused some groups to move on, but that Belgic and particularly Teutonic peoples were also thrusting southwards. We really know so little about these vast migratory movements in the ancient world, but we do know that they had crucial 'knock-on' effects which caused wholesale disruption in their wake. The very fact that the Gauls/Celts moved as tribes and clans, including women and children, strongly suggests that their expansion was not of a straightforward military nature. But although this expansion began as a series of migrations, the evidence is fairly clear that in time it took on an increasingly militaristic character.

It is interesting, therefore, to compare the Gallic/Celtic experience with those of other, rather earlier, peoples who were also on the move, though in a somewhat different sense. In this case we are thinking about the early Greeks and their colonizing activities throughout the Aegean, in the Mediterranean, and even as far afield as the lands bordering the Black Sea. Here there was a mixture of motives. Land hunger was one; some states just could not sustain an increasing population, and in a number of cases emigration became compulsory. Also there was a spirit of adventure. In those days of precarious sea travel, ordinary people did not know very much about what lay overseas. No doubt many felt that in founding new settlements abroad, they were going to embark on a whole new and exciting future.

But what of the indigenes? Most of these colonies were to be set up in territories that were already occupied. In these circumstances, the migrants usually tried to come to terms with the 'natives' who were often not as culturally advanced as the would-be colonists. But the indigenes were often understandably reluctant to give up any of their lands. So if persuasion or bribery did not work – and it frequently did not – they were elbowed out and the colonists took over, a situation which often made for further conflict.

We are not exactly sure when these colonization movements began. It may well be that the ancient story of Jason and the Golden Fleece contains vestigial elements of an actual expedition to Colchis on the far shores of the Black Sea. If so, this would suggest exploratory journeys that went back to at least 1000 BC. Certainly by the eighth century, or even a little earlier, colonizing ventures were under way, and it is no exaggeration to say that by the sixth century some hundreds of such expeditions had taken place – not all of them, of course, wholly successful. These colonizing movements were rarely joint affairs. The separate city states sent out their own expeditions, and once a colony was founded it remained in touch – or was supposed to remain in touch – with its mother city. Not infrequently established colonies founded their own colonies, and sometimes relations between 'mother' and 'daughter' (or 'mother' and 'granddaughter') were not that amicable. This was very much the case, for example, with Kerkyra (Corcyra or Corfu) which was founded by settlers from Corinth.

We can probably assume that the primary impetus behind these movements was demographic pressure, and all that this entails. Our certain knowledge of the Greek 'Dark Ages' (i.e. between *c.* 1100 and *c.* 700) is somewhat meagre, but it is inferred that it was a period of relative peace with a consequent increase in population. We learn, however, from Hesiod and from the Athenian political leader, Solon, that there was widespread economic deprivation which inevitably gave rise to political conflict (stasis). Also a tradition of sharing land between some resulted in an increase in uneconomic plots which led to poverty and debt (where there is a system of primogeniture with the eldest son only inheriting the land, the end result is much the same – at least, the rest of the children go without and consequently leave in order to find their fortunes elsewhere). In short, the shortage of arable land and what it could produce, and the relative lack of development of even the most rudimentary industry fostered the idea – in some instances, the compulsion – to seek out new lands. There were, of course, other precipitating factors, not least, invasion by enemy states, but this was something of a rarity. Defeat in one of the interminable internecine wars between Greek states did not usually result in occupation. What was probably more pertinent was colonization that was consequent upon initial exploration, possibly in search of metals or markets – the Greeks were quite adept at establishing trading centres (emporia) at suitable sites, e.g. Marseilles (Gk, Massilia) began this way. It is interesting that some seafarers could be both traders *and* pirates – as the opportunity arose.

The most active colonists at this time were from Chalcidike, who, the evidence suggests, were definitely motivated by land hunger. In the eighth century, Greek attempts to settle in Asia Minor were both facilitated and hampered by the breakdown of some of the petty kingdoms in that area. This let the Greeks in, as it were, but at the same time they were menaced by the dominant power of the Assyrian Empire which also pressed for control of cities on the Mediterranean seaboard. It is perhaps because of this that according to tradition the first Greek colonies were set up in the West in southern Italy from *c.* 775 BC. From there the Greeks ventured to Sicily where the Corinthians founded Syracuse after having first driven out other Greeks who had got there before them. It may well be that it was the Greeks who brought a form of the alphabet to Italy (which, as far as we know, originated among the Semitic Phoenicians) where it passed from the Etruscans to the Romans.

The Greeks expanded in Italy where they founded a number of prosperous cities. They also established several cities on the coast of Sicily, and it was here that they encountered another perennial problem, they had to share the territory – in this case, the island – with another formidable power, the Phoenicians, with whom they achieved an on–off modus vivendi. When the Greeks established their colonies in Sicily, the indigenes whom the intruders regarded as barbarians, either fled into the interior or remained on what had become Greek territory and were reduced to the status of serfs. The Phoenicians, who had settled there earlier than the Greeks, occupied the western part of the island from where they were in touch with their other settlements in Sardinia and the Balearic Islands, and not least their powerful sister community at Carthage on the North African coast (modern Tunisia). They were a powerful presence as far as the Greeks were concerned, a people that the incomers dared not push around as was their wont in other situations.

While other venturesome Greek states were sending out their colonists, Sparta which was developing into a powerful state militarily (though regarded by many Greeks as backward in other respects), decided to solve its population problem in other ways. Sparta had a virtually unique system for selecting and training its young men. Infanticide was practised, especially where children were regarded as weak and sickly – though, in fairness, it should be pointed out that infanticide was certainly not peculiar to the Spartans (the Greek geographer, Strabo, on visiting Egypt, was surprised that they reared all their children). But more pertinent to our discussion, we find that apart from one colony, Taras (Tarento) they had no settlements in the west, but instead decided that there were easier pickings nearer home. They invaded and took possession of the neighbouring state of Messenia which took many years to subdue, and reduced the population to serfs (helotes).

The colonizing efforts of the Greeks were far more adventurous in the north (Thrace) and in the east, that is the Hellespont and the Propontis. Much of this was the work of Aeolian and Ionian Greeks, though – surprisingly – little was done by way of colonizing by the Athenians who may have been one of the cities least affected by the depredations preceding the 'Dark Ages'. A few colonies were established on the North African coast, and it is from here that we have a particularly interesting extant inscription concerning the city of Cyrene which more than hints at the degree of desperation which must have obtained on the somewhat barren island of Thera. This 'State of the Founders' which apparently relates to the original founders from the island of Thera, says that their Assembly had agreed that colonists should be prepared to give the experiment five years, and if they could not make a go of things they could return to Thera and continue to enjoy full citizenship. However, it makes clear that colonists should be *free*men, and that

> one son be conscripted from each family (and) that those who sail should be in the prime of life ... But he who is unwilling to sail when the city sends him shall be liable to punishment by death and his goods shall be confiscated. And he who receives or protects another, even if it be a father his son or a brother his brother, shall suffer the same penalty as the man unwilling to sail.
> (Quoted by Fine: 1983, p. 89).

It seems reasonably clear from this and other evidence that certain states needed, for whatever reason, to reduce their populations. They probably first called for volunteers, and if these were insufficient then compulsion was introduced. The expeditions set out, presumably with the blessing of the gods, and once the colony was successfully established and allotments of land (kleroi) made, these original inhabitants became the founders of the colony's future aristocracy. These colonies were then regarded as independent entities (Gk, apochiai = away homes), no longer under the jurisdiction of their mother cities, although they usually retained their traditional political and social institutions. The links were supposed to remain close; at least, this was the ideal, but it was not always followed out in practice. It was a bold and imaginative undertaking – probably born of necessity – but it was a loosely organized programme of expansion that often meant the repression of others.

CHAPTER SEVEN

Militarism: The Economic Factor

Probably all wars, especially 'successful' wars, have an economic dimension. Economic necessity – whether culturally determined or not – is probably the commonest motivation for war. It follows, therefore, that it may also be an important generating factor in the use of militarism in any one society. Whereas many peoples have learned to maintain themselves by productive labour, and supplemented this by trading and exporting goods, others have lived by the forceful appropriation of others' lands and property. And this parasitic activity can actually come to be regarded as the 'right' of militarily superior people. Confiscation has been the 'trade' of bandits and pirates at one end of the spectrum to military conquerors at the other. Indeed, military conquest can be seen as a kind of institutionalized banditry. For over a thousand years the people of Sicily supplemented the produce of their island by preying on unwary merchant vessels, and it became effectively their way of life. The ravages of predatory peoples such as the Ottoman Turks or the Norsemen were much the same thing, though on a grander and more devastating scale.

Economic theory has long toyed with the ideal-type conception of the 'economic man', i.e. the rational individual who is assumed to seek to maximize his returns (satisfaction, utility or profit) from economic activity. In reality, of course, this achievement of economic aims is not always possible or even desirable. But this does not mean that the model is based on unreasonable assumptions. Actually, it is indirectly related to the economic interpretation of history, a theory – or set of theories – closely associated with Marxism. This view assumed the perennial economic determinism of social forms, although some versions of the theory do allow for humanistic and voluntaristic agencies in the whole process of social change. For some theorists this idea constitutes a method rather than a finished theory, although the emphasis is still on the primacy of economic factors in any kind of historical explanations (Jary and Jary: 1991). However, for the fundamentalist Marxist, the idea of historical materialism, the key to which is the mode of production (including the forces and relations of production) is regarded as the primary determinant of human behaviour and therefore plays a constitutive role in human consciousness in producing and reproducing social life.

Many studies of war and militarism stress, too, the role of political factors, but recognize that underlying the political issues are conflicts of economic interest. One extreme form, found in the Soviet analysis of war emphasized the 'fact' that war had its roots in the division of society into economic classes, and that violence – or the threat of violence – was one way in which one class was able to impose its will on another. An early variant of the economic factor view was that because wars were fought for economic reasons, war in an industrial age could not be profitable, and should therefore be outlawed (Angell: 1910) – a view that would hardly be endorsed by those who definitely made money from the two World Wars.

We can summarize the main versions of the economic factor thesis as follows:

1. At the intrastate level, wars/revolutions within societies come about because of conflicting economic interests. Witness the seemingly interminable struggles between demos and aristoi in many of the early Greek city states.
2. Wars between states are sometimes little more than a diversion in so far as they direct people's attention away from internal economic/domestic problems and concentrate on the 'bigger issue'. The ongoing tension between Cuba and the USA may, in part, be fostered by the Cuban government in order to take citizens' minds off the effects of their failing economy.
3. Interstate conflicts arise because powerful economic groups profit from armament production and the like. That certain industries can flourish in such circumstances is without question. But the idea that war is really a matter of this nation's industrial output versus that nation's output, though cogent in certain circumstances (for example, the burgeoning US industrial capacity to produce aircraft and tanks compared with that of Germany in the Second World War) tends to discount a range of other factors.

War is a very complex phenomenon which has many dimensions and many causes. Economic motives are very important, but they are not the only reasons for war or for the generation of the military ethos. Raymond Aron argues that wars must be analysed 'in the forms in which history presents them' (Aron: 1965, p. 201). After all, there are colonial wars, religious wars, tribal wars, national wars and so forth. And there are the relevant theories to go with them, not least the view that war and militarism are really about the establishment and perpetration of power. But, it could be argued that power cannot be maintained unless there is the economic wherewithal to sustain it.

Case study

There are so many societies that one might choose to exemplify the economic factor argument. The issue is further complicated by the fact that most societies do not fit neatly into any one category. The Aztecs, for instance, could well serve as an example of a militaristic culture which went to war for ritualistic reasons, but there was a marked economic dimension to their predatory activities (Carlton: 1990; Fagan: 1984). Similarly, the Crusader knights could be said to have been inspired by religious motives, but material aggrandizement was also an important factor in their agenda. In this section of the discussion, however, we are going to look at the Norsemen, also known to us as the Vikings and later in France as the Normans. They are perhaps not the most attractive of peoples, but they did play a critical role not only in British and Irish history, but also in the development – or in some cases, lack of development – of a number of other cultures, as well.

There were several predatory peoples intent on pursuing their expansionist aims during the period we term the Middle Ages. The Mongols and later the Tartars under the leadership of Tamerlane (Timur-Leng) ravaged parts of Asia and Eastern Europe and, from the fifteenth century, these were matched by the conquests of the Ottoman Turks. But of all the peoples in the West who attacked what was left of the virtually defunct Roman Empire, none were more ferocious than the Scandinavian Norsemen/Vikings. They are a good example of the poachers who eventually became gamekeepers. In their early days they were little more than pirates, hardy and merciless, but with considerable gifts for seamanship. They introduced a number of interesting technical innovations into their seagoing craft, not least the efficient 'balance' and the development of the steering rudder. But they also had an eye for trade, and when they were finally assimilated, showed a considerable flair for organization and administration. Having once been a scourge comparable with the earlier Huns, Goths and Visigoths, once settled, they built up appreciable realms in England, France, Sicily and even Russia.

Some observers might be tempted to see these people in heroic – even romantic – terms but, as one historian comments, they were a people who 'raised ... valour to a murderous cult and those religion was a weird blend of fatalism and anthropomorphic fantasy, akin to, but without the grace or humour of, Greek mythology ... The jolly idea of them as gallant and colourful masters of the waves would have been unintelligible to their victims' (Bowle: 1980, p. 189).

They were extremely skilled navigators who appeared from the far north – regions unknown to antiquity – and were able to strike 'out of the mist', as it were, with speed and ruthlessness. Their favourite targets were coastal towns which were rarely heavily defended, and there they would pillage and burn, usually before any defensive force could be mustered. When they saw that an area was particularly vulnerable and that there were rich pickings to be had, they sometimes made base camps with palisaded fortifications. They then ravaged the surrounding area, using their long-handled battleaxes and two-edged slashing swords to kill most anything in sight – save sometimes for young girls who they would take as slaves, for 'warrior comforts' and perhaps for sacrifice. In the tenth century, as part of the elaborate Viking burial rituals, it is attested that slave girls were sometimes plied with drink, then ritually violated by a succession of warriors. Their agonies would be ended by being either strangled or knifed by an old woman called the 'angel of Death'. It may be that these unfortunate girls were simply additions to, or surrogates for, a favourite wife who was also supposed to go uncomplainingly to her death to accompany her warrior (possibly royal) husband. It is noteworthy that even after conversion, the Church did not witness any significant or immediate change in their heathen rituals.

Viking warriors could be anything from 18 to 60. Although reputedly undisciplined socially, they complied with the rigorous demands of their military profession. They were supposed to observe strict discipline in their boats, never to flinch before the enemy, always to avenge the death of a comrade and to bring all loot unprotestingly to their leader for the appropriate distribution. Their oaken ships, anything up to 120 feet long and propelled by both sails and oars, were able not only to sail the seas but also navigate most sizeable rivers, giving the raiders access to the interiors of the territories they attacked. What is particularly remarkable about the Norsemen is that unlike most earlier maritime nations, they did not confine themselves to coasting voyages, but were prepared to face the open oceans (though even they were apprehensive about sailing at night lest they fall over the edge of the world).

The dissension and fragmentation in the extensive Frankish kingdom after the death of Charlemagne in 814, roughly coincided with the Viking onslaught. Indeed, it probably made the Viking invasions that much more tempting, and a good deal easier. However, there is no generally accepted reason why the Vikings should have launched their attacks at this time, but once these raids began, it seemed that no part of Europe was safe from them. Everywhere they went their destructiveness was a byword. England was an early victim (787), then it was the turn of the Hebrides and Ireland. Soon afterwards they ventured along the Seine and the Loire. Rouen and Bordeaux were destroyed, as were also Antwerp and Aachen. In the middle of the ninth century, they destroyed many of the old Roman cities in Provence, and also decided to help themselves to some of the riches of Spain and Italy where Pisa in particular was plundered. On the other hand, their fortunes in Sicily were mixed. They conquered the island from the Arabs – a brilliant military achievement – but, in this case, their success was short-lived.

Other Viking groups ventured as far as Greenland and Iceland, and – as we now know – actually reached the coastal area of America. And Swedish Vikings, using the river valleys, penetrated the western plains of Russia where they finally settled in force. According to the saga of Eric the Red, America was first discovered by Norse seamen who had sailed from Norway to Iceland, and then – really by accident – had ventured further still. Eric the Red had already led some 500 colonists to Greenland, and it was his son Leif, possibly late in the tenth century, who first encountered the country they called Vinland. They were probably daunted by the huge emptiness of the new land, although we are not at all sure how much or how far they investigated the interior. This, plus the understandable inhospitality of the natives, added up to one of the Norsemen's rare failures. The prospects for settlement were hardly attractive.

In the East, the omens were much more auspicious. The land was rich and the cities were even richer. The Swedish Vikings (known to the Russians as the Varyagy) established control over vast areas of land from Novgorod to Kiev, and had trading relations with the important city of Byzantium (modern Istanbul), the last remaining bulwark of the old Eastern Roman Empire, and with Hungary and Bavaria. By 988, Vladimir, Grand Prince of Kiev, on condition of obtaining a Byzantine princess in marriage, agreed to abandon his pagan gods, his five wives and 800 concubines – 'an extravagant number even for a Viking' (Bowle: 1980, p. 192) – and accepted conversion to what was to become the Russian Orthodox Church. His successors became so powerful that they were able to arrange advantageous dynastic marriages with the royal houses of Norway, France and Hungary. Norse rule had at last become respectable – and decadent. After two centuries it eventually succumbed to the even more rapacious onslaughts of the Mongols from Central Asia.

England was one of the first Norse targets. Attacks took place from 787 onwards with savage raids on towns in Northumbria, and further assaults on the Isle of Sheppey and other areas on the Kent coast where

Athelstan defeated a Danish fleet. And in 851, Ethelwulf trounced a Norse army which had taken London and Canterbury (the Norsemen are *said* to have sailed up the Thames with 350 ships). But their attempts at complete occupation were thwarted by Alfred the Great of Wessex who defeated their main army in Wiltshire in 878. From England where the Danish Vikings in particular had secured more than a foothold in the Eastern counties, the invaders made their way to the Low Countries where they sacked Charlemagne's palace at Aachen, but their forays into the Netherlands were countered by the Eastern Franks. From there they besieged Paris where they were bought off by the aptly named Charles the Fat (886), but finally settled in the rich lands which were ceded to them as the Duchy of Normandy ('the place of the Northmen'). Here they prospered, with Rouen as their capital (910), and again cast covetous eyes across the Channel to England.

England at this time was divided into a number of somewhat disputatious kingdoms, some very much more important than others. Northumbria was by far the most powerful kingdom in the north. Wessex and, to a lesser extent, Mercia were dominant in the south. The Church, however, gave these divisions some semblance of coherence and unity. Much of eastern England was in the hands of the invaders. York was taken in 866 in an invasion by Danes led by warriors with the unlikely names of Halfdan, Ubbi and Ivar the Boneless. The English, we are told, put up a strong resistance, but the invaders were able to hold on to considerable tracts of land from which it seemed impossible to eject them. In 865, the Norsemen first accepted Danegeld, a huge political bribe to cease their ferocious raids. The English scholar, Alcuin, had earlier expressed his shock at such attacks, and had written 'never before has such terror appeared in Britain as we have now suffered from a pagan race, nor was it thought that such an inroad from the sea could be made' (quoted by Wilson: 1970, p. 72). The English were bedevilled by the lack of a united front, and had the added disadvantage of a long coastline and an inadequate navy. It was not until Alfred that the Scandinavians finally met their match, but even he ceded all of north-eastern England to the Danes on condition that their attacks should cease. When Alfred died in 899, he bequeathed a considerable legacy in cultural and legal reforms, yet the Danes had still not been ousted. The frontier of their English kingdom was extensive, and was marked by the garrisoned towns of Leicester, Lincoln, Nottingham, Stamford and Derby, though later all these boroughs (burhs) were recaptured. The menace had not been dispelled – but it had been checked. There was a modus vivendi. The Norsemen settled for what they could get, while their fellow warriors had greater success elsewhere, not least in Normandy where the nobility was merely biding its time.

The Norsemen were hardly in agreement with each other. Different groups had rival intentions even within a single culture zone. The Danes who were reasonably settled in the north-east and in eastern England still made occasional forays in the south. And this, in turn, was punctuated by incursions from the Continent. They would still attack towns, especially in Cornwall and Gloucestershire, pillaging and taking off well-to-do people for ransom. If the pickings were meagre, they would sometimes break off, sail westwards and try their luck in Ireland. In a somewhat purple passage, a twelfth century writer said that

> an hundred garrulous, loud, unceasing voices ... could not recount or narrate, enumerate or tell, what all the Irish suffered in common, both men and women, laity and clergy, old and young, noble and ignoble, of hardships and of injuring, and of oppression, in every house, from those valiant, wrathful, purely pagan people.
> (Quoted by Wilson: 1970, p. 70)

Alfred's son, Edward, was successful in combating any full-scale incursions, but had to contend not only with 'English' Norsemen, and raids from Normandy and Brittany, but also predatory assaults from those Vikings who had established themselves in Ireland. Under their leader, Ragnald, they had already had noted victories in Scotland and Northumbria, and in 919 took York also, where Ragnald was accepted as its king. According to the Anglo-Saxon chronicles, Edward was succeeded by Athelstan, but the record of his reign is deplorably thin. It would appear that the period was characterized by continual military toing and froing, still with no final or satisfactory outcome. What we do know is that it was during Athelstan's reign that he received a goodwill visit from the Norwegian king, Harald Fairhair, and there is reason to believe that Harald's fosterson, Hakon, was brought up in Athelstan's court.

Then history began to repeat itself. After Athelstan died in 939, and was succeeded by his brother, Edmund, the Viking raids started all over again. The English suffered ignominious defeats, and were forced to surrender a number of eastern shires to the Norsemen. The wars continued, and victory went to one side and then another. Edmund was killed, and the councillors in the north pledged themselves to his successor, but then reneged with the arrival of the Norseman, Eric Bloodaxe, whose reputation as the unifier of Norway had gone before him. He ruled in York until he was quietly murdered two years later – a deed that was matched by the periodic regicide in the English royal family. It was clear that the English were not going to let the invaders settle permanently even though they had now occupied much of the country for over a century. And the Norsemen now had one great advantage, their bases in Normandy. It was from here – as every schoolboy used to know – that they planned and finally achieved the victory they desired.

There was something of a revival of monastic life towards the end of the tenth century, and with it new forms of art and architecture, and a greater interest in learning generally. But all this did little for the English monarchy which was dogged by ill-fortune, regardless of the fact that some of the sovereigns were endowed with a reputation for saintliness which they probably did not deserve. Edgar, one of Athelstan's most notable successors, died young – and suddenly – in 975, and the factions supporting various of his young sons squabbled about the succession. Edward (probably about 13) pressed his claim in opposition to his younger brother Ethelred who was probably no more than 7 or 8, and about whom suspicions regarding suitability were already being entertained. Three years later, Edward went to visit his brother at Corfe Castle in Dorset, and was promptly set upon and stabbed to death by some of Ethelred's retainers. The murderers hurriedly buried the body, but it was later disinterred and reburied with appropriate rites, by the young king's supporters. It should surprise no one to learn that soon Edward came to be seen as a martyr, and that his bones were subsequently regarded as holy relics. The cult was such that even Ethelred – complicit or not – was forced to acknowledge that his brother was a saint. The cult of the beatified Edward became the focus of opposition to Ethelred's rule.

Ethelred 'the Unready' (the term is a corruption – perhaps a joke – and simply refers to the possibility that he refused to accept wise counsel) was indeed indecisive, and certainly ineffective as a general. Within two years of his accession, the Danes were again on the warpath. They were again intent on plunder, and although much of the flower of the English nobles fell at the battle of Maldon (991), Ethelred still had enough silver to be able to bribe them to cease their attacks – at least for the time being. But when they returned in 1009, they were no longer thinking of loot or even enlarging their landholdings; this time they wanted the whole country. First, they carried on with their raids as part of a preliminary 'softening-up' process. After three years, another immense payment of Danegeld was made, but before they left, among their many outrages they murdered the Archbishop of Canterbury. One of their leaders, Thorkell the Tall, obviously had qualms about this and deserted to the English side. Not that it did the English any good; on the contrary it brought over the Danish king himself in 1013 who received submission and hostages from so many of the shires that he was eventually given yet more tribute and made king. Viking aggression had at last paid off, though not as far as the new king was concerned. Sweyn died within a year and bequeathed a chaotic situation to his son, Cnut.

Ethelred, who had abandoned the struggle, fled with his queen to France where her brother was Duke of Normandy. Within two years he was back, though not to everyone's satisfaction. The real challenge came from Cnut and from Ethelred's son Edmund 'Ironside'. After a certain amount of sparring, they met in battle at Ashington, and – almost coincidentally – Edmund died (1016) the same year as his father. This left Cnut undisputed master of England; he was also not only king of Denmark and Norway, but also ruler of part of Sweden. In fact, when he died in 1035, aged about 40, he was the most powerful figure in the northern world. He was remembered as a 'splendid Viking', whereas, in reality, he was no better than adverse Norse tradition deserves. He eliminated and mutilated the hostages his father had taken, and he saw to it that anyone who might endanger his position was also killed, including Ethelred's family. As a final irony, he married Ethelred's widow – a reunion of Danish and Norman Vikings which still failed to avert the conflict to come.

After Cnut's death, there was yet more disputation and assassination in the struggle for power, but finally in 1042, Edward, often known as the 'Confessor', a son of Ethelred, came to the throne (the term 'Confessor' is usually associated with his known piety, but it seems more likely that the story of his unconsummated marriage and incipient homosexuality had occasioned more than a little priestly counselling). He was not the kind of man who by aptitude or training was really suitable for kingship. He was not dominant enough to shape circumstances to his liking, rather he was very much shaped *by* the circumstances obtaining at the time – almost a king by default. It was not particularly strange, therefore, that he invited his nephew, Harold, to help maintain the kingdom for him. Harold was very much the military man, and led Edward's armies on campaigns in Wales. He was also ambitious, and it may be significant that when the king summoned another nephew (his namesake) from Hungary, the young man died mysteriously en route. All Harold had to do now was to face the potential threats to his rule by Tostig, his brother who was the Earl of Northumberland, by Harald Hardrada, king of Norway, and the Normans themselves.

It was during Edward's and Harold's reigns that the Vikings really cemented their rule in Normandy. The dukes of Normandy, although influenced by prevailing European norms and values, were, in many ways, still very much the Vikings of old. The earliest recorded presence of Vikings in France dates from the end of the eighth century when raids were made on Aquitaine. These appear to have been little more than piratical excursions. Then there was something of a lull. Much more serious attacks began in the middle of the ninth century when, as we have seen, the Norsemen sailed up the Seine and plundered as far as Rouen but failed to take Paris (845). They also explored the resources of the Loire and sacked Nantes. Further south, they attacked Lisbon and Cadiz, but the Moorish forces in Spain were able to hold out against them. This was only a temporary setback, they continued their raids in the Mediterranean area, and in 881 returned to France but were yet again unable to take Paris. They failed, too, in Brittany where it is said that only a few hundred survived out of an invading army of several thousand. French resilience had proved quite remarkable.

However, in a few years they were back. Viking leaders were famed not only for their ruthlessness, but also for their obduracy. They were just not going to give up. Motivation, on the other hand, is uncertain. One commentator has observed that the springs of action may have been hunger induced by pressure of an excessive population, or possibly the spur to adventure was born of a sense of technical superiority in shipbuilding and navigation. Whatever, 'it is difficult to resist the feeling that a good deal of Viking enterprise ... was due to an acquired sense of metier ... The apparatus of conquest was available, and a Viking's leader's professional instinct was to make use of it' (Linklater: 1966, p. 23). So in the early tenth century, a compromise was decided upon. The French Charles the Simple came to terms with the Viking chief, Rolf (or Rollo), and the province later called Normandy was ceded to the invaders on condition that they ceased their incursions, renounced their gods and accepted the 'true faith', and promised to defend Charles's kingdom against further attacks. It was Rolf who was the patriarch of the dynasty that produced William the Bastard, Duke of Normandy, who led the invasion of England (1066).

Like the Anglo-Norman royal house in England, the Norman ruling family experienced its fair share of intrigue and violence. Succession to office was rarely without its problems. Factional groups of nobles supported their own acclaimed candidates, either because they really believed in their suitability or because they thought they were pliant enough to serve their particular interests. The future William of England had his own candidature contested by his cousin, but although he was not yet 20 he showed his skill in battle by routing the opposing forces, and thus proving his eligibility for office. Fortunately, too, he had the backing of Henry I of France, who in a temporary and uncharacteristic fit of brotherly love decided to support William's claim to the dukedom – something he afterwards regretted (1047). It was a time of ambitious princelings wishing to enlarge their domains and Henry decided to capitalize on their aspirations by leading a confederacy against William in 1054. Much of Normandy was laid waste by the invading army, but by a mixture of cunning and military competence – and, not least of all, patience – William was able to defeat his enemies.

Authorities unsurprisingly differ considerably in their estimates of the Conqueror. Some speak of his skill at arms, his moral courage and imagination. A ruler whose 'most striking qualities and interests grew slowly to maturity ... whose ideas did not come by intuition ... [but] by experience' (Brooke: 1971, pp. 146–7). Others recall his ruthlessness, a pious churchman who was also a relentless military leader who conquered by fire and sword, and who ruled by fear. In England, in particular, he is remembered for the 'ravaging of the North' – a campaign of confiscation and destruction that left the northern counties destitute for years. His claim to the English throne was tenuous at best, but he was able to exploit to his advantage a promise made by Edward the Confessor at a time when the English king was in a position to indulge his proclivity for patronage. (There may be some truth in the story that Edward was in exile at the time, and that the offer was only made half-seriously to the young William who was probably no more than 15. Edward may even have forgotten that he said it, but it is obvious that William did not.) The 'obvious' successor was Harold supported as he was by the leading factions among the English nobility. Harold's 'election' seemed a mere formality. His candidature had even been endorsed by Edward. But the king either changed his mind, or his promise to William was one of those idle and expansive 'I'll see you right' kind of promises. What is probably more pertinent is that William had the support of Pope Leo IX who had initiated a series of important papal reforms. And once he was ruler of England, William had the additional support of the Italian monk and scholar, Lanfranc of Pavia who became Archbishop of Canterbury. He seems to have approved William's prerogative to choose his own officials, even within the Church – a legacy which is still operative in our own time.

It is perhaps not without significance that William's marriage, which was considered a sin by the Church because he and his wife were third cousins, was later condoned and confirmed on condition that he and his wife endowed two abbeys in Normandy. It was all a matter of quid pro quo, plus – of course – a little cash. William's wife, Matilda, was a princess of English royal descent, and marriage may have been his first positive move in obtaining the English crown.

The conquest of England was not a particularly difficult affair, but there were certain preliminaries to deal with first. William's main adversaries on the Continent were Henry, King of France, and Geoffrey of Anjou. Fortunately for William they both died in 1060. Now he was able to go on to complete the conquest of the neighbouring state of Maine. Then he had the most incredible stroke of luck. Harold, his greatest rival for the English throne was shipwrecked on the coast of Ponthieu, and the Count of Ponthieu duly surrendered him to William who treated him well, but also made him swear a solemn oath of fealty which was tantamount – at least in William's eyes – to an agreement to forgo his claim to the English throne. What caused Harold to set out for France in the first place is something of a puzzle. One tradition has it that he was intent on securing the release of some relations who were being held as hostages, while another tradition has it that he was on a mission for King Edward. It is possible to reconcile these stories; there may be some truth in both of them. Whatever, it appears that William was able to exact some kind of promise which would give him a free hand in England. If the story is true, and is not a post-Conquest Norman fabrication, then according to the mores of the time, Harold had forfeited his inheritance. One wonders just what pressure was brought to bear in order to get him to relinquish what he believed to be rightly his.

After Harold's release, he returned to an England which was undoubtedly in a state of confusion. Edward was dying, Harald of Norway was threatening an invasion, and William of Normandy, who had very few supporters in England, had already prepared the way for a takeover. Ignoring the legal implications of the Norman detainment episode, Harold was anointed king in January 1066 with the full approval of his thanes. This spurred William to action. Against the advice of his nobles, he immediately began mobilizing the men and equipment he needed to mount an invasion. Legally, if not morally, he now felt (or rationalized) that he must oust the usurper. His ambitions were territorial, but in no way could it be said that he and his fellow Normans (a corruption of the word Norsemen) actually needed the land. It was more a question of status honour than land hunger.

It now seems fairly clear from the records, that if Harold, who was in the south of England anticipating the Norman armada, had not been drawn away to the north to deal with crises there, the Norman invasion might not have been so successful. Harold defeated the Norwegian forces commanded by Harald Hardrada who died in the battle of Stamford Bridge. Only two days later the Norman army landed in England unopposed. Harold hurried south with a relatively small army, and recklessly offered battle before he had time to augment his forces. It was a fatal mistake, and before the day ended Harold was dead and the battle was lost. William then made his way towards London laying waste the land as he went – a foretaste of typical Norman 'pacification'. Within three months he had been anointed William I of England. He rewarded his senior officers with the lands of the English thanes who had fallen at Hastings. And when a rebellion broke out in the Midlands and the north, he put down the revolt with his customary ferocity. It is said that his treatment of Yorkshire in particular was extreme even by eleventh-century standards. William was thus able to confiscate yet more lands that could be reallocated to his supporters. These anti-Norman insurrections were not just the work of Anglo-Saxons but of Anglo-Normans and sometimes other Norsemen. It was often a question of Viking against Viking. Furthermore, the Normans felt no kinship in the Dane law (Danish England).

William did not die a happy man (1087). He was no longer the virile warrior of yesteryear. At 60 he had grown bald and fat, but still had a commanding presence. His preoccupation with England had meant neglect of his dukedom in Normandy which inevitably spelled trouble. His eldest son, Robert, had rebelled against him and he was forced to bequeath the throne to his less effective – and somewhat unprepossessing – younger offspring. (Robert later had his eyes put out by his brother, Henry, who then had him incarcerated in Cardiff Castle for 30 years – Pine: 1966, p. 23.) William's riches were left to his sons, to the poor and, not least, to the Church – possibly as a kind of insurance policy (he is said to have cried copiously – as well he might – when praying for divine mercy).

Must societies expand or die? This would seem to have been the Viking belief, though they probably did begin their voyages as pirates, then became explorers and traders, and finally militaristic conquerors and settlers. There are many instances of small-scale societies that have not been swallowed by large-scale societies and which have survived and retained their identity for many hundreds of years. Expansion is not always the key to survival. Note, for instance, the case of Tibet. The interesting thing about so many expansionist peoples is that in time the conquerors become the conquered. They become absorbed by the cultures they try to suppress. The Normans undoubtedly made an impression upon the conquered peoples, more so in England than in most places. But where are the Normans/Norsemen in Sicily and Italy? Can they still be found in Turkey? And where are the Vikings in the Ukraine? Their architectural achievements are everywhere evident in England and to a lesser extent Ireland, but in those far-off places where they ventured, there is little or no legacy of their presence.

CHAPTER EIGHT

Militarism: The Political Necessity Argument

To say that militarism arises for political reasons is not really saying very much. After all, it could be argued that all reasons are in some sense political. Economic imperatives, status considerations and so forth can all be seen as being broadly political. We are here dealing with a dishearteningly inclusive term. What we can say with reasonable confidence is that militarism, as we have defined it, is not peculiar to any particular kind of polity. All types of society can be – and have been – militaristic in the sense that they have been prepared to wage wars of aggression and/or to intimidate by force of arms in order to further their interests and ambitions.

However, if we think instead of political *necessity*, it does put a slightly different complexion on the matter. The notion of necessity connotes such things as the fear of national and cultural extinction – a 'them or us' scenario in which a state is either prepared to fight or go under. In the internecine conflicts that once took place between many of the ancient Greek city states, a few of the poleis made it their business to try to be better at war than others. And once successful, as was the case with Sparta, the next step was logical, that of developing a sociopolitical system that was devoted to war, a system in which the young were schooled for military service from their early years. Athens, too, did much the same thing in order to retain her small but important maritime empire, and later still Thebes followed suit, though on a rather more modest scale.

Until Alexander none of the Greek states went very far afield. This cannot be said of Rome which began its career of almost unbounded conquest as one tiny state struggling to survive among a number of other warring states which threatened to crush her military ability. But as we have seen, once having tasted victory against the Samnites, the Etruscans and later the Carthaginians, it was difficult to stem the Senate's desire for further expansion.

This story could be repeated time and time again, especially in relation to small nations/states that have 'made good' either by intimidation, persuasion, negotiation or outright conquest. This was often accomplished in adverse circumstances, either within confined territorial areas, as was the case with certain medieval Italian city states or, as in the case of Great Britain, by accumulating vast territories abroad. So much depends on the political culture obtaining in a given state at any particular time. How does this or that state play the political game? The norms and values – not to say the beliefs of a society – affect the ways in which it responds to critical situations. This may well have been shaped over a long period of historical development, and will have given our hypothetical society its distinctive character. Alternatively, a society may undergo change when an altogether new – or seemingly new – political ideology has been imposed which is alien to its previous traditions.

Some may be inclined to argue that this is what happened in Nazi Germany in the 1930s, but a brief look at the militaristic norms which prevailed in Germany and Austria in the nineteenth century – not to mention the racist undercurrents – show that the Nazis exploited sentiments that were already there. Here political groupings, often styled *militias*, were organized on military lines for the purpose of intimidation (e.g. Nazi SA). This might be compared with Russia under the Soviets, although this too with its authoritarian system and repression of the peasantry bore an uncanny resemblance to Russia under the Tsars. A better example would be the Soviet satellites who found a system thrust upon them which was not consonant with their earlier traditions. Such systems imposed not only a political but also a cultural and ideological *hegemony* which had not formally existed in these societies. This was facilitated by the existence of *cells* which consisted of carefully selected, highly motivated individuals who sought to further the interests of the party, if necessary by subversive means.

Political culture inevitably involves political socialization, the inculcation and internalization of the required political norms. Once these norms are acquired and accepted unquestioningly, they may be formally codified, and this endows them with the *status of legitimacy*. In Max Weber's well-known typology, legitimate authority can be one of three ideal types:

1. *Traditional*: resting on established beliefs and values, and the sanctity of custom. This is characteristic of all societies to some extent, particularly simple and complex pre-industrial societies where there was a largely passive acceptance of both the traditional ways in which the society was governed, and the kinds of persons suited to the task, kings, autocrats, oligarchs and the like.
2. *Charismatic*: where a special respected or revered person is/was regarded as having been endowed with certain qualities which make them fit to lead and to rule, such as a religious or priestly individual

(Dalai Lama) or a 'chosen' individual who is given dictatorial powers (priest-kings). According to Weber there can be a further phase, the *routinization of charisma* where the leader may die or be removed, but the system continues in a rationalized form.
3. *Legal-rational*: where authority resides not in a person or office, per se, but in enacted rules which call for legal representatives to carry out the will of the people – a system which is theoretically characteristic of modern democratic societies.

As ideal type of legitimate authority they may not have existed anywhere in a 'pure' form. They are simply models which may be compared with reality. In practice, these types actually overlap; for instance, all three are represented in the authority structure of Nazi Germany. Here was an essentially revolutionary system with a charismatic leader who was keen to give his authority legitimacy, but was also careful to retain certain traditional values and customs. Such a system can have a remarkable potency, and is tailor-made for unquestioning military adventure.

Case study

In recent times, people have tended to associate the interests of Austria with those of Germany. They share a common language, were allies in the First World War, and as part of the Greater German Reich after the Anschluss of 1938 Austria's fortunes – or misfortunes – were linked with those of Nazi Germany in the Second World War. But it has not always been so. In the eighteenth century Austria fought Prussia in the War of the Austrian Succession (1740–48), when she was supported by Britain, possibly to thwart the designs of Frederick the Great, and to check the ambitions of the old enemy, France, who with Spain was allied to Prussia. It was a time of monarchical politics and shifting alliances, and of treaties and settlements which were occasionally abrogated or tenuously maintained.

Austria and Prussia were at war again in the following century, and this resulted in a defeat for the Austrians at Sadowa (Königgratz) in a campaign lasting less than three weeks (1866). Prussia became the established hegemonic power in Germany, with Austria excluded from the German federation. Prussia went on to further victories especially over France (1870–71), and Austria, having consoled herself with the defeat of Italy (to which she was afterwards forced to cede territory) carried out constitutional reforms and established a Dual Monarchy with Hungary (1867). Thus was born a heterogeneous hotchpotch of German and Balkan states termed the Austro-Hungarian Empire. It seems to have been doomed to dissension and fragmentation almost from its inception. How can any state successfully contain Austrians, Czechs, Serbs and Magyars? And to complicate matters yet further, in 1878 Austria-Hungary took over administration of Bosnia and Herzegovina, which she later annexed (1908) with the tacit agreement of the Russians but opposed by the British and the French.

By this time, it was obvious that outright conflict in Europe could not be delayed for very long. A naval armaments race was in full spate; Germany called up more conscripts, and there was considerable sabre-rattling on all sides. Meanwhile, the Balkans – as ever – was in turmoil. Italy, having lost the battle of Adowa over Ethiopia, decided – for no really adequate reason that anyone can discern – to attack Turkey. The Italians attacked Tripoli and threatened the Dardanelles, and this prompted a motley combination of Bulgars, Greeks and Serbs to combine to throw off the Turkish yoke which they had endured for too long. In 1912, they almost succeeded, and after mediation by the Great Powers, the Turks were left with a modest strip of territory bordering the Black Sea.

Then, true to form, the victorious Balkan conglomerate fell out among themselves. How should the victors share the spoils? This argument precipitated the Second Balkan War (1913). The Serbs and the Bulgars fought each other over Albania and Macedonia. It was a case of anyone can join, and the Bulgars were defeated by an alliance of Greeks, Serbs *and* Romanians. Amidst the confusion, the Turks made a temporary comeback, but when the dust had settled, it was the Serbs who emerged as the most successful militant people in the Balkans. It was then that the government of Austria-Hungary determined that the Serbs must be put in their place. With German consent, they decided to provoke a war with Serbia, barely realizing that they were about to ignite a European conflagration.

The first ten years of the twentieth century had been turbulent and heavy with pessimism over prospects for a European peace. Britain, in particular, now at the high water mark of her imperial glory, had carefully avoided too many European entanglements after the Napoleonic Wars. There was the Crimean War, of course, but other than this Britain had been able to sit back and enjoy her industrial achievements and her colonial acquisitions. For Germany too, it had been a relatively prosperous period, but for Austria-Hungary it had been rather different.

In the pre-First World War years 1900–13 there had been two Moroccan crises, and the Continent had survived a revolution in Russia

(1905) and the two Balkan Wars (1912–13), yet in the months immediately preceding the Great War there was apparently a certain air of tranquillity. Admittedly, nations were fiercely arming, but this was ostensibly in the interests of peace. One eminent German banker, Max Warburg, assured the Kaiser that there was no cause to 'draw the sabre' in the near future as in three to four years Germany would be undisputed economic master of Europe. Yet a special representative of Woodrow Wilson, the American President, viewed events with a more detached and dispassionate eye. He made a visit to Europe that spring and said that in London, Paris and Berlin he detected 'jingoism run stark mad' and warned that soon there was likely to be 'an awful cataclysm' (quoted by Herwig: 1997, p. 8).

In Austria-Hungary, 1914 was to be a year of decision. Things were getting out of hand in her Balkan dependencies, and the very point at which members of her government were contemplating just what to do about it, fate played a two-faced card. In June, a Serbian student assassinated Franz Ferdinand, heir-presumptive to the Austro-Hungarian throne while he was on a state visit with his wife to the Bosnian capital, Sarajevo. In one sense it was a disaster for the Dual Monarchy. Not that the Archduke was that popular – it was noted that there was no great display of mourning in Vienna. In another sense, however, it was a golden opportunity for the government justifiably – so they reasoned – to move against the Serbs. At last, an acceptable reason had been found for settling accounts with a people that was becoming increasingly troublesome.

There should have been no problem for a state as powerful as Austria-Hungary to crush the relatively small state of Serbia, but the Emperor Franz Joseph and some members of his government were worried. Would the Russians, no great friends of Austria-Hungary, come to the aid of the Serbs? They might also think it an opportune moment to humble an unwelcome rival. In order to guard against such an eventuality, the Austrians sought a 'blank cheque' from the Kaiser. With German backing, the government felt sure that the Russians would hesitate, but if they did not and there was a wholesale European conflict, then at least they would have the support of the most powerful military machine on the Continent.

Austria-Hungary made much – probably too much – of the 'Serbian menace'. Hungarian officials were not quite so keen and made representations to Vienna, but the Austrian military were adamant that it was now or never. As one statesman argued retrospectively, 'only a war [can] save Austria ... I am also quite sure that two or three years later war for Austria's existence would have been forced on us by Serbia,

Romania and Russia and under conditions which would make a successful defence far more difficult' (quoted by Fellner: 1995, p. 14). With such convictions – perhaps sincerely held – it was almost inevitable that the Austrians should opt for a pre-emptive strike.

That the Germans were willing to endorse such a policy was in itself rather ominous. It appears that the Kaiser was actually ready and waiting for war, but for no other reason than that he would like to demonstrate the superiority of his military machine. There are hints, yet again, of an underlying Social Darwinism, the sort of thing that one can read into the works of people such as Herbert Spencer, de Gobineau and Houston Chamberlain (and resurrected later by the Nazi ideologue, Alfred Rosenberg), that the nation could be tested and refined by the 'fire of war'. Consequently, not only did Austria-Hungary issue a patently unacceptable ultimatum to the Serbs, but her officials were instructed to break off relations with Serbia no matter what the response. And the Austro-Hungarian Foreign Minister warned that unless his delegates made it clear that war was what was intended, the Allies (France and Britain) might spoil things by suggesting some kind of peaceful solution.

The evidence is now reasonably clear that Germany had plans of her own, and that these included the support of Austria-Hungary in protecting her eastern borders against Russia while she made a preventive strike against France. The plans of the German military were obviously nothing like as 'parochial' as those of Vienna. A Serbian war was seen as small-time stuff compared with the sort of operations that Berlin had in mind. Perhaps the German military were just that much more perceptive than the Austro-Hungarian strategists in that they realized that any hostile moves against Serbia were bound to bring in other interested parties, and that a full-scale war would be inevitable. If this was so then a preventive strike by Germany would make some sense even if it did result in the violation of the neutrality of smaller buffer states such as Belgium. Some historians have suggested that the western Allies – and possibly even Russia – would have been prepared to make concessions to solve the Serbian problem, but that these possibilities were ignored because Germany deliberately wanted to escalate matters so that a European war would ensue.

In short, what the Austro-Hungarians thought would ensure a localized conflict, the 'blank cheque' of a supportive ally, had been turned by that ally into an opportunity which was certainly not to Austria-Hungary's advantage. The outcome was an alliance in which the friends, Germany, became the masters and dictated events from now on. As the Kaiser wrote in a telegram to Austria-Hungary,

it is of the greatest importance that Austria directs her chief force against Russia and does not split it by a simultaneous offensive against Serbia ... as a great part of my army will be tied down in France. In this gigantic struggle ... Serbia plays a quite subordinate role which demands only the most absolutely defensive measures.
(Quoted by Fellner: 1995, p. 22)

The Germans had obviously planned for a European war which had no part in Austro-Hungarian intentions, and which eventually led to the destruction of the Habsburg Empire.

Different and conflicting impressions remain of the Austro-Hungarian Empire. James Joyce, writing to a friend, said, 'It was a ramshackle affair, but it was charming', and went on to add that he had experienced more kindness there than anywhere else in his life. Frederic Morton, originally Fritz Mendelbaum and born in Vienna, in his excellent attempt to recapture the elegant decadence of Emperor Franz Joseph's Vienna and the backstage dynamics which precipitated the Great War, admits that 'Imperial Vienna has become a byword for melodious decay' (Morton: 1991, p. x). However, there were those on the Austrian General Staff who entertained ambitions for a revival of Austria's greatness, certainly as a military power. (How great Austria ever was is itself open to question: was it not Napoleon who once said that the Habsburg forces were always one year and one idea behind?)

The evidence is clear that in 1914 Austria-Hungary was not ready for war – certainly not a European war. Taking on Serbia was seen as a parochial affair that was surely within the Empire's capability. Austria-Hungary trained a smaller percentage of its militarily eligible population than either its allies or its adversaries. Each year it trained an average of 25 per cent of its young males, just about a quarter of those who were drafted in France. The army of less than half a million had fewer men than the Imperial bureaucracy had civil servants. Admittedly, both Austria and Hungary had reserve formations, but these recruits trained for only eight weeks a year, and were hardly ready for service in the field. Its General Staff of some 700 officers under their chief, General Baron von Holtzendorf, were forever drawing up contingency plans of one kind or another. But one is left with the overall impression of an underequipped army in magnificent uniforms relishing their display of disciplined ceremonial; not an army that was intended to fight, except perhaps against one of those small, ill-equipped recalcitrant states that bothered the Empire from time to time.

Dissension within the Empire was endemic. Its various peoples and ethnic groups took the broad framework of the Empire for granted, but instead of doing their best to make it work as a system of mutual interdependence, they contented themselves either by quarrelling or fighting with each other, or – in various alignments – conflicting with the central authority. The whole situation was aggravated, especially as far as Czech–German relations were concerned, with animosities arising from industrialization and the migration of poor peasants to the towns. Austrian liberty may have been, as one politician put it, a 'hybrid creature' but this does not mean it was egalitarian, yet Austria-Hungary did have a notably liberal legislation for the time (Crankshaw: 1995).

Perhaps the most serious division, both potentially and actually (depending on which circumstances were opportunely exploitable) was between the governments in Vienna and Budapest. Their different cultures, best exemplified in their different languages; different histories and ultimately different ambitions hardly made for unity. There was an ongoing distrust, particularly between the respective military establishments, and it did not help the future prospects of the Dual Monarchy that proud and outwardly impressive as the military was, it no longer commanded the esteem that it once had among the nobility of either state. As in most modern states, service with the military was no longer seen as a necessary prerequisite for those in social and political authority (nobles on the General Staff had declined from 60 per cent in the mid-nineteenth century, to a mere 11.5 per cent on the eve of the Great War).

Circumstances, then, were not exactly propitious when on 5 July Serbia rejected the ultimatum which would have meant the loss of its sovereignty. In Vienna the news was received with delight. Crowds paraded the streets into the small hours singing patriotic songs in anticipation of the military action to come. Franz Joseph was informed – quite erroneously – that Serbian troops had actually fired on Habsburg forces on the Danube so that the attack on Serbia could be depicted as a defence against Serbian aggression.

It is probably fair to conclude that Austria-Hungary went to war in 1914 to save itself. It was essentially a political decision. Fear as well as a determination to seek an advantage surely motivated their military planners: fear of Pan-Slavic nationalism, fear of losing German support, and fear of status humiliation in relation to the other great European powers. Each possible scenario predicated one thing – war was the only solution to the state's problems. 'Austria-Hungary had to emerge from the crisis as the dominant force in the Balkans' (Herwig: 1997, p. 18).

It hardly needs to be reiterated that the planners were wrong. There is usually a political solution short of war. As it was, the worst-case scenario was realized; the attack on Serbia culminated in a full-scale European conflict. Even the 'localized' attack on Serbia proved to be disastrous. This campaign which ended on 12 August 1914 ended in defeat and the loss of about 100 000 men. Almost simultaneously, the Habsburg forces also launched an expedition against the Russians which resulted in an even more catastrophic failure. It is estimated that on their Eastern front the Austro-Hungarians lost the best part of half a million men. These were losses of regular soldiers that they could not possibly make up. It was left to the Germans to come to the rescue. Under General Erich Ludendorff and General Paul von Hindenburg tremendous losses were inflicted on the Russians between 1914 and 1916, resulting eventually in the surrender of Russia and the Treaty of Brest Litovsk with the Soviets in 1918. The strategists on the Austro-Hungarian General Staff had completely misjudged the situation. They did not ideally relish the prospect of a war on two fronts, and had hoped that their numerically superior forces could defeat the Serbs before the numerically superior forces of the Russians could be mobilized. They reckoned, too, on a short war, perhaps no longer than six weeks, in which they would hold the Russians while the Germans would deal with the French. But it did not work out this way.

The General Staff had settled on a flexible approach to the deployment of their forces, but the initial thrust against the Serbs prevented the military from using their main force against the Russians in time. The fervent enthusiasm of the public, and the all too willing patriotism of Austria's young men were not enough to offset the catalogue of mistakes made by those in command (at first there was just not enough equipment or clothing for the mass of volunteers who came from various parts of the Empire). In the first battles against the Serbs, both armies fought for ten days in rain and mud. Exhausted and dispirited they halted the carnage which was further exacerbated by the outbreak of malaria and typhoid fever. The Empire's casualties ran into thousands including over 23 000 dead. Against the Russians, the losses were even more severe. Initially, the Habsburg armies had some success, but eventually they were overwhelmed by superior forces and, despite almost incomprehensible bravery on certain sectors of the front (in one case a regiment, in desperation, mounted a bayonet charge against an entire Russian division), soon the Austro-Hungarians were doing their best to evacuate 22 000 casualties a day with a transport system that had all but collapsed. They abandoned *matériel* in their retreat, and in the upper echelons of the military, men were so depressed and ashamed that several generals actually suffered mental breakdowns. There was talk of courts martial for those held to be responsible, but in the end Baron Holtzendorf simply ordered a few timely dismissals.

The European war had hardly begun, yet by a combination of inadequate preparations and ill-judged strategies against the Russians in

Galicia, the Habsburg forces had lost a third of their effective combat strength. At this stage these losses numbered nearly half a million men including 100 000 killed. Disease did the rest. The hope of a short 'lightning' war was now a thing of the past. Indeed, the situation was now so ominous that there was talk of moving the state archives and of trying to negotiate a separate peace with Russia. The old guard, including the aged emperor, found it all too much to take; for them the war had changed from chivalrous engagement to mass slaughter. Someone had to take the blame. Much rested with Holtzendorf who was very largely responsible for starting the war in the first place. But there was also a strong temptation to blame the Germans whom, it was felt, had not come to Austria-Hungary's aid soon enough. Yet accusing an ally, especially one as valuable as Germany, was an altogether unwise expedient, especially as her help was going to be sorely needed in the coming days. Furthermore, the Austrians were reluctant to surrender the initiative to their allies, powerful as they were (a similar situation arose with the British and the Americans in the Second World War).

Serious complications arose also on the Western Front. Things had been going well for the Germans against the Allies until the debacle on the Marne in which both sides suffered severe losses. Indeed, the war on both the Western and Eastern Fronts was becoming a matter of who could afford to sustain the greater losses; who had the larger numbers of cannon fodder (or perhaps more pertinently machine-gun fodder). If anything, numbers were becoming more important than skills. As both sides settled down to a trench-bound war of attrition, it was largely the numbers employed in the great set-piece battles that tended to decide the day.

It was not, however, unrelieved gloom for Austria-Hungary. Aided by large reinforcements of German troops they still met with some success in southern Poland, but the generally poor performance of the Habsburg armies brought a torrent of complaints from the German military. When Field Marshal von Hindenburg was appointed Commander-in-Chief of the German Eastern Front assisted by General Ludendorff, the tide began to turn against the Russians. In November 1914, they launched an attack against numerically superior forces near Lodz in Poland, and netted 136 000 Russian prisoners. Once the severe winter set in, fighting virtually ceased, though by this time the Habsburg manpower situation was so acute that many army companies were down to half their normal establishment. Unsurprisingly, victory brought more problems. The Germans and Austro-Hungarians met in December to review the situation, but still could not agree on a unified command or even a common strategy. With so much Polish territory now in the hands of the Central Powers, disputes also arose as to which victor went the spoils. Germany, Austria and Hungary all had different 'solutions', and the debate continued until the end of the war when they all lost out and Poland was declared an independent state.

In the Balkans, the Habsburg forces were initially doing much better, although both they and the Serbs also had to contend with extremely hazardous – and frustrating – weather conditions. The advantage came and went until, finally, the Austro-Hungarians were forced to abandon Belgrade which they had so recently captured (15 December). Both sides had sustained horrendous casualties; the Balkan army of the Austro-Hungarians was now down to about half-strength. But, in some ways, the greatest blow to the Habsburgs was their loss of prestige. It was unthinkable that the army of the Dual Monarchy should have been defeated by the inferior Serbs. Yet Holtzendorf had to concede that his armies were dispirited and exhausted, and were so depleted in numbers that their future effectiveness as a fighting force was seriously in doubt. He argued that if the Russians, in particular, could not be defeated by February 1915, then the Dual Monarchy could no longer master the situation. Indeed, although it was still only the first year of the war, the Austro-Hungarians had been virtually eliminated as a viable military force. The War Minister estimated that the state had already lost close to a million men including 26 000 officers. No wonder a kind of fatalism was beginning to permeate the ranks.

Despite these frightening losses the majority on the General Staff were undeterred. It was still believed that the war could be won. If anything 1915 turned out to be worse than 1914. In the East the Habsburg forces were haemorrhaging at the rate of 170 000 a month. For the entire army the losses totalled over 2 million. This included 775 000 taken prisoner. However, the military took heart from the fact that not only had considerable numbers of the wounded returned to the fray, but some 3 million new conscripts had been drafted into the forces. The General Command could now make new plans for further carnage. Having failed lamentably against the Serbs and the Russians, they decided to chance their arm against a new enemy, the 'honourless' Italians.

This offensive began in May 1915 with a heavy bombardment, but the Dual Monarchy's superior forces soon became bogged down in the Alpine snow and mud; supplies failed to reach the troops, and after a month's fighting both armies retired exhausted by both the conditions and the slaughter. Holtzendorf did not regard this as an irredeemable setback. He blamed his subordinates, and declared that his war aims were still the annexation of areas of Poland and Galicia. Furthermore, that Serbia – which he regarded as the real cause of 'this gruesome war' – should be 'crushed and conquered', its citizens 'pacified' (a convenient euphemism) and Belgrade governed by an Austro-Hungarian military regime.

In 1916 he was forced to reassess the situation when in June the Russians launched a massive attack against the Habsburg forces at Lutsk in which the Russians lost something in the order of a million men. Perhaps they could afford to do so, but the Habsburg losses of about 750 000 were so catastrophic that Austria-Hungary never really recovered. Holtzendorf's reputation was now tarnished beyond repair. He made what excuses he could to the emperor, and lamely protested to the Kaiser that he had been taken completely by surprise, and now needed German help. He said he wanted time to 'calm his nerves', but one of his military critics commented that Holtzendorf and his staff had been incapacitated by 'winter sleep, females, hunts and tennis' (quoted by Herwig: 1997, p. 211). It was a charge that was levelled as much against the Archduke Joseph Ferdinand who was known to debauch himself with other playboy members of the nobility. The Archduke was commander of the Austro-Hungarian Fourth Army which, perhaps because of poor leadership, had performed so badly at Lutsk. He and his staff had believed that the Fourth Army had occupied invincible defensive positions, but the Russians literally tore through their entrenchments and retreat turned into a rout. It lost over half of its original strength, and the Archduke was relieved of his command.

It was now high time for a complete re-evaluation of the situation as far as the Austro-Hungarians were concerned. The truth is that they wanted out, but hardly knew how to justify this to their military 'controllers', the Germans. They realized that in all probability the war could not be won, yet if it had not been for them it might never have started. They were on the horns of an acute political dilemma. They deeply resented their growing dependence on Germany, besides which they already owed 2.5 billion marks in war loans to German bankers. How could they possibly extricate themselves from these difficulties and still retain a modicum of pride?

Real power now resided with the German High Command. Effectively, this meant Field Marshal Hindenburg and to a lesser extent General Ludendorff because by this time even the Kaiser had been somewhat marginalized. From September 1916 onwards the Austro-Hungarians had only one independent army group left, and even this was commanded by the German Chief of Staff, and 'leavened' by a cadre of German NCOs. Surrendering control to the Germans meant that the Polish issue went unresolved. Italy, 'the snake', could not be dealt with, and a separate peace with Russia could certainly not be negotiated from strength. Most ironically of all, the Serbian problem was still an open question.

The Germans must have been fully aware of their ally's reluctance to continue the war. Indeed, to the observer it seems as though they should have been considering something similar themselves. In the high summer of 1916, the German High Command had plenty of problems of their own. Their Fifth Army had suffered huge losses on the Western Front, especially at Verdun, and then to complicate matters even further, Romania decided to enter the war against the Central Powers. The conflict was escalating. The Greeks had joined the Allies, possibly in the hope of getting a slice of Bulgaria, but Bulgaria had also opted to join the Central Powers, considerably increasing the size of the forces at their disposal. They again went on the offensive and largely destroyed the Romanian capacity to make any effective contribution to the war effort by confiscating their valuable resources.

In November 1916 the Emperor Franz Joseph died having given up hope of ever securing a victory over the Allies. Although in theory Austria-Hungary's military potential was not exhausted, the million or so combatants still at her disposal were ill fed and ill equipped, and – some argued – poorly led. To pay for the war the state had resorted to issuing war bonds and – more contentiously – to money inflation which had simply generated ever higher prices and had adversely affected personal savings. Costly as the war was, it could hardly compare with the profligate waste of lives. As the pacifist philosopher Bertrand Russell put it, the whole enterprise had become one of 'maximum slaughter at minimum expense' (cited in Hardach: 1977, p. 53). The true Austro-Hungarian statistics were kept from the Germans; Holtzendorf made things look worse than they actually were, presumably in order to support his case for some kind of negotiated peace. The Habsburg military was still a viable force despite its numerous desertions, but Holtzendorf insisted to Hindenburg that the army had really reached its limits. It was also clear that there was low morale not only in the army but also the civilian population. Not least was the problem of how to mobilize support among the ethnic minorities within the Empire who were by no means whole-hearted in their commitment to the cause.

The Germans, however, were determined to continue with the war, and Austria-Hungary had very little choice both politically and morally but to honour its obligations to their superior ally. So the General Staff resolved to try again, and persisted with the task of recruitment and training, even to the point of 're-classifying' those previously categorized as unfit and unsuitable for army service. Standards generally were lowered both for the ranks and for officers. Hence although the army was strengthened in quantitative terms, the qualitative conditions for service were hardly being met. The General Staff also did their best to ensure that the war industries met the technical standards and production schedules which were required of modern warfare. (It was not until late in 1917 that the Habsburg army was issued with steel helmets – and these were supplied by the Germans.) The Austrians and the Hungarians were not exactly as one in all of this. Budapest was particularly incensed because Vienna was demanding a disproportionate recruitment effort on their part even though they needed extra agricultural labour in order to feed both the army and the civilian population.

All sorts of raw materials were in short supply, especially metals and suitable coal for smelting. Austria-Hungary did, however, enjoy plentiful supplies of oil, even though the Russians had done very considerable damage to many of the oilfields. Everything was mobilized for what now became total war, but many felt that the price was inordinately high while the rewards were minimal. Almost unbelievable privations at the front were nearly matched by the sufferings of the civilians at home. Disease ravaged many communities, various civil buildings were converted into hospitals for the sick and the wounded. But probably the most general problem was the acute shortage of food. There were riots at certain stores, and sometimes supplies ran out altogether. Women in particular, were irate at the exorbitant prices charged for staple foods such as bread and milk; and meat, for many, was becoming no more than a distant memory. All sorts of ersatz commodities were concocted for public consumption, but it was obvious that people were not going to put up with these substitutes indefinitely. As an extreme resort the government introduced a form of military discipline in the factories, and there were various punishments for those who were deemed guilty of quasi-traitorous acts. Industrial workers who became too voluble with their complaints were often heavily fined, and in some cases they were swiftly transferred to the army for less conducive duties.

With such frantic mobilization of labour and resources, the state had to rely on the recruitment of women and youths who were usually paid only about 60 per cent of the wages normally paid to men. Many women supplemented their low wages with a little occasional prostitution. It is estimated that there were over 30 000 prostitutes in Vienna alone, not surprising as prostitution was always a trade that flourished in wartime. Working hours increased and double shifts were introduced, all in the hope that further output might bring victory, but as the days wore on it became all too clear that the chances of coming out of the war with anything other than grief and hardship were well-nigh minimal. Strikes and unrest followed. The police had to escort some workers back to their factories, and civilian courts had their work cut out trying to deal with the thousands of cases requiring judicial decisions. Little wonder, therefore, that there were further secret soundings as to how the war might be ended.

Death and disease were rife both among civilians and those wounded at the front, and medical services could hardly cope. Matters came to a head towards the end of 1918 when the menace of Spanish flu began to decimate a population already seriously undernourished (it is estimated that some quarter of a million Germans died of malnutrition alone). If anything, the situation was even worse in the army where many of the ethnic minorities whose allegiance to the Dual Monarchy was uncertain at best, were effectively in open revolt and deserted en masse. In October 1918 military leaders called for an armistice in order to prevent further anarchy. The Italians launched a *coup de grâce* following which about 10 per cent of their 300 000 prisoners died in labour camps. The horrendous cost of the war for Austrian-Hungary was that, of the 8 million men mobilized, 1 015 000 were killed, nearly 2 million were wounded and another 3 748 000 taken ill and hospitalized, and about half a million of those who were taken prisoner also perished (Herwig: 1997, p. 439).

Prussia and its legatee, Germany, can be seen as militaristic societies par excellence. They did not just play at war. They fashioned war machines of formidable effectiveness; indeed, in 1914 Germany probably had the most powerful army in Europe – perhaps in the world. What other nation could have taken on the combined forces of France, Britain, Russia and eventually the USA and held out for so long? Austria-Hungary, on the other hand, was something of an albatross around Germany's neck. She was a decaying empire made up of none-too-cooperative ethnic minorities who were looking for independence. These heterogeneous elements made a not altogether willing contribution to the war effort, especially when things started to go badly for them. The main constituents of the Empire, Austria and Hungary, were themselves often at loggerheads about policy and practice. In both societies there was a tendency for the military to play at soldiers. The officer corps in particular relished the pomp and grandeur that went with military display, but – by and large – they had not the professionalism and know-how that characterized their German counterparts. Even more disastrously, the rank and file were ill equipped and poorly trained, and were just not prepared for wartime exigencies. True, the army was an effective unifying factor in a multinational state, but it was cumbrously organized and inefficiently administered (Joll: 1984, pp. 71–2).

The Dual Monarchy was quite ready to pounce on a suitable victim such as Serbia which, admittedly, was a thorn in its side. This was supposed to be a swift campaign against a much weaker enemy. But when the government made spurious allegations against Russia, and declared war on her in August 1914, it was a misjudgement of monumental proportions which led – almost incomprehensibly – to the incalculable carnage of the First World War.

CHAPTER NINE

Militarism and the Ethical Implications of Aggressive War

In modern society probably most people would agree that ideally war is wrong or at the very least undesirable, and that if at all possible it is something to be avoided. Militarism, depending upon how it was defined, might fare a little better. So much would depend on the circumstances. Would military posturing à la Vagts be permissible, something that would intimidate and therefore deter a potential aggressor? Or would military aggressiveness depend for its acceptance upon its degree of success? After all, one has only to witness the overwhelming approval that greeted the early victories of the Axis powers in the Second World War to see how expansionist policies and practices can receive the endorsement of their own peoples. Even onlookers – the so-called neutrals such as Sweden and Switzerland – were duly impressed and, to some extent, morally compromised. Was it not Hitler who once observed that no one asks questions of the victors?

Of course, it can always be argued that it makes all the difference if we are talking about a 'just war'. Normally this would be defined as a war that is initiated to defend others. The sort of thing the British and Americans were said to be engaged in with the Gulf War, though even here there was a mixture of well-intentioned and self-interested motives. It is argued (Fotion and Elfstrom: 1986, pp. 107ff) that the 'just war' must be:

- declared by a legitimate authority such as a sovereign state
- initiated for a just cause
- waged with the right intentions
- conducted by the correct means.

It needs only a superficial glance at these 'conditions' to see just how fallible they are, and how easily each one can be rationalized to suit the interests of the aggressor. It is always possible to justify armed force as 'intervention' or as the need to remedy injustices. It is rarely a problem to redefine one's goals.

The question of *means* is particularly interesting because it raises the highly contentious issue of what is meant by 'total war'. Some theorists argue that because all societies formulate rules for the regulation of social conduct, including warfare, there is therefore no reason why these should not be extended to cover those situations which attend conquest and subjugation. In some societies these rules may not be codified, but they are, nevertheless, recognized and observed by those concerned. So, in developed societies, there has been tacit agreement with the articles of the Geneva convention covering such issues as the outlawing of poison gas and biological weapons, and the humane treatment of prisoners and defenceless populations (Best: 1980). But we all know that there *are* infringements. Obeying the rules can be – and often is – partial and selective. Starvation, deprivation, torture and execution may not be on the official agenda, but they have been widespread, even in what we like to call 'civilized society'.

The realist school, however, takes a much more sceptical view of affairs. They maintain that it is all very well concocting codes to reduce the amount of pain and suffering, as utilitarians might argue, but such good intentions are based upon a conceptual confusion between the *formulation* of the law and the *application* of the law. Rules may well be based upon the seemingly sound Utilitarian principle of the greatest happiness for the greatest number, but the application of those rules may have nothing to do with the principle. In some ways this is analogous to the Roman *jus ad bellum*, the law governing going to war, and *juo in bellos*, what you do when you get there. It is a matter of theory and practice. The rules may be drawn up by legislators for the very best motives, but the reasons they are then applied by military authorities and observed by military personnel may have little to do with common morality but everything to do with military expediency. 'No one is suggesting that there should be no attempt to make such rules, but these may well prove to be worthless in situations where they can be changed, rationalized or simply ignored' (Carlton: 1992, pp. 179–80).

It follows from what we have said so far that what is considered to be a 'just war' is still a matter of some debate (Walzer: 1980). So much depends upon the perspective of the observer. Similar questions are also raised about the question of 'total war'. Does it mean what German Propaganda Minister Goebbels called for in the ominous days of 1943, that the nation must mobilize *all* its resources to achieve victory or, at least, prevent ignominious defeat? Or does it mean all-out war – the kind of war where anything goes, the sinking of unarmed vessels, the saturation bombing of cities, the killing of prisoners, even the deliberate massacre of defenceless civilians? A war without mercy – the sort of war that Hitler commanded his generals to wage in Russia in 1941? Thoroughgoing realists argue that in modern war we can no longer distinguish between combatants and non-combatants, all contribute in some way to the war effort, and therefore none are immune. All are fair game. All participate, therefore all must suffer the consequences. Indeed, some would go so far as to say with extreme relativists that to speak of a war of moderation is a kind of imbecility and that the so-called rules of war lie outside the realm of ethics even in a nuclear age.

We know that, in practice, this is how so many wars – past and present – have actually been conducted. Even in early, more limited, wars the innocent have suffered, if not from atrocities and wounds, then from starvation. Perhaps the crime, as the Nuremberg judges agreed in 1945–46, was not only the way in which war was conducted, but the fact that it was initiated at all. This is aggressive militarism at its most dangerous.

Cast study

The Second World War was total in the sense that by late 1943, at the latest, the main combatants had mobilized what were near enough their total resources. In Britain this was largely done by consent. An electoral truce was called at the beginning of the war in 1939, and a coalition government was formed which remained in power until 1945. This meant that although key issues were decided by an inner caucus – the War Cabinet – under Winston Churchill, much that was done was validated by parliamentary consent. Similar and effective conditions also applied in Britain's allied democracy, the USA. Yet there had to be a considerable degree of centralized control even by these governments in order to deal rapidly with wartime exigencies. (In Britain, for example, it was not until the end of 1941, that the country could really be said to have a coordinated economy.) By contrast, the more authoritarian governments of the Axis powers were able to act without recourse to popular consent, as was also the case in the Soviet Union which had central planning from 1928 onwards.

In Nazi Germany – our special concern here – after the spectacular military successes in Poland (1939) and France and the Low Countries (1940), there were initial moves to wind down production levels, and even demobilize certain military personnel. But the intention to invade Russia changed all that. For this Hitler assembled the largest and most formidable war machine the world had ever seen. Yet it was not until the reverses of late 1942–43, that the nation was put on a thoroughgoing wartime footing.

Military activity among the belligerents had to be supplemented by rigorous social measures such as rationing, direction of labour and by increased taxation and compulsory savings (Britain was able to cover something like half her wartime expenditure out of current revenue – something not achieved by any of the other nations, but she was still on her financial beam end by the time hostilities ceased in 1945). Militarization was vital for all the competing nations, and science and technology were harnessed in ways that were able to produce the most effective and destructive weaponry that human ingenuity could devise (Farrar: 1978).

The Polish campaign which opened the Second World War on 1 September 1939 began after some hesitation by Hitler who was uncertain as to whether Britain and France would actually honour their treaty obligations to Poland. On the basis of past experience, especially the takeover of Czechoslovakia (completed in March 1939). Hitler felt that he could take the risk. This was a serious miscalculation. But the Allies''intervention was too late and too inadequate to make any difference to Hitler's plans. The ostensible reason for the Polish campaign was to resolve the question of the Polish Corridor, that narrow strip of land which, quite irrationally, separated most of Germany from East Prussia. This gave Poland access to the sea via the 'free city' of Danzig. A more cogent reason was to restore Germany's borders, that is, the borders she enjoyed prior to the First World War. These had been 'redrawn' by the Allies partly to re-create the Polish state, but largely as a way of punishing Imperial Germany for helping to initiate that terrible conflict by divesting her of some of her territory. The German leadership wanted revenge, *and* the effective obliteration of Poland. The Corridor issue could probably have been solved by negotiation, but all the signs were that Hitler wanted his war.

The German onslaught on Poland was devastating. Polish forces at every level were no match for the Wehrmacht, and certainly had nothing to compete with the Luftwaffe in terms of numbers and technology except the skill of her pilots, many of whom were later able to display those skills in service with the Royal Air Force (RAF). The Polish army consisted of 42 divisions plus ten reserve divisions. This was not inconsiderable, but its weakness was that only two divisions were motorized, and its tank and armoured brigades were woefully short of up-to-date equipment. The German army with its 60 divisions (including nine armoured divisions) was able to slice through the Polish forces with little difficulty. The German plan was to fold up the Polish army by a series of enveloping manoeuvres which trapped the Polish units by sheer speed of movement – 'blitzkrieg' (lightning war) as it was dubbed by an Italian journalist. It was a triumph of cooperation between infantry and panzers, aided, of course, by the devastating dive-bombing of the Luftwaffe's Stukas. The Polish Air Force was effectively neutralized within the first few days, so the destruction of the Polish military could be carried out at will. It also allowed German bombers to range freely, and to carry out the gratuitous bombing of Warsaw. There was brave but rather hopeless resistance until 17 September when the Soviets, by prior agreement with the Germans, cynically invaded Poland from the East. From then on the war was lost.

German losses were a mere fraction of those of the Poles who lost 66 000 dead, at least 200 000 wounded, and about 700 000 who were taken prisoner. But this was simply the overture. The real agony of the Polish people was yet to come. Some hundreds of Polish officers were callously murdered by the Soviets in the Katyn Forest – a crime which was originally thought to be the work of the Nazis. But then Hitler had his own plans for the Poles, especially the Polish intelligentsia. These were put into practice by Hans Frank, a one-time lawyer to the SS, who was appointed Governor-General of the rump state of Poland. Code-named AB Aktion (Extraordinary Pacification Action), this misleading euphemism disguised the liquidation of some 2 000 Polish leaders and intellectuals, both men and women (including a high proportion of Jews) who were summarily executed between September 1939 and June 1940. Frank kept meticulous records of this 'action' in a 42 volume journal – a record that eventually led to his own trial and execution.

Between them the Germans and the Soviets had disposed of just about anyone who could possibly lead a revolt, indeed, anyone who might voice any serious opposition to the 'new order'. In the German sector the territory was divided into areas largely peopled by *Volksdeutsche*, and the Government-General which was Frank's special preserve. Frank established the headquarters of the Government-General at the one-time royal palace at Cracow, and ran it as though it were his personal fiefdom. This was intended to be a 'service state' for the Reich. It acted as a repository for Jews and other undesirable *untermenschen* such as Slavs, and it was from here that people were later turned over for 'treatment' by the SS/SD – in other words, consignment to the death camps.

Despite subsequent disclaimers, the generals whose expertise had made the Polish campaign so successful were fully in accord with Hitler's invasion plans. There were a few on the General Staff who had voiced their doubts, not so much because they were opposed to the invasion, per se, but more because they were afraid that it would precipitate a world war. They were right, of course, but Hitler had been willing to take his chances. A few did demur, but these officers were either ignored or marginalized. The principal architects of this entirely gratuitous offensive were the army Chief-of-Staff, General von Halder, and the Führer himself, who was prone to interfere with the army planners, sometimes concerning himself with quite minor details. The actual campaign was operationalized by Generals von Bock, von Runstedt and von Kluge, all thoroughgoing professionals. Later they were to modify their views of Hitler the strategist, or the 'first soldier of the German Reich' as he liked to call himself (Humble: 1976, p. 47).

The generals seem to have had few moral reservations about the quite unnecessary war against Poland. And it is unbelievable that at the highest echelons the military did not know what was going on in the country now that the war was won (Bethell: 1976). The state was quite obviously being dismembered and much of the population effectively enslaved. The generals took the view that their troops had done everything that was expected of them, and their tactics and planning had been thoroughly vindicated. Now it was to be the turn of the West.

It would appear that Hitler and some of his closest associates really believed that the Allies (France and Britain) would now come to terms. But when they did not, and even went to the point of downright rejection of Hitler's 'peace' overtures, the generals became more than a little nervous, especially when in October, only a matter of days after the completion of the Polish campaign, the Führer demanded an assault not only on France, but on the Low Countries as well. True, Britain and France had taken the initiative and declared war on Germany two days after the attack on Poland began, but Holland and Belgium were surely a different matter. At least this was the position taken by some of the generals. Only a day after Hitler issued his Directive No. 6 detailing his ideas as to how the attack in the West should be organized, General von Leeb, in charge of Germany's defences on the Siegfried Line, replied with a memorandum expressing his moral objections to the proposed attack on the Low Countries. This was backed by General von Brauchitsch, not the most forthright of men in the presence of the Führer, but both were ignored. They had all given an oath of loyalty to Hitler, and presumably felt (or rationalized) that this took precedence over some 'higher ethic' concerning aggressive war. It was altogether easier to comply. Any reservations they might have had were duly set aside once Hitler had awarded 24 of them the Knight's Cross of the Iron Cross, an exceptional honour for so many.

The offensive in the West was postponed more than once late in 1939. This was partly because there were genuine hesitations about a winter campaign, and partly because Hitler was not entirely satisfied with the battle plan which he felt was simply a rehash of the old

Schlieffen Plan which had failed in the First World War. Hitler's view was that the dominance of the aerial factor combined with the development of mechanized armour made for a quite new situation and demanded a bolder approach. Runstedt's Chief-of-Staff, General von Manstein, now considered one of the Wehrmacht's most innovative strategists, came up with a blueprint for an attack through the Ardennes forest which had much more appeal to the Führer. This called for a feint in the north that would entice the allied armies into a trap which would be sprung by panzers driving through the mistakenly believed impenetrable Ardennes.

There was a delay caused by another campaign in Scandinavia in April 1940 to thwart Allied landings in Norway, and a simultaneous bloodless occupation of Denmark, both of which went virtually without a hitch. But this was no more than a hiccup to Hitler's overall plans, and the offensive in the West began on 10 May. The generals, possibly heartened by another victory, now apparently had little compunction about invading the Low Countries which had desperately wanted to remain neutral. Again, the whole operation, meticulously planned, was a brilliant success. The speed of the enveloping pincers of the panzers completely outmanoeuvred and demoralized the Allied armies, and the French were ready to capitulate before the end of June, and the relatively small British force could do nothing but scramble on any craft that would carry them in the amazing escape from Dunkirk. There were recriminations, of course, on both sides. The French felt that the British had deserted them, and the British countered that the French army, the largest in Western Europe, had collapsed, leaving the British with no alternative but to get out while they could and hope to fight another day.

For Hitler it was another outstanding victory. He was so pleased with his generals that he created 12 new General Field Marshals, an honour indeed. This was the highest rank in the armed forces (it was awarded very sparingly during the First World War when only five generals were so honoured). It probably strengthened Hitler's hold over the often distrusted military caste, and surely further anaesthetized the generals' moral scruples. What did it matter that his armies had overrun yet more countries, and that his officials were now confiscating their treasures and rifling their bank deposits? Who was asking questions now? Everyone was surprised; even Stalin was impressed – and worried. The British were alone. No one looked like joining them, least of all the USA where isolationism and anti-Europeanism were still strong. It was obviously time again for the Führer to make more enticing overtures to Germany's racial cousins across the Channel and get them to see sense and acknowledge the Reich's unchallenged hegemony in Europe.

But the British were stubborn. They could not admit defeat, and what is more they did not trust any of Hitler's promises. They had seen what happened when countries surrendered to the Nazis. People and gold reserves and – not least – liberty disappeared. Against common sense – so it seemed – the British hung on, hoping against hope that eventually the USA would come to their aid. Ultimately, help did come – but from an unexpected quarter. Hitler had decided to relegate the prospect of invading Britain to the sidelines (Operation Sealion) and instead take on the Soviet Union in the greatest offensive in terms of men and *matériel* that had ever been assembled. It transpired that this possible campaign had been on the cards for some time, certainly since the French debacle. Indeed, Hitler had promised as much in *Mein Kampf* written way back in the 1920s when he was in prison following an abortive putsch in Bavaria. One can only conclude that incarceration had expanded his conceptual horizons. Now he intended to deal with what he regarded as the 'Communist menace' once and for all, and give the German people the Liebensraum that they deserved.

Regardless of the casuistic rationalizations made at the time, the invasion of Russia (Operation Barbarossa) was another of those gratuitous undertakings to which Europe was becoming accustomed. True, Stalin had been incautiously nibbling away at strips of territory in the Balkans and Scandinavia which Hitler regarded as being within his own sphere of influence. Furthermore, the build-up of Russian military might did pose a possible threat to the Reich but, as in more recent Cold War days, there was no clear evidence that the Soviet Union actually intended an attack. And when Germany did forestall such an eventuality – if, indeed, it ever existed – Stalin and his military planners seemed genuinely surprised even though they had been alerted by British Intelligence that such an attack was imminent.

After their unparalleled victories in the West, the generals seemed to think that there was very little left to fight about. There was still Britain, of course. Her air force and navy precluded the possibility of an easy invasion, but there was always the possibility that Churchill and the War Cabinet would see the hopelessness of their situation, and settle for some kind of negotiated peace. So surprise is hardly what they felt when Hitler brought them together for what was misleadingly called a 'conference' at the Berghof, his Bavarian retreat, in August 1940, where he announced that he had further plans for expansion. He told them that Poland had been little more than a dress rehearsal, and that he intended to crush Russia despite the fact that he and Stalin had a ten-year non-aggression pact which – as a cynical stratagem – was signed in August 1939. In completing the diatribe he evinced all the signs of the dictator in a hurry by insisting that there was no time to be lost: 'War must come in my lifetime'.

Preliminary planning had already begun at OKW (Oberkommando der Wehrmacht), the new High Command set up by Hitler in 1938, and which was his special preserve as Supreme Commander of the Armed Forces. The generals raised no serious questions of principle; most subsequent discussion simply revolved around details in the planning with which the Führer liked to be intimately involved.

Somewhat like Mussolini, Hitler was a great believer in the idea that war was good for a nation. This was grandiloquently expressed by a well-known writer of the time, Ewald Banse, a professor of military science. For Banse, national sentiment was a form of self-respect, and internationalism led to 'degeneration of the tissues'. War derived its 'nourishment' from a country's spiritual and economic strength; peace, although an ideal state, carried with it the 'risk of stagnation and somnolence'. Military action, for Banse, was a 'grand stimulant', and the warrior was the man who never shirked a fight, but 'greeted it with joy' – a characteristic he associated with the 'original Nordic aristocracy'. On the other hand, the pacifist endures humiliation to avoid war, and is thus listless and servile, and values honour and renown less than his own inconsequential life. In summary, Banse took the view that there had to be a renaissance of the essential 'German soul' and that this meant the reclamation of German territory. This could only be achieved by war, and this meant not just the development of the requisite technology and a totally efficient army, but the training of the minds of the whole people for military action and sacrifice (Banse: 1934). As an explanation of the Nazi credo, it is doubtful if Hitler himself could have said it any better.

It was envisaged that the Russian campaign would last a mere five months beginning in May 1941. Hitler signed his Führer Directive No. 21 in December 1940 to the effect that Russia would be attacked on three fronts, and that the onslaught would be such that the enemy's will to resist would be completely broken before the onset of the formidable Russian winter. The generals acquiesced and agreed that the plans were feasible. Did they also know what Hitler had in mind for the pacification of the Russian people behind the lines? Was it clear that this was to be no ordinary war, and that Hitler intended 'to destroy Russia altogether – to crush her government, pulverize her economy, enslave her people, and eliminate her as a political entity' (Stoessinger: 1993, p. 26)?

We now know, of course, that the whole timetable went awry because of events which neither Hitler nor his planners could easily have foreseen. Mussolini, having declared war on the Allies on 10 June 1940, had squandered little time in trying to secure what pickings were left with the French on the brink of defeat. He then sent an army to North Africa which, as we have seen, put up such a lamentable display that they had to be reinforced by Germany's Afrika Korps under General Rommel who had played a notable part in the French campaign. Not to be outdone by his Axis partner, Mussolini then decided on another 'master-stroke', he invaded Greece. Hitler, who had not always divulged his own plans to the Duce, was furious when Mussolini met him on the station at Florence, and said, 'Führer, we are on the march'. Hitler had his own ideas for the Balkans where states were very largely dependent on trade with Germany. And when the Italians stumbled to a halt within a week of the attack (3 November 1940), the Führer was left with very few options. He left the Italians to stew for a few weeks, but then felt he had to intervene, even if it meant upsetting his timetable for 'Barbarossa'.

The British felt that they had to help the Greeks and thus get a foothold in Europe, but they had to deplete their forces in North Africa in order to reinforce the Greek army. Again, the panzers supported by the Luftwaffe were able to make short work of the opposition. The German 'Operation Marita' (obviously already worked out by the General Staff as a contingency plan) was mounted from Austria and Hungary, as well as from Bulgaria and Romania, and simply scythed through the resolute Yugoslav, British and Greek armies in a matter of days. The offensive included the entirely callous mass bombing of Belgrade as a 'punishment' for daring to abrogate a previous commitment to the Tripartite Pact between Germany, Italy and Japan. The Nazi flag was soon flying over the Acropolis in Athens, but the Greeks fighting in Albania were never completely subdued. The British managed to execute another 'Dunkirk' in getting many of their own and Commonwealth troops away from the mainland to Crete and North Africa. The German airborne attack on Crete which followed (20 May–1 June), although successful, inflicted such serious losses on these elite troops (over 6 000 killed and wounded) that the German Airborne Forces (an arm of the Luftwaffe) were never used in this role again.

As soon as the Greek/Yugoslav operation was over, the German forces moved back to their jumping-off points for 'Barbarossa', but the Balkan diversion had cost at least four weeks, a setback which was arguably crucial to the success of the Russian campaign. Three powerful Army Groups under Generals von Leeb, Bock and Runstedt invaded the Soviet Union on 21–22 June in a massive offensive which Hitler prophesied would cause the world to hold its breath. At first, it was almost unbelievably successful. For weeks the Russians retreated on all fronts, and the Germans took literally hundreds of thousands of prisoners, very many of whom were so badly treated that they did not survive. But then the Russians' greatest ally came to their rescue – the weather. German armour and transport became bogged down in the mud and slush, and then some froze up altogether. The General Staff, anticipating a short campaign, had not arranged for the troops to be kitted out with winter clothing, and the casualties from frostbite began to approach those caused by enemy fire. It is still a matter of debate whether the Army Group Centre (von Bock) would have been stopped in the outskirts of Moscow *if* they could have made an earlier start. As it was, German troops were halted there and would have retreated had it not been for the Führer's order that they must stand fast. It is now known that the advance on the capital had been stopped by the arrival of fresh Russian reinforcements from their Far Eastern Army, and that this had been made possible by clever espionage work by Richard Sorge, a Soviet spy. Sorge had established that there was no danger of an attack in the Russian rear by the Japanese who were just entering the war as a Tripartite partner.

The Germans commenced their ruthless persecution of Jews and Slavs almost as soon as they crossed the Russian border. The precedent had been set many years before when at an early concentration camp at Aschaffenberg in Bavaria, some SS men killed a number of Jews, but no charges were brought because it was ruled that the SS were not subject to civil authority. Later by a secret Amnesty Decree (October 1939), Hitler allowed SS formations such as the Einsatzgruppen (extermination groups) to destroy Jewish organizations. Furthermore, it decreed that such units were exempt from army interference. This effectively 'legalized' countless atrocities in the Occupied territories. It must not be thought, however, that most army commanders actually tried to stop the mass killings that took place. Not all were like General Blaskowitz, a career officer since the First World War who became Commander-in-Chief of the occupation forces in Poland. He seriously objected to the excesses of the SS, and sent a memorandum to this effect to Hitler through General Brauchitsch which was promptly 'lost'. (Blaskowitz was indicted as a minor war criminal at the Nuremberg Trials, but before his case was heard in 1948, he died in somewhat mysterious circumstances. He probably committed suicide, although there was a rumour that other inmates of the prison who happened to be ex-SS actually murdered him.)

In Russia, the Einsatzgruppen really came into their own. Admittedly, these men were not from the Wehrmacht, but were personnel recruited from the ranks of the police services and particularly the Waffen (military)

SS. Altogether, they numbered about 3 000 and were divided into four groups, designated A, B, C and D. Each Einsatzgruppe comprised two sections which were divided in turn, into a number of smaller units (Einsatzkommandos) for greater efficiency. Their leaders were actually administrators and intellectuals, as were also their middle-level unit commanders. Together they represented a curious mixture of professionals, about 120 in all, including lawyers, a Protestant minister and an opera singer. This unlikely assortment of officials was required to carry out the mass liquidation of Jews and other undesirables who were nominally regarded as 'partisans'. The whole operation was designed so that up to the last moment before execution, victims believed that they were about to be 're-settled' – a subterfuge that avoided unnecessary commotions. Large batches of people were shot after being divested of their valuables – such as they were. Careful statistics were kept of their operations. They make chilling reading. Each Einsatzgruppe kept meticulous records of the numbers of 'Jews, partisans, looters and Communist functionaries' who were killed, and the numbers run into hundreds of thousands. By the winter of 1941–42, the figures were:

Einsatzgruppe A – 249 420
Einsatzgruppe B – 45 467
Einsatzgruppe C – 95 000
Einsatzgruppe D – 92 000

In total nearly half a million, men and women, young and old were killed.

It was all supposed to be kept very secret, but murder on such a massive scale could hardly escape the notice of surreptitious onlookers – much to the consternation of the execution squads. One member complained that 'rumours from ... areas regarding the shootings have made action considerably more difficult. Information regarding our action against the Jews is gradually filtering through via fugitive Jews, Russians and talkative soldiers' (quoted by Hohne: 1972, p. 331).

As if this was not enough, a second wave of SS/SD units followed upon the first, charged with the task of 'police security in the newly occupied territories'. This was a clear euphemism for more killing. These units were made up of police detachments, Waffen SS and locally recruited auxiliaries (particularly in the Ukraine and the Baltic States where there was already a tradition of anti-Semitism), and were intended to deal with those 'potential enemies of the Reich' that the initial Einsatzgruppen had missed. In time, of course, the whole procedure was to be rationalized with the construction of the extermination camps in Poland from 1942 onwards. The whole ghastly business was mechanized in such a way that it took the strain – as they claimed – from the executioners. At last, murder had become impersonal.

Fairly typical of a senior commander among the second wave was Erich von dem Bach-Zelewski who, after taking charge of a number of 'actions', became plagued by nightmares and had to be admitted to hospital suffering from a 'nervous breakdown'. What may not be entirely typical is that he was reported to be prey to hallucinations, and would wake in the night screaming. Later he was said to have asked Himmler, the Reichsführer SS, if the 'actions' could be halted, but was reminded – threateningly – that the programme had been personally ordered by the Führer. What perhaps should be noted here is that Bach-Zelewski, a one-time professional soldier and afterwards a general in the Waffen SS continued in the task of extermination when in July 1943 he was given the task of quelling an uprising by Polish partisans (it was a practice of the German military to shoot partisans on the spot). Bach-Zelewski was one of Hitler's favourite generals. Towards the end of the war when the Germans were in desperate straits for men, he had the reputation of being able to conjure up armies from nowhere (this usually meant emptying prisons and recruiting anti-Soviet Ukrainians). But for all his ardour as a military criminal, like so many of his kind he did not pay the ultimate price for his deeds; many of the sentences handed out by German courts for mass murder were not only ludicrously light, they were then usually reduced to five years at the most.

It may well be asked how could the military embark upon a highly questionable war with hardly a qualm and, furthermore, how could a self-proclaimed military elite, the Waffen SS, be prepared to engage in a programme of wholesale murder? More still, how could acknowledged intellectuals not only be party to, but actually lead them to such racist extremes when the underlying philosophy was both pointless and biologically fallacious?

Hitler had made it clear to his generals at the outset that the Russian campaign was going to be like no other. He insisted that it was to be conducted without mercy and humanity; without those finer feelings that intrude upon most people's thinking even in wartime situations. This was reinforced by Reinhard Heydrich, Head of the Reich Security Service (SD) and chief architect of the 'Final Solution', when he briefed members of the Einsatzgruppen before they left to carry out their tasks. They had already had a period of indoctrination, and it was very obvious that they were to embark upon a mission of genocide. 'Judaism in the East is the source of Bolshevism and must therefore be wiped out in accordance with the Führer's orders' (quoted by Hohne: 1972, p. 330).

The ideology now had to be realized and it would require unparalleled determination and lack of pity to carry it to completion. There was some murmuring, but no one rebelled. Once convinced that this was a direct order from Hitler their task was endowed with the requisite sanctity. It had both moral and legal approbation.

This section of our discussion is not meant to be a documentation of the war in Russia; this has been excellently treated elsewhere (Downing: 1978; Humble: 1976; Stoessinger: 1993). It is well known that the Germans launched another massive offensive in 1942 which yielded yet more Russian territory. They were more or less stymied on the Northern Front being unable to take Leningrad and, as we have seen, they also came to a halt on the Central Front where they failed to take Moscow. But on the Southern Front they did make appreciable gains until they reached Stalingrad. Here the battle raged for several weeks and degenerated into fierce street-by-street fighting in the outskirts of the city. By early 1943, the Wehrmacht was virtually spent. The Russians gained the upper hand with reinforcements they were not supposed to possess, according to German Intelligence. This was the turning point of the Russian campaign. The Wehrmacht lost some 300 000 men at Stalingrad, and from then onwards it was an almost uninterrupted story of a German retreat. At the same time, they were also falling back in North Africa and the intensive bombing of the German heartland was under way – something that Field Marshal Goering, Head of the Luftwaffe, promised could never happen.

But still the atrocities continued with beatings, burnings and shootings. And the insatiable maw of the Nazi extermination programme was claiming more victims than ever. This was mainly the work of the Security Police (SD) and the SS, including their military arm, the Waffen SS. But the Wehrmacht was also implicated regardless of the fact that some of their commanders made fruitless protests. After all, it was the Wehrmacht which made the atrocities possible. Without their acquisitions of territory, there would have been no one for the death squads to torture and kill. The 'incident' at Babi Yar is fairly representative of the sort of thing that took place. In September 1941, a German Army Group, after hammering away at the Soviet defences at Kiev for 45 days, finally captured the city. A few days later, there were explosions and fires in the Continental Hotel which the Germans had commandeered as their headquarters, and a number of personnel were killed. The military decided, not unnaturally, that it was the work of partisans, and then – quite arbitrarily – that partisan equalled Jew. Consequently, the Jews of the city were herded in batches to the outskirts of Kiev, to a ravine known as Babi Yar, and some 35 000 were shot in reprisal for the German deaths. It was later admitted by the German General Staff that the Jews had not, in fact, caused the explosions but that they had been the work of non-Jewish partisans who had planted landmines in the hotel as part of their resistance operations.

The German military, whether Wehrmacht or Waffen SS must be held accountable for the atrocities committed in the occupied territories, particularly in Russia and Poland and to a somewhat lesser extent in the Balkans. France, the Low Countries and especially Scandinavia (most notably 'Aryan' Denmark) fared rather better, but they were by no means immune, particularly when it came to the taking and shooting of hostages. It should also be remembered that over 50 per cent of the 5–6 million Russian prisoners in German captivity died of disease, starvation and brutality. Everyone was in some way implicated, even the Luftwaffe and the German navy although neither were *directly* involved in the persecutions. But they were making their own contribution to the viability and success of what has to be regarded as an evil system. And because all were in some way involved then no one can be completely exonerated, least of all the commanders (Beevor: 1998, pp. 56–60). It was all very well for them to plead afterwards that they were under oath to obey orders much as they may have disliked them. This was just one way in which culpability could be shifted to the Nazi hierarchy. In this way no one was to blame except Hitler and his immediate subordinates. Even those generals who had turned against their leader, regardless of their vows of loyalty, and had plotted his demise in 1943–44, had gone along with his plans while the going was good. (The courageous and much wounded Colonel Claus von Stauffenberg who had actually planted the bomb in the tragically abortive attempt on Hitler's life on 20 July 1944, had previously been much decorated for his service to the Führer and the regime.) It is therefore little wonder that the conspirators got little backing from the sceptical and mistrustful Allied powers. It is interesting to note that when many of the generals involved in the conspiracy had been apprehended, Hitler appointed Field Marshals Wilhelm Keitel and Gerd von Runstedt together with panzer supremo Hans Guderian to investigate the conduct of their fellow officers. On their say-so the conspirators were expelled from the army and transferred for trial to the notorious People's Court which meant almost certain execution.

At the Nuremberg Trails, the chief American prosecutor, Robert Jackson, summed up the legal and moral aspects of the case, saying:

> the real complaining party at your bar is civilization ... the refuge of the defendants can only be their hope that international law will lag so far behind the moral sense of mankind that conduct which is

> a crime in the moral sense, must be regarded as innocence in law.
> We challenge that proposition.
>
> (Snyder: 1998, p. 181)

The memoirs of the generals are tainted by a talent for misleading history. Many insisted that they had no knowledge of the atrocities – claims that bear no very close examination. Some also insisted, post-1945, that the Führer was militarily incompetent, an 'odious little corporal' and a hysterical upstart; but they did not say these things in 1940–41 when it mattered. They preferred to overlook the dark side of the theory and practice of Nazism, but they were happy with the 'laurels they won and wore with such pride'. Their view was that 'the politics were thrust upon them; they did their duty. The rest was not their business, merely their fate' (Downing: 1978, p. 243). The ethics of militarism – if that is not a contradiction in terms – were lost to them.

CHAPTER TEN

Militarism, Games and Ritual Compulsion

Ritual may be defined as the expressive aspect of religion. Militarism and war are often justified in religious terms, and may actually be waged for what are ostensibly religious reasons. Some states with strong ideological motivations have exhibited an overweening religious fervour and have gone to war either to proselytize or to exterminate the infidels who did not or could not embrace the 'true faith', whatever that faith happened to be. Some were prepared to do both, as was the case with Islam and the Crusader Knights. We are going to discuss this latter phenomenon in the next section of our discussion (Chapter 11), but here we are going to look at another aspect of the same theme, namely, those societies which have regarded war as a kind of ritualized game; societies that lived for war, yet war that was conducted primarily to satisfy what were believed to be vital ritual requirements.

The theory of games has a special and, in one sense, peculiar relevance to militarism. Games theory is concerned with the ways in which a series of operations are designed to provide a solution to a particular situation. This is done in such a way that the participant tries to guarantee himself a certain minimum success or, at the very least, thwart a successful outcome for his opponent. It is concerned therefore with choosing the optimum strategy in anticipation of the possible moves by the opponent. One can think of this in regard to recreational games such as chess or card games, but it is also useful as a tool for describing, and even analysing, more serious concerns such as war and conflict generally.

Games theory also connotes rules and conventions whereby games are played. For instance, it is possible to see espionage and counter-espionage in these terms (Carlton: 1998). Indeed, espionage has long been described as the 'great game'. In effect, games strategies are all about the resolution of certain kinds of problems by collusion and conciliation as well as conflict. Some time ago, Morris Janowitz, writing on the role of the American military, summarized games theory as 'taking into consideration our own reactions to our opponent's response to our moves [for by so doing] we can make him evolve a strategy designed to make him involuntarily choose a course of action favourable to us' (Janowitz: 1960,

p. 343). Such strategies, of course, involve *risk*. There is always a measure of unpredictability about any proposed course of action. Plans can go awry. Incomplete predictability involves *uncertainty* which, in turn, can generate indeciveness. Respective disciplines see these terms in different ways. In economics, for example, risk is all about the probabilities and possibilities of the market, of risk premiums and what is and is not insurable. On the other hand, psychologists are more concerned with subjective or affective uncertainty, than inner doubt which is only indirectly related to external events, and which may well lead to the adoption of avoidance strategies.

Whether or not risk is calculable, or the degree of uncertainty in any sense measurable in politico-military situations, is a moot point. Undoubtedly, theories of games of chance (probability theory) and particularly theories of games of strategy have considerable relevance to military intentions. Both have arisen out of the study of autotelic activities, that is, games which are undertaken simply for pleasure; activities such as sports which are pursued because they are enjoyable *in themselves*. We all know that such games can become too serious, especially when factors such as money and status come into play, in which case the intrinsic pleasure of the game takes second place to less laudable considerations. There are accepted rules governing most autotelic pursuits, and it is acknowledged as 'bad form' if these rules are contravened. Yet we all know that this takes place especially, say, in professional sports where winning is everything. What is particularly interesting is that when the rules are broken, they are broken according to yet further unwritten rules.

This, of course, mirrors much more serious social behaviour. We cannot maximize our own interests without taking into account how others are likely to respond. At the same time we are aware that they are doing the same to us, so we have to take this into consideration too, and possibly have to adjust our behaviour accordingly. And so it goes on; we are all involved in a tortuous complex of relations, and possibly neither they nor us can begin to understand exactly how we do it (Moore and Anderson: 1965).

In studying models of this kind it is important to distinguish between interactional games and non-interactional games. In games the rules and conditions are set; it then is a matter of skill for the competitors. In puzzles – the one person game – the conditions are also set, but the key difference is that once they are set they do not change, no other person or team is there to thwart the attempt at a solution. In some ways this reflects the difference between the physical and social sciences. In the social sciences, in the study of people, we have what is effectively a kind of game. And the game changes in the very act of investigation – witness how people respond to questions in front of cameras. In contrast, in the physical world (leaving aside the uncertainties of quantum mechanics) the conditions are ready for investigation, and to the best of our knowledge nothing is going to thwart our attempts to elucidate its mysteries.

In some games, where the outcome is ultimately unpredictable, one can differentiate between the *agent*, the person who initiates the action, and the *patient*, the person on whom the agent's actions impinge. The agent's actions will be directed towards certain predetermined goals, and these, in turn, will be related to a given system of values. But implicit in all this is the *reciprocal perspective*, that is to say, the imaginative ability of both agent and patient to put themselves in the other's position. In the real world it is difficult to see how society could run if this reciprocal perspective did not exist. Finally, there is the umpire or referee, the person who ensures that the rules of the game are observed, and who may – depending on the game in question – invoke certain sanctions if the rules are not kept.

It does not take much imagination to see how all this can be relevant to international politics and their military implications. It can certainly apply where a militaristic society is intent on pursuing its expansionist policies. Even war in conducted according to rules which – admittedly – are all too frequently modified, rationalized or actually broken. In a sense, there is also a referee, the international community, public opinion and the media. And given that people are looking on, it can lead to strange, anomalous situations. Even some of the Nazi concentration camps were tidied up in readiness for inspections by teams from the International Red Cross. One can hypothesize a number of possible reasons for this, but one surely is that in a totally uncharacteristic way these brutal Nazi officials were conscious of public opinion.

Militarism and military activity can be viewed as a game – a very serious game of skill, in which the participants are trying to outwit each other in an activity where the outcome is initially unpredictable. But what concerns us in this section of the discussion is ritual motivation and the *autotelic character* of much military activity, preparing for and going to war for the intrinsic pleasure that it brings. Given the horrific nature of modern warfare, many may regard this as a kind of lunacy. Perhaps it is, but there is ample evidence to support the fact that some societies have gloried in war, and their warriors relished the prospect of seasonal campaigns. It is as well to remember, too, that in many ways pre-modern warfare was more demanding than its modern counterpart. Much of it was hand to hand, an exhausting and bloody effort to overcome an opponent. And with little in the way of first aid or any really effective kind of medical treatment, even small wounds could be fatal, and death was often slow and agonizing.

Some rare societies such as the Dani had 'pretend wars' which involved simulated violence and amounted to little more than an exchange of abuse by warriors who were egged on by their women who wisely kept to the sidelines. These organized engagements kept injuries and fatalities to a minimum. Other societies actually played at war when no serious campaigning was in the offing. Medieval knights made a sport of jousting and in so doing honed their skills in readiness for the real thing. In Aztec society, war games became more serious still. When their gods became even more ravenous and more sacrificial victims were required, the military in conjunction with the priests contrived tournaments to ensure that supplies were maintained. They organized 'Wars of the Flowers' which were festivals of fighting held in honour of the deities. These ceremonial combats sometimes escalated into genuine hostilities if there was some underlying political rivalry. Contests of this kind helped to display warrior prowess besides providing more sacrificial fodder for the gods.

Case study

Although the Aztecs are a prime example of a society which combined warfare as aggrandizement and warfare for ritual purposes, they are also typical of those who appear to have got an autotelic buzz from the whole process of military enterprise. Perhaps this was because if they took captives for sacrifice they were honoured for their bravery, and if they themselves became victims, it was also an honour to be dedicated to the gods. Belief was everything. It was ideology that 'lubricated' the system and made the whole thing work. But the Aztecs were not the first or the only Meso-American culture to applaud militarism in this way, or to place it at the service of such a repugnant ritual system. It may also have been a feature of the little-known Olmec culture, perhaps the oldest of the Meso-American 'high cultures', which flourished in the Vera Cruz area of Mexico in the first millennium BC. Militarism and ritual sacrifice were certainly characteristic of the much later Toltec culture which was located at Tula (Tollan), just north of the capital of the Aztecs, Tenochtitlan (present Mexico City), who were their immediate successors on the Mexico scene.

Our concern, however, is with the Maya whose great days coincided roughly with the European 'Dark Ages'. Our knowledge of the Maya comes from the still not completely understood carvings on extant monuments at their ceremonial centres, and from the writings of some Spanish priests soon after the Conquest by the Spanish conquistadores which began in AD 1519. Many illuminated Mayan manuscripts were destroyed on the orders of Bishop Diego de Landa of Yucatan who displayed an understandable bigotry concerning what he felt to be a fundamentally evil religious system. Only a few, therefore, have survived. By an irony, an important but forgotten work by Landa – paradoxically a great student of Aztec culture – dated 1566, turned up in the Royal Library of Madrid in the nineteenth century giving some details of Mayan calendrical calculations which are reputed to be more advanced than those of the ancient Babylonians.

The Maya occupied territory in the arid Yucatan peninsula, in the highlands of Guatemala, and in parts of what became British Honduras. Their culture dates from c. 400 BC, but its full flowering was not reached until the Classic period c. AD 300–600. There was a post-Classic phase when Mayan culture was at its most flamboyant which ended c. AD 900. After this its ceremonial centres were abandoned, possibly with the incursions of the aggressive Toltecs, but that is sheer speculation. Both had similar military-cum-religious systems involving taking captives for sacrifice, though neither practised this on the scale of the later, expansionist Aztecs.

Mayan class structure took a fairly conventional form. The ruling class or nobles occupied the most important offices of state. They also comprised the richest farmers and merchants, as well as being the most esteemed warriors. The priests, too, who were particularly influential members of Mayan society, all belonged to this elite. Commoners, needless to say, comprised the vast majority of the population. They were the peasants, fishermen and artisans, and were regarded as free citizens. There is some evidence of a social category below that of commoner but above that of the more menial slave, in other words labourers with a status somewhat like that of a medieval serf. At the bottom of the social ladder were the slaves. They were extremely numerous and were frequently commoners who had been captured in war. Usually, they were held by nobles, although some might be owned by more wealthy commoners. They could be men, women or children, and may, alternatively have been enslaved for some offence (say, theft during a time of famine). If they were enslaved for minor crimes such as failure to pay their debts, it was possible for relatives to pay the fine to redeem them. It was common for people to be born into slavery, but there is no evidence of breeding slaves for profit, as in ancient Greece and Rome. If free citizens were rash enough to impregnate slaves they too could then be enslaved.

As we have already seen, one of the commonest causes of war was the need of slaves for sacrifice. Nobles, too, could be sacrificed if taken prisoner, but they were also often ransomed – a much more profitable alternative. Yet because nobles were usually also leading warriors they could end up on the sacrificial stone because they were a potential danger if left alive, and such practices were not stopped until the time of the Conquest. It is ironic that if the country had not been divided by internecine war before this the Conquest would not have been so ridiculously easy. The Maya had been engaged in fratricidal strife for about 70 years before the Spanish arrived. This was not primarily over the need for sacrificial victims, but over boundary and lineage honour issues.

Mayan society was based on a double-unilineal kinship system. Landa reported that there were some 250 patrilineages in the Yucatan at the time of the Conquest. These patrilineages were strictly exogamous and constituted mutual protection groups inasmuch as all members were under an obligation to help one another when necessary. Some property and land were held in common, and the patrilineage determined the pattern of inheritance arrangements for its members. The matrilineal factor, on the other hand, primarily determined preferential marriage arrangements. Lineages were important, and there was strict ranking within the system. Status and the timocratic (rule of honour) factors were greatly esteemed. Noble lineages provided the territorial rulers (the 'real men'), who normally lived in the capital towns of their districts. These were supported by the products of their own lands in addition to the tribute which was regarded as their due. Lesser members of the nobility ruled as provincials through the respective town councils where even the rich were 'chaired' by an annually elected commoner, although nobles had magisterial and administrative duties besides acting as war leaders.

Class distinctions also extended to religion. Caciques (principal men) were 'related' to certain gods who could not be directly approached by commoners. If ordinary people wished to supplicate these normally inaccessible deities they had to do so through their lords by bringing gifts every 20 days. It was a strictly hierarchical system which reinforced social dependency and control. It is possible that these rules were not part of the original Mayan culture but were introduced by Mexican invaders *c.* 1450 in order to underline their own authority. The area and degree of jurisdiction enjoyed by the lesser nobles was shared by a 'narcom' – a feared individual who acted as a kind of priest. He held office for three years, and it was his duty to perform the ritual sacrifices. In this he was assisted by four older men who were drawn annually from the laity. These religious functionaries were also complemented by a diviner (chilan) whose task was to prepare and consult the appropriate oracles in order to discern the will of the gods.

We have here then a rigidly stratified society with a strong patrilineal emphasis. It was non-monarchical (though it is believed that the early highland Maya did once have kings), and it worked largely through elected lay councils. But it is evident too that it was imbued, as we shall see, with pervasive hierocratic tendencies.

It would be tangentially relevant here to say something about Mayan sex roles because these do have an indirect bearing on militarism. Children were 'baptized' sometime between the ages of three and 12, something that astounded the Spanish friars who came with the conquistadores. The children also underwent purification rites involving incense and holy water. Early in life there was a separation of the sexes. Girls stayed at home with their parents partly for domestic training and partly as a precaution against unchastity for which punishments were severe. Exogamous marriages were arranged and monogamy was the custom, although polygamy was common among the nobles. Dress and decoration 'declared' and reinforced sex roles. Both sexes had frontal teeth filled, sometimes with jade plaques, and both sexes practised tattooing and scarification from the waist up after marriage. Curiously, crossed eyes were greatly esteemed, and parents often tried to induce this by hanging small beads over their children's noses! Painting the body was also common for men, and always for warriors, before marriage. Black was the usual colour, and was believed to have some kind of religious significance. Infringements were very frowned upon, and sanctions were particularly unpleasant. In fact, adultery was punishable by death.

Boys, by contrast, were separated from their parents, and in a system somewhat reminiscent of the ancient Spartans, were housed together in communal blocks. Here they learned the arts of war which was destined to be their main preoccupation when they were fully mature. They were allowed some diversions including the pleasures of prostitutes. But their main recreation was the ball-game. This was not, as it sounds, a kind of baseball, but a game – with variations – that was played throughout Meso-America. We are not too clear about the rules, but it appears to have been a sort of mixture between basketball and volleyball except that the rubber ball had to be knocked through a ring high on a side wall with the hips, wrists or elbows – a very difficult task. Winners could claim cloaks of feathers and jewels from the spectators, but for losers the result was very different. It may be that as with the Toltecs the game was played 'for keeps'. There is reason to suppose that the losers were actually decapitated. Certainly, the huge ball court at the main Mayan ceremonial site at Chichen Itza was lined with skewered skulls.

Sex roles were also reflected in the religious system. The Mayan pantheon had a bewildering assortment of deities. A late (eighteenth-century) manuscript lists 166 deities, several of whom had a variety of aspects – always a source of confusion to the investigator. Furthermore, a number of the gods had 'consorts'; in this case the consort of the supreme deity, Itzamna was Ix Chel (the Rainbow Lady), who was the goddess of medicine and childbirth. Also, as in a number of pre-scientific societies, the Moon goddess was the consort of the Sun god. In general, the Mayan deities were either nature gods such as the rain god (Chac) and the Sun god who was often represented as a ravenous jaguar (a favourite emblem of the Olmecs), or they were gods of professions and classes. The chief deity of the ruling caste was the culture hero, Kulkulcan, better known under his Aztec title, Quetzalcoatl ('feathered serpent'). It was the nature deities and war deities that were almost always male, and were characterized by a certain degree of ferocity. (This may be compared with other early societions where they are sometimes depicted as female, note the Greek Athena and the revengeful Egyptian Hathor.)

The priests, who were also often members of the military order, appear to have been exclusively male. No women seem to have officiated in any way in the sacrificial rituals. Self-mutilation was common among the religious functionaries: stingray spines were inserted into the ears, lips, cheek and tongue – even the penis. The blood was collected and used to anoint the idols. Animals were sacrificed, and towards the latter days of Mayan society – possibly under the influence of the Toltecs – human sacrifice appears to have increased. It took three main forms: removing the heart, shooting the victim with arrows, and drowning them in the sacred well. Usually the victims were prisoners of war who were pinioned on the sacrificial stone by the priests while one opened the breast with an obsidian knife, cut out the heart and offered it to the Sun. The heart was then handed to another priest who smeared its blood over the image of the god. Then often one priest would dress himself in the flayed skin of the victim and dance before the assembled tribespeople. If the victim was deemed to have been a brave warrior, his body was cut up and his flesh was eaten by the warriors and the aristocracy, presumably on the assumption that his enemies would be partaking symbolically of his laudable qualities. The rationale – or philosophy – for this was that the Sun god needed to be refreshed and reinvigorated after his nightly journey across the arid wasteland of the dead (night) in order to continue to sustain the land during the day (Hultkrantz: 1980).

Those sacrificial victims who were drowned were usually young virgin girls who were cast into the sacred well (cenote) at dawn just as the Sun was rising from the 'realm of the dead'. They were thrown or forced to jump from a ledge some 65 feet above the well which is said to have been about 60 feet deep. It was almost certainly a fertility rite associated with rain, and it is known that precious objects of gold and jade were also sacrificed to the 'powers of the well'. On other special occasions the victims might be hunchbacks or otherwise deformed people whose sacrificial death was thought to avert accidents. Again, it is thought that some of the practices were introduced in post-Classical Mayan times by the Toltecs who were associated with the ceremonial centre at Chichen Itza. Before the sacrifices took place ritual taboos were observed such as sexual abstinence. Subsequently, however, there was considerable licence involving drunkenness and sexual excess, possibly as a kind of psycho-social catharsis.

Even a superficial overview of Mayan religion shows us that the people lived in an orderly fatalistic universe. Life was not easy. Like the Incas of Peru and the later Aztecs of Mexico, they had no wheel, no technology as we have come to understand it, yet they were able to construct architectural marvels such as their ceremonial centres with their complexes of temples and plazas. This was facilitated by a large labour force which was presumably both politically and ideologically motivated, and by their fascination with mathematics (they had the concepts of place, number and zero, and had even calculated the length of the year to three decimal places). As far as their monumental achievements are concerned, it is a wonder that they were able to do so much with so little.

Their delight in war was intrinsically bound up with religion. As in a number of other cultures, it was believed that the warrior who died either in battle or as a sacrificial victim of the enemy went straight to paradise. Here he would be in the company of those brave women who had died in childbirth, and those who had committed suicide (old and infirm people who were likely to die from their illness often chose to kill themselves so that they would receive the anticipated post-mortal rewards). The ideology, therefore, was such that the warrior could not lose. Indeed, the weaponry the Mayan military used was hardly calculated to inflict serious losses on their enemies. It was much more important to take prisoners who would end their days on the 'stone' than it was to kill them in battle (it was this religiously motivated strategy that largely led to the downfall of the Aztecs in the early sixteenth century who insisted on trying to capture their Spanish enemies instead of killing them).

It is a little surprising, given this generally optimistic view of death, that the Mayan god of death (Cizin), who is mentioned frequently in the extant Mayan codices, is depicted as a terrifying skeletal figure. The war god was a companion of the death god who, together with other Mayan deities and their daemonic minions, controlled the destinies of the people. It hardly goes without saying that the war god was closely associated with the sacrificial knife as it was also with the later Toltecs and Aztecs who before the Conquest are believed to have sacrificed several thousand people a year. Indeed, no other society is known which claimed human victims on such a scale. The evidence suggests that Mayan society became more militaristic in its later phases. Competition between polities obviously played a part. In a sense it all became a kind of game with different local rulers vying with each other, and warriors competing to see who could bring in the most prestigious captives. Land and resources were also important factors, but prestige and power were the critical issues.

During the late Classic period (c. AD 750) warfare became 'endemic' and the primary objective became not so much the annexation of territory, as the demonstration of dominance and the taking of tribute and captives for sacrifice. The greatest coup for a ruler was the capture and sacrifice of another ruler. This was a comparatively rare event, but when it happened it was usually celebrated in stone. As in other early societies, e.g. Egypt, it was the monuments and stelae that proclaimed the victories of the ruler. When a Mayan polity lost its ruler it was considered little short of devastating, because he was the living link with the supernatural world, and it was his well-being that was believed to sustain the whole community. If he was not sacrificed but simply confined by a rival ruler, he was deemed to be in a state of suspended animation and became increasingly powerless. How such strange and irrational ideas developed is difficult to know, but they certainly existed in many other pre-scientific cultures which might be as primitive as eighteenth-century Dahomey and as sophisticated as the Egyptian Old Kingdom.

Written language has long been a problem for scholars of Mayan civilization. The enigmatic symbols have proved to be all but impossible to decipher. It is now believed by some Mayanists (for example, Schele and Freidel, 1990) that the code has been cracked, but there are still some uncertainties about what is decipherment and what is speculation, especially about specificities. Having added this cautionary word, we are told that sometimes one ruler would actually usurp the territory of another. So, for instance, when the war leader of Tikal (with what is said to be the exotic name of Smoking Frog) wished to take over the city of Uaxactun during the reign of Tikal's Great Jaguar Paw in AD 378, war ensued, and so did a great deal of bloodletting. If scholars have understood the text correctly, this was the first known instance in the Mayan lowlands of the extermination of one ruling family by another. According to one authority (Sharer: 1994, pp. 187–9), this and many other Mayan aggressions were timed to coincide with certain positions of the planet Venus, especially Venus as the Evening Star, as well as other celestial bodies.

At Dos Pilas in Guatemala, archaeologists have located double defensive palisades which were erected to trap the attackers and leave them at the mercy of the defenders. This is borne out by the discovery of the buried skulls of decapitated young males who were presumably sacrificed after capture probably in AD 761. At Bonampak in Mexico are some of the most famous, though damaged, Mayan murals, many of which depict battle scenes of hand-to-hand fighting, while elaborately dressed war leaders stand by holding pathetic captives by the hair. The aftermath of the battle is also shown including the royal entourage on the stepped pyramid, with musicians and dancers performing below. The victors liked to record how their captives were tortured and bled prior to sacrifice and decapitation. It is not all sites, by any means, which support events with such graphic archeological accuracy. Only some events can be reconstructed or surmised by the puzzling Mayan glyphs. But the general nature of the society is clear, and its military-cum-religious system reasonably incontrovertible. Conflict between rival polities was 'endemic'. All sorts of reasons and motives were present, but there is little doubt from the nature, frequency and ritual aftermath that militarism and war had an autotelic quality.

Excursus: The Phenomenon of Blood-Sacrifice

To moderns the idea of blood-sacrifice probably seems offensive, and the notion that it somehow brings spiritual cleansing strikes many as being faintly ludicrous. Sacrifice in the broader sense of giving up something – possibly something of value – so that somebody else can benefit makes more sense. And even the practice of forgoing something – say, certain kinds of food (as per Albert Schweitzer) – because other less privileged people cannot enjoy similar delights has a kind of resonance with some people, even though it is of no *direct* benefit to them. It is only a gesture, a token of identity, but at least it is comprehensible. But blood-sacrifice as a religious act seems to be totally irrational, yet it has been practised by many peoples both past and present.

There are many theories of blood-sacrifice from piacular notions that it actually facilitates communion with the divine, to substitution or scapegoat theories which hold that the gods require a victim (blood) to compensate for or 'bear' the sins of the people. The idea is that a life has to be given, be it that of a bird, an animal or, most efficacious of all, a human being. And nowhere was this more believed and practised than among the tribes of Central America.

The term 'sacrifice' literally means 'to make holy' and not only connotes the idea of propitiation, but also that of an honorarium to secure the continued favour of the offended deities. Among primitive tribes which practise some form of totemism (which, strictly speaking, cannot really be classified as a religion) the totemic object may or may not be violated. It might well be something inanimate such as a rock or a stream but, if it is an animal, killing may only be allowed at certain times or under certain conditions. In this case the special properties of the victim, especially if it has been duly consecrated, may then be consumed by the priests and the people in the belief that they too may share these qualities, and/or that the gods will be generous enough to grant an increase in the species concerned. There is reason to believe from the evidence of the cave paintings at Lascaux and Carnac that practices like, or similar to, this go back at least to the Upper Paleolithic period, and were practised in order to facilitate an adequate food supply by indulging in a little 'hunting magic'. On the other hand, the artists may have been simply trying to brighten up their living quarters with some much needed interior decoration – a much more mundane explanation.

Blood sacrifice, symbolizing the pouring out of life was in many societies the occasion for very elaborate ceremonial. There is reason to believe that in some early communities, the priest or shaman wore an animal mask or actually dressed in the skin of the sacred animal and performed mimetic dances in order to invoke the required deities or spirits. Implicit in the ritual would probably be not only the idea of appeasing the spirits but also that of a quid pro quo, in effect a kind of bargain, if not actually a bribe, which 'declared' that, if we are dutiful to them, they might just be kind to us. In early Roman society, the blood of the victim was sometimes sown into the ground to ensure a fruitful harvest. Similarly, though more poignantly, among the Pawnee in Mississippi in the early nineteenth century, warriors were known to steal girls from the other tribes and sacrifice them to the Morning Star in ways reminiscent of the Maya. There is on record the instance of a young Sioux girl being treated like a goddess for six months, and then two days before she was due to be sacrificed, was painted half red and half black as part of her preparation. On the central day of the ritual, she was roasted over a slow fire and then – possibly to put her out of her agony – shot with arrows. Her heart was then torn out and eaten, and the rest of her body was cut into small pieces, taken to a cornfield where the blood was squeezed into the new grains and the flesh rubbed on potatoes (James: 1962, p. 85).

A very similar practice obtained among the Khond people of Bangladesh. A youth was consecrated to the Earth goddess, often in childhood, and on the appointed day his hair was cut off and he was given a new garment and tied to a post where he was anointed and revered by the people. After this he was strangled and his body was cut into pieces which were then distributed throughout the local villages and used to promote the fertility of their fields. This is not dissimilar to the one-time practice of taking human heads as war prizes, as happened in widely different societies such as Burma, Borneo and the Philippines, because they would stimulate the growth of crops.

As we have seen from the Central American experience, such practices were not peculiar to undeveloped societies. In ancient Egypt, there is some evidence that human sacrifice may well have been known in pre-dynastic times (i.e. before *c.* 3000 BC). Indeed, it seems also to have been practised during the first two dynasties (Emery: 1972), although during the more developed phase of the Old Kingdom, say by the fourth Dynasty *c.* 2500 BC (the principal Pyramid Age), the evidence becomes more ambiguous. It may well have been passé by this time, although there are some hints in the records which suggest that there was some ritual killing of prisoners of war as an offering to the gods. The abandonment of human sacrifice as a society becomes more developed can also be seen among the early Hebrews. In fact, it may be that the story of the near-sacrifice of the child, Isaac, by his father, Abraham, and the substitution of an animal, was originally an aetiological folk tale which signifies the change from human sacrifice to animal sacrifice.

About some other early societies we are not altogether clear. Too little is known about the Indus Valley civilization in what is now Pakistan. In early Mesopotamia we know that at Ur, retainers and perhaps wives were killed and buried with at least one ruler, and the same was apparently done in early China during the time of the Shang dynasty (1500 BC). We have comparable examples too in Classical society. Both the Romans and the Greeks practised blood sacrifice and appear not to have been averse to the occasional human sacrifice when the situation demanded it, but here too it seems to have been discontinued when these societies reached their more developed phases. This is not, however, to suggest that 'more developed' necessarily means 'more humane'. We surely know too much about the horrors of modern history to believe that. But it does mean that as societies became more 'cultured' the practice of human sacrifice as an institutionalized part of religion has been generally discontinued. Yet there were exceptions. Here, probably the best example is the Phoenicians, particularly their colony on the North African coast, Carthage, where children were fed to the 'fire of Moloch'. The god 'demanded' his quota of victims until the destruction of the city by the Romans in 146 BC. It is understood that there was actually a minor holocaust of victims to try to avert this disaster, but nothing could save the Carthaginians from the ferocious onslaught of their enemies who were determined to end the series of Punic wars for good.

Nothing, however, compared with Central America for both the variety and scale of human sacrifice. What can match the ceremonial slaughter ordered by the Aztec ruler, Ahuitzotl, at the dedication of the temple of the war god, Huitzilopochtli, in 1487, where we are told that the sacrifices lasted from 'dawn to dusk' for four days? The carnage involved some hundreds of war captives and slaves, and was witnessed by dignitaries from all over the Aztec empire at a cost of a year's tribute from the subject states. Monumentally impressive as Tenochtitlan was, the sheer imbecility of the prevailing militarism-for-sacrifice culture still tends to be minimized by relativist anthropologists (e.g. Fagan: 1984; 1998) who are overawed by other Aztec achievements and rightly disgusted at the subsequent treatment of the Indians by the Spanish conquerors.

CHAPTER ELEVEN

Militarism as a Religious Imperative

Militarism and aggressive expansionism have often been associated with what the 'trade' terms 'high' or world religions. These are the religions that have claimed impressive numbers of adherents, and which had – and in many cases still have – an appeal which marks them off from the defunct religions of the past such as, say, Osiran religion in ancient Egypt and Olympian religion in early Greece. High religions have a number of interesting characteristics which, while not always that distinctive, when taken together constitute relatively unique systems.

1. *High religions often have a universal appeal,* not only in the sense that they can attract people of different nationalities and cultures, but they are also frequently 'classless' in that, in the strict sense, everyone can be included. There are, of course, important exceptions to this. Judaism tends to exclude those not born within the 'family', but even so it is prepared to accept sincere and duly instructed converts. Similarly with Hinduism. Everyone except outcastes (scheduled castes) had a social position within the caste system even if it was a particularly modest position. Although it was virtually impossible to change castes, there was some upward mobility *within* castes from one sub-caste (jati) to another. Much as the caste system has been criticized for its inequalities, it lasted for at least 3 000 years, and traditionally each caste and sub-caste had its place in Indian society; almost invariably it had some kind of occupational or otherwise functional contribution to make to the system. For good or ill, this system which undoubtedly favoured a special elite (Brahmins), has now broken down with Westernization, although there is still evidence that in some areas and at certain levels the new orthodoxy is being ignored.

   By contrast, the Judaeo-Christian and Islamic traditions have been uncompromisingly universalistic in their appeal and in their 'marketing'. As we are surely all aware, these systems too have their hierarchies and inequalities especially in their modes of organization. They also have their disputes and divisions. But what is most interesting from the standpoint of this particular discussion is that although purporting to be religions of love and goodwill to all, they – of all religions – have been the most militarily active in propagating their respective beliefs. But whether it is the religious ideology that inspires military action or whether the ideology – appropriately interpreted – provides a convenient justification for the action is a moot point. After all, military compulsion can only bring nominal acquiescence or acceptance, it cannot actually inspire *belief*, as such. The injunction to submit, pay the necessary tax or die, is hardly likely to bring about anything but a mere token conversion.

2. *High religions often claim to be revealed religions*: social scientists will frequently suggest that religions arise and are accepted for a combination of socio-economic and psychological reasons. But the movement itself will almost invariably justify its existence in apocalyptic terms. The faith is seen to have special insights which have been 'revealed' or communicated by supernatural means to a founder or founders and thus to society at large. If the founder or founders are regarded as divine or otherwise chosen or 'anointed' persons, the revelation will be seen as irrefutable, a unique social phenomenon. Its message then becomes doctrine (what should be believed) or dogma (what *must* be believed). It is the kerugma – the 'preached thing' – and is therefore not open to contradiction or modification. However, we know that in practice this is often far from the case, and that religions fragment and divide into sects under charismatic leaders (e.g. the Shia and Sufi movements in Islam). The problem with revealed religions is that they are always susceptible to newer and higher revelations.

3. *High religions are frequently 'religions of the Book'*. After a period of oral tradition, the 'message' or corpus of belief is committed to writing. This is done for a number of reasons. Most commonly the writings or scriptures act as aids to the respective rituals which are sometimes designed to function as 'acted truths'. The idea that scripture says what ritual does has a certain cogency. The writings also help to preserve the tradition so that it can be transmitted to future generations. In this way the revelation can be communicated in an ostensibly indelible form.

Just as important is the fact that a written tradition serves to refute criticisms. The message becomes 'set', as it were, for all time. What began as a codification of the tradition for convert instruction, becomes a means of perpetuating 'everlasting truths'. These are not only inspirational but also educational in that they act as 'apologias' for the faith, reasoned defences against hostile attacks of critics and heterodox adherents who threaten to undermine the unity of the movement. What some regard as the downside of written traditions is that historically they have given rise to the apparent necessity of literate priesthoods who have acted – and to a lesser extent continue to act – as guardians of the tradition. The rationale is that infallible scriptures require infallible interpreters. Inevitably, these functions have served to increase priestly status and authority.

4. *High religions are sometimes militant and expansionist in orientation.* High – and especially revealed – religions are sometimes polytheistic (having many deities) or henotheistic (having many deities of whom one is supreme) and these tend to take a rather relaxed and tolerant approach to adherence. After all, what does one god more or less really matter? This was the Roman attitude towards the religions of their conquered peoples. Conquerors are usually not too worried about belief as long as its expression is kept to a minimum and is in no way subversive. Monotheism, on the other hand, tends to breed militancy on the mistaken assumption that people can be made to believe when they can only be made *to say* that they believe. This was probably also the case with many recanting heretics. Militancy may be justified on the basis that people must be converted 'for the good of their souls'. In the medieval Inquisition this meant that the body might be tortured and subsequently destroyed in the interests of the soul. Immortal concerns outweighed temporal discomforts. One wonders if it seriously occurred to anyone that these interests were not necessarily incompatible.

Compulsion exhibited by some religions, while ostensibly for spiritual purposes, not infrequently had a covert political function. Movements which try to establish earthly theocracies by force rarely act out of pure motives. In sociological terms, we must distinguish between structure and agency, between the system and its doctrines, and the human agencies by whom this is expressed. Governmental authority which is created in the name of religion has to be exercised arbitrarily by men. There is no form of control more efficient and inexpensive than that exercised by belief (Carlton: 1977).

Case study

Probably most people are aghast at a religious system that can impel people to commit acts of wanton carnage, and may even feel either that the ideology must be seriously flawed, or – more likely – that its adherents are grossly mistaken in their interpretation of that ideology. There is nothing entirely new in this. Intolerance and persecution have been the outcomes of several religious systems and of sub-systems within those systems. In the modern world, the most ominous developments are those within Islam. The Muslim fraternity, like the Western Church, is hopelessly divided within its own ranks. More to the point, is there any difference today, as opposed, say, to the medieval world, in that extremist elements within Islam seem to be prepared to go to any lengths to achieve their aims. And this is only part of the problem. Extremism is on the increase, so much so, in fact, that it is no longer confined, as once it was, to radical brotherhoods, but has expanded to include whole nation states such as Iran and Afghanistan.

Has Islam always been like this? Was fundamentalist Islam, as we have come to understand it, always a potential possibility? And if so, is extremism inherent within Islam, or is it the result of an outrageous heresy which has afflicted the 'religion of the Prophet'? Or, to pose the question in terms of our theme, has Islam always been militaristic, and if so is this a logical outcome of belief in its ideology?

These are not really issues that can be simply answered in today's terms. They go back to the rise of Islam in the seventh century AD, and the original inculcation of a faith that taught that unbelievers were infidels who must submit or face the consequences. Such a faith impelled its adherents to conquest, although this is not to argue that the only motivation that Muslims have ever had was the propagation of their beliefs. There has always been an admixture of mercenary – even carnal – interests as well as more lofty religious reasons for launching campaigns against the 'infidel'. Today, Islamic extremism is directed largely against the West and ostensibly Western values (though notably not against Western money or Western technology – especially armaments). In earlier days it was also very much about power and territory as well as religion. Indeed, it has been argued that the earliest conquests in Arabia itself would not have been carried out had it not been an attractive solution to certain economic problems. Furthermore, it is maintained that these first tentative military actions were mere raiding parties in search of plunder, and that wars of conquest only followed when it was discovered just how weak the enemy really was (Lewis: 1958).

Ironic as it is when considering modern Israeli–Arab relations, it is almost certain that both cultures derive from the same Semitic stock which can be traced back to early pastoralists in the second millennium BC. Arabia was hardly touched by the great warring empires such as the

Assyrians, Babylonians and, later, the Greeks and Romans who all had such an influence on Syria-Palestine. It therefore remained very much a pastoral society well into the first millennium AD. The situation was not much different when *c.* AD 600 Muhammad, an obscure and rather tormented idealist, began to preach a monotheistic religion to an essentially polytheistic people. Muhammad's claimed revelations resulted in the Koran (Qu'rān) containing a series of laws and injunctions which were not actually codified until about a century after his death (AD 632). This came as a fervent and revolutionary message to his early converts; it constituted a mission which eventually found military expression. From their initial base at Medina, the tribes subdued Mecca and then the rest of Arabia. Their unifying principle which built on the traditional tribal structure was that of the brotherhood of believers, the possessors of *the* truth. Typically, as with revealed religions – 'religions of the Book' – the belief demanded operationalization. It was a call to action.

The early leaders of Islam ('submission') were related in some way to the Prophet. These initial caliphs (khalifa or deputy) were castigated by many of the rank and file for their wealth and their overbearing and despotic style. In 644 the Caliph Umar was assassinated by a Persian slave, and in 656 a party of mutineers from the Arab army in Egypt went to Medina to present their grievances to the Caliph and then murdered him. Ali, his successor, the last of this series of Caliphs led an army out of Medina – an event which spelled the end of Medina as the capital of Islam – and launched an attack on his fellow Muslims in a civil war that established an ominous precedent for the unity of Islam. In 661 he was deposed and killed by conservatives who felt that their leaders were guilty of abuses of office. In a very real sense this marked something of a turning point in the history of the movement because many felt that this sort of internecine strife did nothing for the faith and weakened the religious and moral prestige of the Quraysh Caliphate.

The first century of Islam was probably its most eventful. The Quraysh Caliphate was succeeded by the Umayyad Caliphate with its capital in Damascus, but the struggle for ascendancy within the movement continued, and it was eventually displaced by the more famous Abbasid Caliphate based on Baghdad (AD 750) with which we are going to be primarily concerned. During these momentous years, the Muslim armies were victorious virtually everywhere they campaigned. Once Arabia had been brought under the authority of the Crescent, the armies, now considerably reinforced, moved north and took Syria, Palestine and Iraq. The whole of the Middle East was now at their mercy. In two separate campaigns they conquered Egypt in the West and Persia (Iran) in the East. Their forces were then augmented by a navy, and they ventured along the North African coast taking Libya and the ancient city of Carthage.

This initial tide of conquest came to an end in the middle of the eighth century. Muslim forces, until now almost always successful, were stopped in the remoter regions of Anatolia and the Caucasus, and the unsuccessful sieges of Byzantium (Constantinople, now Istanbul – an almost impregnable fortress which was not taken by Muslim armies until the fifteenth century) halted the Muslims in the Balkans. They carried out impressive campaigns in Afghanistan and took Kabul in 664, then on to Hindu Kush and the invasion of Sind which ended in 711.

These were incredible military achievements, reminiscent in some ways of Alexander's campaigns a thousand years earlier – though he did it in even less time. This was the high water mark of Islamic success. By the 730s, their armies were overstretched. They had extended lines and communications were difficult, so when they ventured into Europe proper it was a different story. Having reached France they came up against the powerful kingdom of the Franks. Until now they had been virtually irresistible in the Mediterranean, having taken Gibralter and capturing Cordoba and Toledo in Spain. With forces composed principally of Arabs and Berbers (who later revolted) they had also taken Seville and Merida (712). It should be noted that at this time Spain was in a deplorable state. Under a series of despotic Visigothic princes, its armies consisted mainly of serfs and slaves who had neither the ability nor the will to withstand the Muslim onslaught. The serfs and the Jews (who had been intensely persecuted at this time) had nothing to lose and actually aided the Muslims in the fight against the oppressors. The Muslim army was finally halted in France by the augmented Frankish forces under their leader, Charles Martel, at the battle of Poitiers (732). The Muslim leader, Abd-al-Rahman, was killed, and the Arab armies retreated, though it did not stop them from making dangerous forays in other parts of France such as Avignon (734) and Lyons (743). It still remains that 100 years after the Prophet, Islam held sway from France to the Chinese borders.

The fortunes of Islam waxed and waned. Much depended on the location and strength of the Caliphate. It is probably beyond dispute that one high water mark was reached with the establishment of the Abbasid Caliphate and the ascendancy of Baghdad under the authority of Caliph Mansur. His armies and bodyguard were composed largely of men from Central Asia, although he did retain a number of Arab warriors. In addition, Abbasid leaders often imported Turkish mercenaries – an expedient that was not always to the Caliphate's advantage – especially in the fratricidal wars between those who were jockeying for more power as well as in the ongoing conflict with the Byzantines. These ethnic problems continued to beset Islam. In 834, for instance, when there was trouble with his Persian subjects, the Caliph Mutasim moved from Baghdad with a huge bodyguard composed of Turkish slaves and set up court in Samarra. It would appear that he had a marked distrust of certain ethnic groups, including Arabs, who were taken off his payroll in Egypt (Levy: 1971, p. 417). As the original recipients of the 'message', Arabs could and did react when others assumed supremacy.

It was obviously in the interests of the Caliph that he kept on good terms with the army. Their interests were paramount and had first call upon the imperial treasury. It was quite common for those who were not that ideologically committed to riot if payment was not forthcoming – and sometimes they could not be trusted even when it was. At one stage a Caliph was murdered by one of his Turkish chiefs, who was later assassinated by rivals. For a while the Caliphate was run by the guards, and Baghdad was at the mercy of rampaging bands of mercenaries who terrorized the inhabitants. Once power was restored by the Caliphate and discipline was imposed, the military assumed its rightful role and operated with its well-known efficiency.

The Caliph was ultimately responsible for military policy, while his chief minister (vizier) assisted in other matters of state. Much depended on the nature of the campaign in hand. If it was a relatively minor problem the standing army together with the bodyguard might be sufficient. But if a large-scale operation was called for against 'foreign infidels' such as the Byzantines, then – something the Caliphate eventually came to regret – the army was enlarged by the recruitment of additional and somewhat motley bands of tribesmen. The actual tactical command of the army was in the hands of the Caliph's generals who were usually his relatives, possibly his sons. There were sometimes murmurings about this, but the really powerful rulers such as the Abbasid, Harun-al-Rashid (786–809), made it clear to his subordinates how things had to be.

It is generally acknowledged that during the Abbasid dynasty, Islamic culture reached what was perhaps its most brilliant cultural and intellectual phase. This Baghdad Caliphate comprised ten successive rulers in all, the most notable of which was the fifth Caliph, Harun-al-Rashid. His rule has undoubtedly become embellished with time, but it is known that he ruthlessly rid himself of his rivals among the Persian intelligentsia, 'people of the pen', at his court. Most of them were cast into prison, and their property confiscated, but one personable individual – whom one assumes had been particularly presumptious – was decapitated and his body then halved and the portions impaled on the gate of the city. It is a reflection of the irreconcilable divisions within Islam that al-Rashid's greatest rival other than the still powerful Byzantine state, was not Charlemagne in Northern Europe but fellow Muslims, the Umayyad dynasty, in Spain. The Caliph had already distinguished himself in successful encounters with the Byzantines which had earned him the title, 'follower of the right path' (al-Rashid). It was customary for the Muslim forces to carry out three campaigns a year, if for no other reason than keeping the army in trim. How far the ideological impulse was present here, we do not know. There had been many expeditions against the 'infidels', and there were to be many more (al-Rashid won several engagements in 806), but none of the sieges of Byzantium (Constantinople) succeeded until the Ottoman victory in 1453.

The court of al-Rashid was a fabulous place according to the chroniclers. But then history and legend have become conflated in the Arabian Nights' world of the Abbasids. The riches of the palace were something to behold, especially on festival occasions and during the visits of foreign dignitaries. We are told that al-Rashid's wife refused to use tableware that was not made of gold or silver and studded with gems. It is said, too, that at the nuptials of al-Rashid's successor, his son al-Mamum (825),

> a thousand pearls of unique size were showered from a golden tray upon the couple who sat on a golden mat studded with pearls and sapphires ... [and] balls of musk, each containing a ticket naming an estate or a slave or some such gift, were showered on the princes and dignitaries.
>
> (Hitti: 1970, p. 302)

The list of wealth and munificence goes on. The Caliph is seen as the acme of Islamic kingship, and the incomparability of his court is extolled with its poets, dancers, singers and musicians all in attendance. Beautiful girls perform in 'rhythmic unison', and at a dinner the Caliph is served a dish of 150 fishes' tongues. There may be just a hint of exaggeration here and there (and there is little mention of the welfare of ordinary people), but as one authority states, 'Even when stripped of the adventitious glow cast by oriental romance and fancy, enough of the splendour of court life in Baghdad remains to arouse our astonishment' (ibid., p. 340). The irony is that al-Rashid's sons fought one another for the succession in a disastrous civil war, and when the victor entered Baghdad in triumph, half the city lay in ruins.

The revenues needed to finance the luxury of the court and its officials, the palaces and the harem, and for payment to the considerable

Muslim armies was raised in a number of ways. There was a legal tax which was obligatory on every Muslim. In theory, all money collected from believers was disbursed to believers, especially the poor and needy. But it was also recognized that some – an unknown proportion – was used to finance the 'holy war' (jihad) which could mean any campaigns against unbelievers. Tithes were also levied on merchandise, and not inconsiderable payments accrued from capitation taxes on non-Muslims within the empire. In addition there was truce money and tribute exacted from defeated enemies and, not least, confiscations (al-Rashid took 50 million dirhams from one man alone whose estate is said to have provided a *daily income* of 100 000 dirhams). The bureaucrats at the state audit office ensured that these monies were duly collected and allocated to the appropriate agencies, not least to the court treasury and to the military and police without which the Caliph was virtually impotent (all too many rulers have been toppled because they neglected the autocrat's golden rule of maintaining generous donations to the armed forces, especially the bodyguard). Military pay was reasonably good. At its height, the state paid the infantry soldier 240 dirhams a year, and a cavalryman twice that much. (A dinar was a gold coin weighing about 4 grammes; 1 dinar was worth 10 silver dirhams.) This may be compared with a master builder's wage of 1 dirham a day, and a labourer's at only one-third of a dirham. (These money values are impossible for us to assess, but they are interesting for purposes of comparison. The construction of Baghdad involving thousands of workmen cost nearly 5 million dirhams, but how disproportionate this is when compared with a set of three ornate barges for 3 million dirhams; and al-Rashid's mother who had an income of 160 million dirhams.)

Although the Abbasids are credited with introducing science into the art of warfare both in offensive operations (naphtha as a weapon) and in relation to troops' welfare (rudimentary field hospitals), it was during the later Caliphs that decline set in. The incorporation of certain cadres of foreign troops did not help, and the decentralization of commands and payments to provincial governors exacerbated the problems, even though decentralization was an inevitable consequence of having such extensive territories to control. In time this led to the virtual autonomy and increased power of some of the governors, and a diminution in the power of the Caliph. There was also the problem of women and the military. Surprisingly for a notably patriarchal society, royal women – who were often ennobled slaves of some ability as singers, musicians and dancers – came to exert a considerable influence on affairs of state, even to the point of assuming positions in the military, positions for which their beauty alone hardly qualified them.

The Abbasid Caliphate had come into power on the promise of returning to Islamic fundamentals, but eventually imitated the autocratic style of its predecessors. With the decline of the Abbasid dynasty, the empire became fragmented – a situation not helped by the fratricidal war between al-Rashid's sons. Power became more concentrated in Persia, and other provinces, notably Syria. Egypt, Morocco, Tunisia and Spain, became autonomous states under local dynasties. Added to this were the amazing victories achieved by a coalition of Bedouin tribes which in 871 captured and sacked Basra. Soon the Caliph's authority extended no further than Iraq, and principally only in the capital itself. And before the end of the tenth century, Baghdad fell to the Persians, and they – and later the Turks – took charge of the empire. The Caliph retained an honorary position as 'leader' of Islam, but he was no longer able to exert any real power. Islam was now irrevocably divided politically and theologically, and, except for certain extremist groups (Hiro: 1988), would never again be able to display the same fire and fanaticism that it had in the initial days of expansion.

The purpose of war for Islam was, of course, to increase wealth in terms of lands and goods (one-fifth of all booty went to the Caliph), and to prevent rebellion by those who would deprive the state of such things. But it was also to obtain slaves. One tenth-century Caliph is said to have had 11 000 Greek and Sudanese eunuchs, and another a harem of 4 000 concubines (it was customary for governors and generals to give presents of purchased or captive slave girls to the Caliph). Not least it was to promote the religion of Islam. This presented difficulties. Which other religious communities must be forced to submit to the teaching of the Prophet, and which should be recognized as kindred spirits? The Zoroastrians of Persia, for example, were so numerous that the Caliph deemed it expedient to allow them to continue to practise their own faith. Other dualists though, such as the Manicheans (followers of the third-century Persian teacher, Mani) were proscribed and persecuted. Some very minor sects were also largely unmolested, and Muslims found it impossible to eradicate polytheism in those parts of India that came within the empire. Many – perhaps too many – of the 'conversions' were forced on large segments of the conquered populations. It was proselytization by order. And it paid 'converts' to comply and avoid the humiliating tribute and other disadvantages of refusal.

The concept of jihad – war for ostensible religious purposes – was, and still is, a central tent of Islam. Injunctions to conquer and to slay are particularly directed against polytheists; 'seize them ... wherever you find them ... encompass them, and ambush them; [but] if they repent and observe prayer and pay alms, they may go their way' (Qu'rān quoted by Gibb: 1969, p. 45). So it might well be argued that it was the Prophet himself who had originally pointed the way to all faithful Muslims, and – as we shall see – had actually set them a personal example.

Muhammad claimed to have had certain psychic experiences which he at first attributed to a spirit or jinnee. But it was not until he was 40, while meditating in a cave near Mecca, that he said he was visited by the angel Gabriel in a dream and commanded to go forth and proclaim that Allah was merciful. After a period of soul-searching and acute depression, the visitations resumed, and he was told to tell the people that:

- they should abandon their beliefs in spirits and give up their animistic practices
- they must recognize Allah (the all-powerful) as a sovereign deity
- hell is a reality
- idolatry is iniquitous
- the faithful will be rewarded in paradise.

After several years of disappointment with the lack of response, he formed a small religious community which operated along embryonic Islamic lines. Non-believers, especially Jews, concluded that there was nothing new in his message, and tended to regard him as a kind of charlatan. This may well account for his increasing antipathy towards them even though he accepted much of the teaching of the Old and New Testament scriptures. The community began to flourish and continued to be governed by the Prophet himself as a seemingly unquestioned autocracy.

The community then began to face the problem not only about how it should be *perpetuated* but also how it was going to be *defended* and *extended*, hence the concept of holy war (jihad). In the very early days of the community, conversion was to be by persuasion, but further convenient 'revelations' condoned and even encouraged violence. First, there was an attack on the recalcitrant city of Mecca to capture the sacred Black Stone which was believed to have fallen from heaven during the time of Adam. (It was probably a meteorite which had once been a focus of idolatry. How it became 'incorporated' into Islam is an interesting question.) This was said to be justified in order to eradicate idolatry. Next, certain tribesmen had to be 'subdued', and their victory was ascribed to divine intervention. The following year they suffered a defeat, but this was rationalized as a divine test of their faith – an early exercise in cognitive dissonance.

Muhammad next turned his forces against certain Jewish communities. This seems to have been done to prove the point that he had a divine calling to punish those who would not heed the 'new' message. Some were forced to surrender their goods which were then divided among their attackers, but one tribe, the Koraihda, who were suspected of fomenting opposition to the True Believers were massacred after having surrendered at their discretion. Some 700 or so died at the command of the Prophet, and their goods were taken as the spoils of war. This was all in keeping with the new 'revelation' which taught that the sword is the key of heaven, and that a night spent in arms availed more than two months of prayer and fasting. Indeed, believers were assured that those who died in battle for the cause would have their sins forgiven and – where necessary – their lost limbs restored.

Eventually, jihad came to mean what would-be Islamic conquerors wanted it to mean. Mahmud of Ghazni (d. AD 1330), for instance, was the archetype of the pious Islamic ruler and warrior; when he died his domains stretched from Isfahan in Persia to Lahore in India. But the truth is that he led his armies out of Afghanistan plundering and slaughtering as he went, particularly in his many forays into northern India. He made a special point of sacking the city of Somnath where there was said to be a temple idol that was particularly offensive to a True Believer. In this and his many campaigns it is estimated that at least 50 000 Hindus were killed. Similar sentiments might be expressed about Saladin (d. AD 1193), who became Sultan of Egypt and Syria after engineering the demise of the previous incumbent. He is noted for initiating a Holy War in his campaigns against the Crusaders in Palestine. Apparently he had an ambivalent relationship with their best-known leader, Richard Coeur de Lion (the English king who was rarely in England), although neither protagonist was quite the heroic figure that he is often depicted in storybooks.

The conception of jihad has remained much the same through the ages, from the Prophet himself to various Muslim conquerors, and thence to the suicide bombers of the modern world. (It really did not give Unbelievers much of a choice – either conversion with Paradise to come, or death by the sword and hell in the hereafter.) Jihad is wedded to a radical doctrine of predestination, and a fervent desire for the elimination of the Unbelievers – an entity or community that is now associated with Western culture. Every act of aggression in the cause of Islam can thus be justified. Whatever happens is fated to happen. It cannot be avoided, and was determined from eternity. It was – and is – a doctrine that is not peculiar to Muslims, although in its fundamentalist form it has particularly lethal implications – 'a creed that paralyses the weak, and doubles the strength of the strong'.

CHAPTER TWELVE

Militarism as a 'Test of Manhood'

The notion of militarism as a test of a nation's 'mettle' has a long history, and connotes the virtues of moral and physical courage. This, in turn, may imply initiative and dash – even recklessness – in wartime situations, the sort of thing that could lead to a Victoria Cross or perhaps a court martial. It has been argued that war is actually good for a society, that internal disintegration is usually greatest in times of truce or peace. One early sociologist maintained that 'In spite of the countless miseries which follow in its train, war has probably been the highest stimulus to racial progress ... the most potent excitant known to all the faculties' (Brinton: 1901, p. 76). The idea here is that great conquests have destroyed what was effete and have opened the way for advancement – a view that can be found in one form or another among many of the Conquerors of history from Alexander to Hitler. There is, of course, an element of truth in this idea, but if war is a necessary ingredient in the process of social evolution, what appals us is the frightful waste that it entails – a 'waste that has made the evolution of civilization so slow' (Sumner: 1968, p. 213).

It is interesting that these observations on war and militarism by social scientists are to be found in such early texts (Sumner's article is really a reprint from 1911). Modern social scientists do not seem so keen on the subject. It is almost as though there is an ideological antipathy to anything that savours of the military and all that this implies. In psychology texts, for instance, there are plenty of references to fear and friendship, emotions and erotica, but virtually none to courage or bravery which are indirectly related to our subject, and are actually interesting in their own right. It seems as though the discipline is not that interested in anything that smacks of what Winston Churchill used to call 'intestinal fortitude' (for a particular exception, see Chapter 13).

Impressionistically, it is easier to display courage as part of a group, especially if it is a question of setting an example, say in a wartime situation (one recalls the reactions of people during the London Blitz in 1940–41). Yet, curiously enough, research done by psychologists on the tangentially related 'bystander effect' have found that an individual will help another individual in a one-to-one situation, but that this tends not to happen when the potential helper is part of a group or has an audience (Baron and Byrne: 1987, pp. 263–6). Of course, people display courage and evince fear in different situations, some of which seem incomprehensible because they are so similar (it is known that some small children appear to show no fear in climbing trees, but will not go on a children's slide in the park). Some studies have shown that it is not so much the anticipation of the amount of injury one might sustain, but the quality of the event itself that engenders fear. For example, there is evidence that people find the possibility of a violent encounter more frightening than that of a traffic accident even though accidents are much more common and the degree of bodily damage may be the same in both cases. Behaviourist research – the methods and conclusions of which are by no means accepted by all psychologists – has indicated that fear is an acquired drive, at least as powerful as the primary drives such as hunger, sex and so forth. Avoidance conditioning works by promoting the learning of new behaviours, and these new behaviours could be extraordinarily and potently persistent.

Complementarily this has some relevance to the question of 'manliness' in military situations. Conditioning of certain kinds is all too apparent, as when, say, Special Air Service (SAS) personnel, Paratroopers and Marine Commandos were periodically reminded that they were elite forces, better than others, and that they must live up to their reputations. Yet one assumes that the natural instinct is to adopt 'minimax strategies', that is, strategies that minimize the maximum harm that an opponent can do to you. In other words, to adopt strategies which promote survival which may mean taking the easier option. Given this, courage and heroism become that much more difficult to explain.

Without doubt the inculcation of a certain *esprit de corps* – a pride in the regiment – plays an important part. During the First World War it was said by a one-time member of a British public school that the senior boys had volunteered for service en masse because they 'didn't want to let the school down'. Very few of them survived. It can be assumed that excitement and bravado played a part, but there was obviously more to it than this.

War can demonstrate certain qualities of manliness – however we define that term – although patently it does not have to. We are well aware that it can trigger the very worst human instincts which can result in atrocities of the worst kind. (It is all very reminiscent of high-minded non-sufferers who maintain that pain is ennobling; there is nothing ennobling about pain, as such, but there can be something noble about a person's *response* to pain, and the way they bear pain.) Similarly, there is nothing *intrinsically* manly about war – ask those who have endured it. But there can be something courageous about the ways in which people react to fear and to danger – war included. As we shall see from our case study, war has little to do with sanity, but it may have something to do with self-revelation.

Case study

The idea – indeed, the theory – that war tests a 'nation's mettle' is associated in modern times with the Italian dictator Benito Mussolini. On this – although not on everything – he was in agreement with his senior partner, Adolph Hitler. Both men had formerly had military experience in the First World War, although Mussolini's contribution was not quite so valorous as Hitler's who as a corporal had won the Iron Cross (the only medal, even as Führer, that he ever wore). In those days they had fought on opposite sides, yet despite witnessing the dreadful carnage, neither seems to have been put off by war, even to the point of advocating it as a true test of manhood.

Mussolini, after a varied career, principally as a journalist and socialist agitator came to power as the leader of the Fascist Party (technically the 'union for struggle') in 1922. Like most European countries at that time, Italy was suffering from the economic privations which attended the aftermath of the war. Its people – or a significant proportion of them – obviously felt that they could give this new party a chance. After all, things were so bad – what could they lose? The Duce did not exactly start as he meant to continue. Although his electoral campaign had been marked by terror tactics, especially against socialist opposition, he actually began quite modestly. It was not until 1926 that elections were suspended and he began to rule by decree. After the first flush of political success, he decided to implement his plans for a greater Italy, and what better than grabbing a share of the defunct Austro-Hungarian Empire as a reward for joining the Allies in the war. What Mussolini actually got, after some hesitation, was official title to the Dodecanese Islands which Italy had already possessed for ten years. And having made extravagant claims for extra territories overseas, presumably to mark Italy's status as a rising power, Mussolini was granted Jubaland (between Italian Somaliland and Kenya) in 1925. The Allies' asset-stripping actually gave Italy little except a consolatory share in the international administration of Tangier – and this was not until 1928. So Mussolini was forced to cast around elsewhere.

It was clear, then, from the early days of Mussolini's assumption of power that Italy needed to be held in check. Inordinately conscious of its image, Italian fascism displayed an incipient tendency towards expansionism, and no matter what form or direction this took, it had to be at somebody else's expense. Africa offered the most promising imperialist possibilities. Italy already controlled Tripolitania and Cyrenaica (reconstituted as Libya in 1934) as well as Italian Somaliland and Eritrea in East Africa. The problem was that expansion along the North African coastline would almost certainly bring Italy into conflict with Spain and France (a nation for which Mussolini had little but contempt and which he insisted was spoiled by alcohol, journalism and syphilis) and possibly Britain which was both envied and feared because of her naval strength in the Mediterranean which Mussolini liked to regard as an 'Italian Lake'.

Mussolini presented different faces to the world at different times. When the occasion demanded it, he was quite prepared nominally to endorse the cause of international peace. Yet he seems to have had an abiding predilection for violence which was often manifested as a kind of posturing aggressiveness. In his socialist days, he had claimed to be an avowed pacifist, but once Italy had joined the Allies (the Entente) in the First World War, he did something of a volte-face and maintained that it was opportune and necessary that Italians should show the world that they were capable of displaying their legendary fighting qualities. Once in power he wanted the national tennis team, as good fascists, to wear black shirts and later the army to adopt the Nazi 'goose step'; women were to give up shameful 'Negro' dances and devote themselves to producing healthy children for the nation. As one writer in a semi-serious vein has argued, the Duce wanted nothing less than to 'transform the Italian people into lean, mean characters who did not dance, shake hands or drink tea' (Large: 1990, pp. 140–41). Yet at times he recognized that the task of changing Italian attitudes was probably hopeless; as he plaintively conceded, 'even Michelangelo needed good marble'.

Mussolini was something of an accomplished poseur. Old newspapers show him with jutted jaw, haranguing the crowds from a balcony and pugnaciously acknowledging their plaudits in his customary self-congratulatory manner. Yet he was generally popular at home, and also had many admirers abroad, especially in the USA. He was seen as a dedicated anti-Communist, and was particularly in favour with the American ambassador to Italy, Richard Washburn Child, who went on to write in a preface to a laudatory text about the Duce that 'He had built a new state upon a new concept ... he has not only been able to change the lives of human beings, but has changed their minds, their hearts, their spirits' (quoted by Large: 1990, p. 142). The high water mark of his popularity was undoubtedly in the 1920s and early 1930s when Italy was just getting back on its feet after the First World War.

Although there was certainly a kinship between Fascism and National Socialism, it is possible that some people came to see Italian power as a counterweight to the growing influence of the Nazis. But when Italy's foreign policy became more adventurous with the Ethiopian campaign in 1935 views began to change, and especially so after Mussolini's partnership with Hitler in helping Franco and the Nationalists in the Spanish Civil War (1936–39). It may well be that one – and only one – reason for Mussolini's more overtly aggressive policy was to satisfy the demands of the more extreme elements of his own party. Ostensibly, the Fascists were a self-proclaimed revolutionary party, but – like so many parties when they came to power – its leaders found that they had to make certain compromises. In Mussolini's case it was primarily to the monarchy, the Church and to some extent to the Senate itself. The extremists would have preferred something more in the nature of a takeover, with more radical solutions to Italy's besetting problems. So for the Duce there was nothing like an overseas adventure to take some followers' minds off domestic and internal political issues. Complementarily, an enlargement of Italy's colonial possessions would demonstrate the efficiency of Italian arms and – in Mussolini's view – put her on a par with Germany with which Italy had a love–hate relationship. The larger, strategic imperative was that Italy should have Great Power status, and an overseas military venture was thought to be able to satisfy all these requirements.

A further rationale for colonial expansion was that it would provide living space for Italy's burgeoning population and presumably employment for her surplus labour. It was thought too – quite mistakenly as it transpired – that it would bring appreciable economic rewards, though, as it turned out, the colonies cost the nation far more than it was ever able to recoup. Added to all this, the Duce wanted a 'proving ground' whereby he could test his military machine which, as we now know, was only ready for a war with militarily inferior peoples. He insisted that war was an ennobling experience that tested a nation's determination and vitality. Recruits were informed that there was no greater glory than fighting – even dying – for one's country. Mussolini was to discover in the Spanish Civil War and more so in the desert war against British and Commonwealth troops that at every level his army was disconcertingly unimpressive.

The Duce's plans for a possible invasion of Ethiopia began to take shape years before the actual campaign. There were a number of reasons why the Italians should target this rather backward and impoverished country. Indeed it was really the only country left in Africa to colonize. The invasion might atone for the defeat the Italians had suffered there in the battle of Adowa in 1896 – a flimsy excuse but better than none at all. Ethiopia also lay in between two of Italy's existing colonies, so its occupation could be considered a 'rational' move to unite them, certainly in terms of ease of communications. At this time (1934) Mussolini still saw Hitler more as a threat than an ally. It was known from an abortive putsch of Austrian Nazis in 1934 that Hitler had thoughts, if not plans, about a reunification with Austria. The Duce therefore wanted to send his rival the appropriate signals. Not least of all, Ethiopia was *vulnerable* with no army or weaponry to speak of. In short, the Italian military considered it a pushover; it would be a campaign that would bring extensive territorial rewards for a minimum of effort and expense. And if all went according to plan, there would also be a minimum of fuss from other powers. The Duce was convinced that as far as world opinion was concerned, it would soon be yesterday's news.

All in all, then, Mussolini felt that Ethiopia offered the most promising imperialist possibilities. He had already sounded out the prospects of territorial concessions in the Cameroons and even in Tunisia, much to the anger of the French. But the Ethiopian venture would not only give him a larger slice of the colonial cake, it would also give him the swift military victory that he craved. His intention was to make Italy great, and by this he meant respected and feared.

In 1934, by which time Mussolini's intentions were becoming blatantly apparent, the League of Nations was beginning to sit up and take notice. The League (of which Ethiopia was a member) had been formed to avert, where possible, any international conflicts, and did their best to head off the impending catastrophe. Britain, in particular was anxious to appease the Duce, and he was offered scraps of territory that nobody really coveted such as parts of the Ogaden which bordered Italian Somaliland. But Mussolini was not to be foisted off with titbits; he made it clear that he was not in the game of collecting deserts (Collier: 1972).

Planning for the invasion had begun in 1932, possibly in the first instance as a 'contingency exercise' – it is interesting just how many annexations start this way. By 1934, Mussolini was becoming almost wholly preoccupied with the project. He had hopes – not entirely ill-founded – that world opinion might condone his action. After all, Ethiopia had not the best of reputations. It was said with some measure of optimism, that the Emperor, Haile Selassie, was trying to bring the country into the twentieth century. Nevertheless, there were still enough reports in the Western press about 'feudalism' and 'frightening atrocities', not to mention slavery, which would seem to make an Italian takeover justifiable and might mollify any hostile outside opinion.

As part of the choreography of war and annexation it is not unusual for the predator to manufacture a *casus belli*. There had to be a reason – or excuse – for what is about to happen. Arranging an 'incident' was well known (the Japanese had already recently worked this manoeuvre in the Far East, and in 1939 Hitler was to do something similar on the eve of his Polish campaign). In Ethiopia there was also such an 'incident' but whether it was deliberately engineered or not is still uncertain. Ethiopian and Somali troops came to blows in December 1934, and the Italians were also involved. This Walwal incident, as it came to be known, left the Ethiopians with some 150 dead and wounded, and Haile Selassie felt sufficiently aggrieved to request that the whole affair be taken to the League of Nations for arbitration. The Duce was 'insulted' by such a suggestion and demanded that the Ethiopians apologize, pay a large indemnity (though no Italians were either killed or wounded), punish the guilty and 'salute the Italian flag'. He did not wait for a response; he had already reinforced his East African garrisons, and now gave orders for the destruction of the Ethiopian forces and the total conquest of Ethiopia.

Before the actual invasion, there were certain diplomatic niceties to be observed. Mussolini wanted to clear the way as far as possible so that any obstacles and recriminations could be kept to a minimum. First, he made overtures to France, and came to an understanding with Foreign Minister Laval (later to be infamous as a pro-Nazi collaborator) whereby Italy would have a free hand in Ethiopia – left conveniently ill-defined – as long as it continued to retain a nominal degree of autonomy. In the same month (January 1935), the Duce sounded out the British on the issue, but received no clear response. It was surmised – probably rightly – that the British took the view that if it came to it, Ethiopia was an overseas pawn that could be sacrificed for the sake of European peace. The problem facing the former Allies at this time was how to contain the rising power of Germany, especially now that Hitler had repudiated the arms limitations imposed by the post-First World War Versailles Treaty. In April 1935, representatives of Italy, France and Britain met to discuss the matter, but did no more than issue the customary 'strong protest' which was simply taken as a sign of weakness.

This was the kind of irresolution Mussolini liked to see. If France and Britain were going to do nothing about Hitler, it probably followed, a fortiori, that they would do very little to inhibit his own expansionist intentions. After all, one could hardly compare the question of stability in Europe with the fortunes of a backward state in East Africa. One British diplomat, Sir Robert Vansittart, a fervent anti-Nazi, suggested at the time that as far as Hitler and Mussolini were concerned, it was a question of balancing one evil against another. So why not let the Duce have his fame and sand – he was going to take it anyway, and no vital British interests were jeopardized.

As the weeks slipped by, however, and the situation began to look as though it could have ominous implications, British political opinion underwent something of a change. It was now felt prudent to adopt a stick-and-carrot approach to Mussolini. Offer him something, but not as much as he wanted, *and* suggest that if he did not accept then sanctions would be inevitable. This line was supported by the House of Commons, but the warning was really all something of a bluff. In the event of hostilities it was most unlikely that Britain would act alone, and it was an open secret that France would not risk a war over Ethiopia. And without some action from the former allies the League of Nations was virtually powerless. The USA, too, did not want to be involved. Americans took the view that this was another one of those colonial disputes which Europeans should sort out for themselves. They, as a multicultural society, claimed to be impatient with colonialism and colonial powers, and this regardless of the *neo*-colonial power that the USA exercised in relation to Latin America.

Italy, meanwhile, was conducting a vigorous public relations campaign to try to convince interested onlookers that she was actually bent on a humanitarian and civilizing mission in Ethiopia. Italians understandably took the view that to deny their country colonial rights was totally hypocritical given the extensive colonial possessions of the objectors. If they could bestow 'cultural benefits' on *their* subject peoples, why make such a fuss about Italy's imperialist demands? So the Duce continued to prepare for war reasonably confident in the assumption that nobody would do anything. And except for the USA imposing an arms embargo on Italy *and* Ethiopia – effectively, 'a pox on both your houses' – he was right. Politicians did what they were good at, they talked. But nobody actually *did* anything.

As we have already observed, relations between Italy and Germany were somewhat strained at this time. Possibly this was because Mussolini had no great opinion of Hitler whom he regarded as something of a 'degenerate', also because there was a sense in which they were rivals, especially with respect to which power was going to act as 'protector' to Austria. With Britain and France making – albeit ineffectual – warning noises, Mussolini was now in need of friends. And it was here that

Hitler, who had always had a certain respect for the Duce, if not for Italians in general, came to the rescue. He ordered the German press to go easy on Italy and its obvious pretensions, and he sent a message to Mussolini assuring him that Germany would do nothing to thwart his expansionist plans in Ethiopia (undoubtedly Austria would have been another matter). From this time onwards, Mussolini began to revise his opinions of the Führer whom, for a while, he came to see as an able but junior partner, although before 1939 these positions were to be reversed. In all this Hitler was playing a subtle – indeed duplicitous – game. It served his purposes to have an Italian–Ethiopian conflict, partly because it would bring Italy and Germany closer together, and partly because it might distract the West from his own expansionist intentions. So, while encouraging Italy to go ahead, he also clandestinely helped to rearm the Ethiopians, though only with a generous consignment of *small* arms and a few military advisers. For these the Ethiopians were almost pathetically thankful as other Western powers deliberately refused to supply arms in the hope that it would force the belligerents to the conference table.

But nothing Ethiopia had in the way of weaponry could possibly match the Italian military effort. Mussolini's generals made meticulous preparations for the war, shipping troops and *matériel*, including tanks, aircraft and hundreds of all-terrain vehicles, to their East African colonies which were to act as jumping-off points for the main invasion. Black troops were also trained and mobilized so that on the eve of the invasion there would be in the order of 300 000 men (one-third of whom were native troops) ready to launch the attack. Furthermore, the Italians attempted to suborn some of the local Ethiopian chiefs in the hope that dissension would make victory that much easier, but in this they were largely unsuccessful. Venality was not unknown among these petty rulers. But it turned out that they were happy to take bribes from the Italians and then do nothing for them.

In their ignorance, the Ethiopians confidently expected to rout any possible invasion even though they were about to confront a well-armed and ideologically motivated foe. Haile Selassie had an inadequately trained army and an air force consisting of only eight outdated operational aircraft. There were also hundreds of American and British volunteers, though few actually went to Ethiopia. (Ironically, the black Americans were not aware that until recently Ethiopian chiefs had kept black slaves.) If the will to win was anything to go by, the Ethiopians could not lose, but mere determination rarely wins wars. From the onlookers' point of view, the whole thing began to look more and more like a tragic farce. The Emperor did not have the same assurance as some of his subordinates, but whatever happened, he was certain that his troops would acquit themselves bravely. What he could admit only to himself was that they would also almost certainly acquit themselves fruitlessly.

The incomparable superiority of the Italian army can be judged by the fact that on the southern front, i.e. the Eritrean–Ethiopian border, there were two divisions of Eritrean troops plus a battalion of Libyans, and by the summer of 1935, these had been reinforced by ten divisions of Italian troops together with an air armada of 150 planes. But this was not all. On the northern (Italian Somaliland) front were another two divisions commanded by Marshal Rodolfo Graziani who had already established an unenviable reputation for brutality. His predecessor in Somaliland, Cesare de Vecchi, had openly attempted to obliterate the cultures of the indigenous peoples, had ruthlessly burned the villages which he considered to be centres of rebellion and had shot prisoners in their hundreds. (But then the Italians had always made a careful distinction between their North African colonies, in which they invested heavily, and their East African colonies where the inhabitants were considered less civilized; see Mack Smith: 1979.)

Both sides now waited for the other to make the first move. And given that the Ethiopian military had inconveniently failed to provoke another incident which would 'legitimize' an attack, Mussolini, impatient for a quick victory, ordered his armies to advance. There was no declaration of war, but on the same day that his forces crossed into Ethiopia, he appeared on the balcony of the Palazzo Venezia in Rome and declared to a cheering crowd that at last Italy was going to achieve a place in the sun. The Duce saw his troops as latter-day Roman legionaries, valiantly extending and securing the empire's borders against the barbarians. It was no longer a war, it was a mission. As a *post facto* justification for the invasion, he ordered his general, de Bono, to drop leaflets to the Ethiopians containing the contradictory message that they had really brought the war upon themselves, but that the Italians had come as 'liberators' to punish those who had been guilty of treacherous attacks on Italian outposts. As far as we know, this charge was entirely fictitious and really fooled no one – certainly not in the outside world.

The leaflets had hardly reached the ground when other planes were bombing the town of Adowa – a cynical but appropriate gesture from the Italian point of view. Meanwhile, Ethiopian troops retreated in the face of the Italian advance, refusing where possible actually to engage in any serious fighting. This may well have been a tactical move to draw the enemy into more inhospitable country which would have the effect of putting an inordinate strain on their supply and communications systems.

The Italian's first objective was Adowa itself; de Bono could not wait to restore Italian honour and reverse the fortunes of those who had been defeated in 1896. When the town was taken, the Italians found a few old veterans from that earlier battle still alive – just. These Eritrean prisoners were incarcerated in cages, and each one had had a hand and a foot amputated as 'punishment' for service with the Italians years before. The Italian troops were more than ever convinced that they were indeed dealing with an uncivilized and barbarous people. A view that was reaffirmed when some Ethiopians made a practice of killing their Italian prisoners.

At first, the Italian advance went surprisingly slowly. On the northern front they released a number of slaves, but slavery was such a given institution in Ethiopian society, that the liberated men did not know how to fend for themselves. On the southern front they discovered just how the Ethiopians dealt with cowardice; men were flogged and their commanding officer bayoneted to death. In general, the Ethiopian warriors showed considerable bravery, enduring lethal machine gun fire in order to get at the enemy. Indeed, they tended to make up in courage what they lacked in skill and unit coordination. Yet despite these obvious Ethiopian deficiencies, the Italians failed to make the kind of progress the Duce expected, and in November after just one month's fighting, General de Bono was relieved of his command.

In the meantime, the League of Nations had not been idle. A 50 to 1 vote resulted in the resolution that Italy was in contravention of the Article which laid down that states should submit disputes to arbitration (Germany was not involved, as Hitler had taken her out of the League). For the first and last time the League invoked Article 16 which called for sanctions against member states that failed to desist from aggression. The intention was not so much a punishment as a rebuke. As far as one can make out, no one wanted actually to expel Italy from the League. It was more a question of getting a cessation of hostilities as soon as possible, and then inviting Italy's representative to the well-meaning but profitless talks for which the League was justly famous. The sanctions consisted of an embargo of arms sales to Italy, together with a restriction on supplies of other relevant materials as well as loans. Also important was a moratorium on Italian imports which would certainly – so it was felt – have a significant impact on Italy's economy. The anomalous aspect of all this was that not all member states applied all the sanctions in the way that was intended, and the whole affair became something of a fiasco. Complementarily, the

Ethiopians who should have been receiving arms supplies were denied the wherewithal to counter the invasion. This was done not because the potential suppliers (especially Britain) were unsympathetic to the Ethiopian cause, but out of a mistaken policy of even-handedness.

Needless to say, the sanctions were roundly condemned by Italian politicians, and the policy had the counterproductive effect of generating a more jingoistic stance by the Italian people who rallied to the flag. Indeed, it is doubtful whether the Duce had ever been so truculent or more popular; or whether attitudes to the British (who were seen as typically hypocritical) and the League were ever more hostile.

With a recalcitrant Italy and largely ineffectual sanctions, a frustrated League of Nations wanted to tighten the screw. But these proposals did not have the desired effect. There were objections, particularly from right-wing politicians in Britain and especially in France. The League then considered an embargo on oil exports which if put into effect would completely cripple Italy's war effort. Much of the country's oil came from the USA where the government was already having to face the implications of Japanese expansionism in the Far East. Consequently there was a sense of outrage at Italy's wanton aggression. But this hardly deterred the oil companies who were only too willing to take advantage of the situation and exports actually *increased*. This was supported again by the right and the isolationist politicians, and – not least – by the vociferous Italian-American lobby. Too many Americans, it appeared, took seriously Mussolini's warning that an oil embargo was an 'act of war'. The Duce admitted much later on that if the League had been able to impose such an embargo, he could not have continued operations in Ethiopia for more than a week.

The Italian forces pressed on in Ethiopia quite indifferent to – or oblivious of – the earnest debates that were taking place concerning the legitimacy of the war. General de Bono's command was taken over by General (later Marshal) Pietro Badoglio who was prepared to employ much more ruthless tactics than his predecessor. Badoglio had something of a mixed reputation. During the First World War he had been under a cloud after the Italian defeat at Carporetta, but he still managed to become Chief of Staff when the conflict was over. He was later appointed Governor of Libya where he built up a reputation for brutality that was confirmed when he took charge in Ethiopia. He made it clear to his subordinates that they could use any means they chose to win the war providing it was not publicized. This included the bombing of hospitals and – if necessary – the use of poison gas. There is little doubt that these extremist measures had the imprimatur of the Duce, because canisters of gas had already been shipped to Ethiopia for such an eventuality. And this regardless of the fact that Italy had already repudiated the use of poison gas as 'uncivilized'. When these methods came to be used, in this case fine sprays of mustard gas, the results were so appalling that the Italian press tried to pass them off as symptoms of leprosy. The gas was used on defenceless villagers as well as on troops. So much for Italy's 'civilizing mission'. An American correspondent, Herbert Matthews, minimized this by reporting that the gas attacks had played only a 'minor role' in the war and did not prevent the native population from welcoming the invasion as they 'burned only a few thousand peasants' (Large: 1990, p. 174). The Church of England openly condemned such measures, but the Vatican, already compromised by endorsing Italy's role in the conflict, was unable to say anything – at least, anything that was credible.

True to his insistence that war was the making of men, Mussolini ensured that his sons Vittorio and Bruno (who was under age) were in the war. Neither were exactly in the midst of the fray. Both were pilots (as was also the Duce's son-in-law, Count Ciano), and the Italian Air Force encountered no appreciable opposition. Vittorio later recorded how delighted he was to be involved, and how 'diverting' it was to drop bombs on enemy tribesmen. Both he and his brother were awarded silver medals for their courage in facing such 'fearful odds' (Mack Smith: 1979, p. 75). Medals were also given to a number of other fascist notables who were also privileged to witness these 'successes' as observers rather than participants.

If possible, the Italians wanted to avoid any kind of guerrilla warfare, but instead bring the Ethiopians into the field so that they could use their overwhelming superiority in a 'battle of annihilation'. Only now and again were they able to do this as, for example when, after a demoralizing artillery bombardment, a unit of skilled Alpine mountain troops scaled a sheer rock face and found some 8 000 Ethiopian corpses (February 1936) or, again, a few weeks later when the Italians were able to cut down a mass Ethiopian attack with devastating machine-gun fire. After this second paralysing defeat at Mai Ceu, the Ethiopian forces began to disintegrate. The Emperor, sensing the mood of his councillors, departed for French Somaliland with his family and entourage on 2 May and from there went to England. This was followed by a riot of looting and killing in the streets of the capital Addis Ababa. No white person was safe until Italian troops entered the capital on 5 May. The havoc in the city again served to reaffirm for the Italians just how necessary the invasion had been.

The Duce was in his element. When he announced the victory publicly on 9 May the crowds in Rome were delirious. Not only was Italy revenged, but its armies had been suitably bloodied and had emerged successful. He could not have been more pleased. He had done in a few months what critics had predicted would take a couple of years. He had successfully defied the League (as had also the Japanese over Manchuria a few years earlier), and had also confounded the Western Allies. Furthermore he had shown Hitler who was top dog in the fascist world.

From 15 July the sanctions which had proved so ineffectual were finally lifted. Mussolini had won, and at very little cost. Italy had lost only 1 537 troops out of a force of many thousands (in the First World War they had 600 000 men killed). They now controlled a leaderless country of warring rival chieftans which would take some time finally to pacify. The whole affair must have given a clear signal to Hitler who also had what he insisted were 'legitimate claims', that the Allies were too spineless and irresolute to challenge any confiscatory moves he might care to make in the near future.

The quality of the Italian military can hardly be said to have been tested in the Ethiopian campaign. The real tests were to come later in Greece and in the Western Desert (1940–41) – both campaigns against pathetically small armies. These debacles sorted out the men from the boys, and in both cases, Hitler had to pull the Duce's chestnuts out of the fire. In the early days in the Western Desert, the British general, Richard O'Connor, commanding a combined force of British and Commonwealth troops, conducted a brilliant ten-week campaign against the Italians in which he advanced 500 miles, and destroyed ten divisions (taking 130 000 prisoners) at the cost of less than 500 men killed (Barnett: 1960). When finally Italian troops became embroiled in the Russian campaign from 1941 onwards, they merely confirmed that either they were not up to it, or – more likely – that they no longer had any enthusiasm for war of any kind.

CHAPTER THIRTEEN

Militarism and the 'Warrior Death'

As we have seen it is almost impossible to think of military action without some consideration of the notions of courage and fear. After all, for the individual soldier this is what war is all about. But such ideas have a logical extension. Military action needs further philosophical underpinning: soldiers need to be inculcated with the idea of the 'good death' – the ultimate in courage. Military obedience requires an acceptance of death as a possibility – even as a probability. It requires a certain cast of mind. As Thomas Hardy once said, 'More life may trickle out of men through thought than through a gaping wound' (quoted by Moran: 1945, p. 120). Such fears and forebodings are often regarded as morbid and should either not be aired, or – when the appropriate occasion demands it – made the subject of uneasy, jocular remarks which smack of bravado rather than courage.

However, it is one thing to accept death as a possibility, and quite another to welcome it as an inevitability. Freud maintained that we all have destructive urges which could also result in *self*-destruction. This death instinct (thanatos), he insisted, was present in all organisms, and arose when organic material developed from inorganic material. He further argued that this death force was inseparable from the life force (eros) with which it was in permanent conflict. As far as human behaviour was concerned, it was Freud's contention that such practices as masochism, sadism, hostility and violence all derived from the death instinct. Critics of Freud – a 'community' that is not exactly inconsiderable – argue that this theory is open to all kinds of objections. Do organisms have instincts? And have they the power or capacity to contribute to the survival of the species? This assumed dichotomy between the life and death instincts is not altogether clear in so far as it seems impossible either to confirm or disconfirm the contention that we are all 'driven' by a death instinct. And what *is* an instinct? Is it a fact at all, and if so how is it acquired? Is it innate or is it learned?

Psychoanalysts have never been greatly taken with the death instinct, and have tended, if anything to regard it as a rather vague expression for the desire to destroy. Modern psychological theory maintains that it is difficult – if not impossible – to identify at all clearly any particular manifestation of an instinct. Does it exhibit a recognizable pattern which is the same for all members of the species? To what extent can environmental conditions qualify or modify this (Farrell: 1981)? The complexities of the issue are legion. And as far as militarism and aggression are concerned, it is difficult to recognize any unambiguous criteria which might show that this arises from a common instinct. Human behaviour is shaped by a puzzling matrix of factors of which the biological organism is one – and even that is very imperfectly understood.

Perhaps what Freud had in mind as much as anything was the notion that in nature organisms die and other organisms take their place. This could be extended to the more deterministic view that organisms *must* die in order that others can take their place. As human organisms, we too require that other things die (animals, plants, etc.) so that we can survive, a law – if it is a law – that appears to obtain throughout the natural world. But this is a far cry from saying that organisms – complex or otherwise – *choose* to die for others. And this is again different from arguing that organisms – and here we are particularly thinking of the human organism – do not wish to die but are *prepared* to die for others. This is, and has to be, a sine qua non of military service. It will be a sorry day for any army when soldiers apply for compensation because they have been traumatized by what they have experienced or witnessed as part of their military duty (as has been the case in the British police in recent times). The possibility of maiming and death is an occupational hazard – it goes with the job.

It has been argued that 'the forceful leader in battle capitalizes on others' fear of death ... but [this is not something] which is deeply understood' (Gray: 1967, p. 116). This seems somewhat specious, and hardly accords with experience. What is perhaps much more to the point is that military leaders are more likely to capitalize on others' fear of fear, and thus being branded a coward. And not just military leaders; it was common, especially during the First World War for subtle pressures to be exerted on young men by their schools (whose honour had to be upheld) and their womenfolk in relation to whom they must never be ashamed. Many a youth bowed to convention and was slain in what must be one of the most savage and unnecessary wars ever fought.

It may be that some men find fulfilment in the military death. The Vikings in their desire for Valhalla, the Muslims in their hope of Paradise, and those of many other cultures also come into this category. Courage was always at a premium, and death in battle was therefore deemed to receive its just reward (interestingly among the Aztecs, women who died in childbirth came into a similar category). But whether these people *sought* death or whether they always secretly hoped to survive, we will never know. Similar attitudes can be found among those who are imbued with certain secular ideologies such as Nazism and Communism. For such people death may be regarded as regrettable but merely incidental to the *cause*. The realization of the cause is what really mattered, therefore anything – even self-sacrifice – that furthered this aim was worthwhile.

All this begs the question, what cause is worth dying for? We may applaud the soldier – or any other individual for that matter – who regards duty and dedication as among his highest values, but for what *cause* is he prepared to lay down his life? And what form will his self-sacrifice take. Nazi Waffen SS men could be recklessly brave in battle. Many effectively threw away their lives when they opted to infiltrate the American lines during the Battle of the Bulge in the Ardennes in December 1944 where they were quickly rounded up and executed because technically they were regarded as spies. The *mode* of sacrifice is equally important. The cause may be felt to be just, but the nature of the sacrificial act may itself be highly questionable. What, for instance, are we to make of Palestinian suicide-bombers who destroy themselves and others in a Jewish marketplace? Both the cause and the mode are critical issues, yet there is also what we might term the *identity motive*. Here we can find examples of what appear to be completely needless sacrifice but which nevertheless, are greeted with both astonishment and approval. Douglas Walton cites the case of Arthur Ambury, an experienced mountaineer who attempted to save an inexperienced climber from falling knowing that this would almost certainly result in both their deaths (Walton: 1986, pp. 138–9). Yet he had to *try*, and both were tragically killed on Mount Egmont in New Zealand. Or there is the case of the non-Jewish music teacher in Nazi-occupied Poland who when the Security Police came to take away his Jewish pupils insisted that he had taught them for so long that he would not think of leaving them even though it meant his death. Supererogatory acts such as these are not entirely unknown, but they do require an inordinate degree of moral as well as physical courage.

The problem of ideology and its influence on behaviour, especially military behaviour, is a complex one. Studies have shown that much depends on the nature of the ideology in question and the culture concerned. Investigations of US servicemen in the Second World War showed that ideological factors had little or no influence on their behaviour. More surprisingly, studies of Wehrmacht soldiers produced similar results (though it should be noted that there was a continued devotion to the Führer and that we are not here talking of SS formations). By contrast, volunteers for the Republican Army in the Spanish Civil War were highly motivated by ideology, as were North Koreans and Chinese in the Korean War (Rachman: 1990, pp. 53–9). But, as our case study will show, these are special cases.

Case study

Military leadership has been defined as 'the capacity to frame plans which will succeed and the faculty of persuading others to carry them out in the face of death' (Moran: 1945, p. 192). But what of plans that will probably *not* succeed, and which will certainly result in death? Recruitment for such ventures, plus persuasion and encouragement were all part of the work of certain leaders in the Second World War. The 'warrior death' ideal finds no better exemplification than in the activities of those who were recruited for suicide missions.

Our discussion will necessarily centre on Japan and the Kamikaze units, although some mention must be made of other forms of 'semi-suicide' operations. Most notable were those involving various kinds of 'explosive boat', especially the midget submarine. The British had the X5 and the X25 class midget submarines and the Italians had their own versions which were used to considerable effect. The Germans had the Biber one-man submarine as well as the Molch and the Seehund (perhaps the best midget craft of the Second World War) as part of their navy's 'small battle units' or K-Force. These normally carried two torpedoes, and their use was regarded as semi-suicidal because once the torpedoes were released, the chances of returning safely to base were minimal. The Japanese, too, had a variety of midget craft which were usually launched from mother ships. There were five main types of midget submarine – something of a speciality of the Japanese – which also carried torpedoes. But towards the end of the war, when desperation set in, one type, the Kairyu (Sea Dragon), developed late in 1943, carried a 600K explosive warhead for ramming purposes. This was a truly suicidal weapon, although it is still not known whether it was ever actually used operationally. The Japanese also developed a 'human torpedo' (the Kaiten) which was also a suicide weapon and used for ramming purposes. Other experimental craft were developed or were in the process of development at the war's end, and would undoubtedly have been used in the final defence of the homeland.

It is not generally known that towards the end of the Second World War the Germans seriously toyed with the idea of using suicide pilots. In their desperation to stop the daylight bombing raids by the B17s and B25s of the USAAF (USA Air Force), they considered the possibility of sacrificing pilots and planes in an effort to break up the box formations (three abreast and five deep) of the Americans. The box formation presented a well-defended front to the German fighters which would be in serious trouble if they approached within 800 yards of a formation. The situation was made worse by the long-range Mustang fighters which the Americans were using to escort the bombers. Consequently an experimental unit was set up by the Luftwaffe in May 1944 consisting of fanatical volunteer pilots equipped with conventional Focke-Wulf 190s reinforced with special armour. The idea was to take the risk of getting in close and attacking each box in line abreast and to delay firing until the very last moment. Once their ammunition was exhausted, there was an *understanding* – though no direct order – that they should ram their opponents. This strategem was relatively successful and a second unit was formed. On 7 July 1944 over 20 B25 Liberators were brought down in two minutes, and on 15 August 40 B17 Flying Fortresses were brought down after a third volunteer unit was set up. In all, by March 1945, they had destroyed some 500 Allied bombers – only ten by actual ramming – for the loss of 150 German pilots.

The idea was also mooted of developing a piloted flying bomb (the V1 'Doodlebug') which was powered by a cheaply produced pulsejet engine – a proposal that came from the intrepid test pilot Hanna Reitsch. A unit was formed known as the Leonidas Staffel and had an unexpected number of volunteers. Reichsmarschall Goering opposed the idea but he was overruled by Hitler and Himmler. Technical problems brought about a change of plan, and it was decided to use FW190s instead, but eventually this idea was also shelved (Hyland and Gill: 1998).

Attitudes of renunciation and resignation can be found in a number of societies, and are particularly marked in Hinduism. But even this is not quite the same as a deliberate act of what can only be described as martyrdom. In this sense, Japan is the culture par excellence. Nowhere else does the warrior death find such institutionalized expression. Certainly in the Second World War, the Japanese Kamikazi, or 'Special Attack' units provide us with a singular example of that rare phenomenon the suicidal determination to obey the code (bushido, the way of the warrior). Put succinctly, this means to die in order to succeed, or to die if one does not succeed. The code demanded loyalty to the nation, to the Emperor, to one's military superior (shogun or military overlord) and, not least, to oneself. There are elements here of Confucianism, and of Shintoism (little more than an elaborated animistic cult) and particularly Zen Buddhism (from *c.* AD 1200 onwards) which in its unadulterated Eastern form stresses rigorous self-discipline, asceticism and, thus, indifference to physical needs.

Historically, this code was most notably associated with the Samurai (knights – though, strictly speaking, military retainers of a local lord). It was said that 'the way of the samurai is death', and was believed to be the only correct philosophy for a dedicated warrior. One 'privilege' of the samurai was hara-kiri (literally, belly-slitting), sometimes more politely termed seppuku. This was a form of suicide either to avoid the disgrace of capture or to obviate or atone for the shame of failure – both of which were incumbent on the true warrior. Sometimes this was actually practised not for personal failure but because of a general defeat, as with many soldiers and some civilians during the war in the Far East (1941–45). For some individuals, suicide was highly ritualized involving disembowelment with a dagger or short sword, or just a token incision with possibly a *coup de grâce* from a retainer or colleague who shortened the agony, traditionally by decapitation. It was regarded as an honourable end for a defeated warrior, especially if he had the responsibility of command. But other less messy forms of suicide were allowed where time and opportunity permitted. In earlier times it was known for wives to follow their husbands by stabbing themselves to death. Whole families actually died together before the final Japanese defeat at Saipan in the Marianas during the Second World War. Sometimes when Japanese were rescued by Allied ships after an unsuccessful engagement, they would kill themselves rather than remain prisoners. In March 1945, 53 naval personnel were going to be picked up after their transports were sunk, but they preferred to swim away and drown. The motivating forces behind such extreme measures were an unusual degree of nationalistic sentiment together with an acute sense of the shame that any survivors would have to endure. As George Santayana put it, 'Nothing you can lose by dying is half so precious as the readiness to die, which is man's charter of nobility' (quoted by O'Neill: 1984, p. 132).

Special attack units, popularly known as kamikazi, although first anticipated as early as 1940, were not actually formed until October 1944. (The name was reputedly coined after the divinely sent typhoon which is said to have scattered the invasion armada of the Mongol, Kublai Khan, in the thirteenth century.) Incidents involving planes crashing into other planes or some other kind of enemy target is known to have happened on both sides, almost invariably when the attacking plane or its pilot were hopelessly damaged. But the kamikazi were different in that they were special squadrons which were formed for the sole purpose of launching suicide attacks on the enemy.

By 1943, the Pacific War had begun to turn in the Allies' favour. The Americans were certainly beginning to win the war at sea after the critical battle of Midway (June 1942). It was at this time that 'special attack' formations were first seriously discussed. The moving force behind the development of kamikazi was Vice-Admiral Onishi, although the whole enterprise is said to have been eventually endorsed by the Imperial General Headquarters (who, at first, were not keen on the idea) and to have had the imprimatur of the Emperor. The impetus, however, for such a radical venture is thought to have come – at least in part – from younger pilots who felt that it was one way in which one man might kill a thousand of the enemy. Recruitment is said to have been organized on an entirely voluntary basis although there is some dispute about this. Some sources (e.g. Pitt: 1979) stress that the amazing thing is just how enthusiastically it was taken up by these young idealists. The Naval Command were actually unable to cope with the response. Sometimes parents wrote to senior officers asking that their sons might be chosen, although it became a general policy that if the young man was the only son, he would not be selected. It has been said afterwards by men who were members of such squadrons but never became operational that there was so special indoctrination to inculcate a sacrificial mentality. In fact, many of these youths were university students, and therefore more like civilians than hardened military personnel. Other sources argue that recruitment was voluntary only in the early stages of the movement. Towards the war's end, it is said that the supply of volunteers dwindled and that pilots had to be coerced into embarking on these suicide missions, and that some – apparently sensing the pointlessness of it all – even returned to their bases claiming that they were unable to locate their targets.

Whatever doubts may exist about the kamikazi recruitment policy, there can be no serious reservations about the Japanese willingness for self-sacrifice. Soldiers bearing satchels of high explosive threw themselves under tanks, others rammed small explosive boats against enemy ships, and it was not unknown for some men to board enemy ships slashing as many of their crew as they could before being cut down themselves. In Japan itself, civilians were also primed to make suicide attacks when the invasion came (Hoyt: 1987, p. 389).

Japan, like Germany – despite the Allied bombing, was actually producing more aircraft towards the end of the war than at the beginning. Their planes were generally inferior in both speed and performance to those of the Allies, and initially it was decided to use the Zero (Zeke) fighters in the kamikazi units. But soon more suitable, tailor-made craft were produced for the same purpose. The Nakajima Ki-115 was a cheap, mass-produced plane with a considerable range of 750 miles but with a maximum speed of only 343 mph and therefore easily open to interception by American Navy fighters. Much more deadly was the OHKA which with a range of only 20 miles had to be launched from a parent aircraft – usually an adapted 'Betty' bomber – at 20 000 feet. It was powered by three rocket motors and had a maximum dive speed of 620 mph, much in excess of any American fighter of that time. With its high (4000 lb) load of high explosives housed in the nose, it was a devastating weapon if it hit its target. The only really successful counter was accurate anti-aircraft fire. Herein lay the real weakness of the 'special attack'. Kamikazi pilots had a severely abbreviated training (normally pilots had a minimum of 100 hours' flying time), so if they were caught en route to the target, their evasive techniques were limited. More critical still, especially for the OHKA, was the fact that once in their high-speed terminal dive, it was difficult to pull out or deviate in any way. In keeping to their 'line' they were sometimes sitting ducks for really good, unflustered gunners.

The suicide strategy had four major aims:

1. Not to win the war, regardless of what the volunteers thought, but in view of almost certain defeat to lose the war honourably.
2. To demonstrate Japan's indomitable will to survive, and thus perhaps to ensure that the Allies would consider a negotiated peace instead of their avowed intention to obtain an unconditional surrender.
3. To delay, as far as possible, the Allied invasion of the Japanese-held island bases so that those on the mainland would have time to prepare for the anticipated invasion, their motto being 'One hundred million will die for Emperor and Nation'. This was something of an exaggeration but was used by the Allies as the justification for using the atomic bomb on Hiroshima. Possibly a million or so US servicemen could also have been added to the huge number of Japanese that would have undoubtedly been *killed* in a mainland invasion. The second bomb on Nagasaki to end the war, though, was possibly inexcusable, although the number of Japanese killed in the fire raids on Tokyo amounted to more than the death toll of either of the nuclear weapons.
4. A more immediate and practical reason for the suicide attacks was the fact that the Japanese were desperately short of oil (one of the ostensible reasons for Tokyo's decision to go to war in the first place). This meant that the military had not enough fuel for their front-line aircraft. (Such fuel as there was had been diluted with alcohol from 1944 onwards.) It was therefore reasoned that certain desperate short-cut measures were justified.

Volunteers for the 'special attack' units came mainly from naval air groups at whose headquarters posters appeared advertising the need for 'divine typhoon' missions. Selection procedures were much like those for normal aircrew duties. Initially, 600 men were chosen and they were led by a veteran commander who promised – somewhat rashly – that he could turn the tide of the war with 300 suicide aircraft. Training was hectic for those who had not, as yet, had any flying hours. It consisted of little more than some familiarization with the aircraft selected, whether it was a conventional Zero (Zeke) fighter or the specially constructed OHKA. Theoretically, the men were then ready for combat duty.

There were several versions of the OHKA; development was necessary largely because of the extreme vulnerability of the lumbering 'Betty' bomber when they were carrying the suicide planes to their targets. Some were being developed at the end of the war which had much larger ranges, and others were designed to be carried on faster bombers. There was even a model from which the pilot – in theory, at least – could bale out at the last minute, but tests proved largely unsuccessful.

There is good reason to believe that the Germans had sent the Japanese designs of some of their own 'revenge weapons', especially the V1 ('Doodlebug') in 1943, the year that their own research facilities at Peenemunde were devastated by the RAF. It may be that the Germans too, *in extremis*, were toying with the idea of a piloted bomb, and it is believed that tests were carried out by Hanna Reitsch, a Luftwaffe test pilot (who had already suffered multiple skull fractures when testing an early jet aircraft, the Me163), but that the whole scheme was later abandoned. It is said that this and similar plans were pushed by the 'commando extraordinary', Otto Skorzeny, but rejected by Hitler who thought that mass suicide missions would have a depressing effect on morale. The Japanese, however, were quick to capitalize on the idea. They had no qualms about suicide weapons, and they quickly developed the Baika ('Plum Blossom'). Like the V1 it was powered by a pulse-jet engine, but this possibly formidable weapon did not progress beyond the formative stage.

The pressure to volunteer for 'special attack' duties when given the opportunity must have been intimidating. It afforded high status and certain privileges for those who were willing to take the step, although it might be many weeks before any individual was called upon to make the ultimate sacrifice. The fact that they often had to wait so long, at least indicates that their willingness to die was not the result of some momentary emotional fervour.

In the initial stages of the kamikazi, attacks were made by just a few aircraft on the initiative of a local commander. These attacks were largely opportunistic, and not the result of some overall concerted policy. Planes crash-dived on their targets when and how they got the chance. Later, the procedure changed. Mass attacks were ordered and the aircraft were directed towards selected targets, the favourite being American aircraft carriers where maximum damage could often be achieved. Once the target was sighted it was the signal for the 'special attack' aircraft to disperse and dive on the target from different directions, thus reducing the effectiveness of the enemy's anti-aircraft fire. Despite this, however, a significant percentage of the planes were brought down by the anti-aircraft (AA) batteries whose gunners soon worked out strategies for dealing with the suicide menace. If, as sometimes happened, Allied radar was able to detect the kamikazi en route and still some way from their targets, interceptor fighters – commonly navy Hellcats – were sent up, usually with considerable success. Perhaps most effective of all once an attack had begun was the large AA shell (usually from a 5-inch gun) fitted with the highly ingenious proximity fuse; with this the American gunners were often able to achieve 'total disintegration'.

Perhaps the two most famous engagements in which the kamikazi were used were in the Philippines and at Okinawa. Japanese sources say that in the Philippines 378 kamikazi aircraft were expended plus 102 escorts which managed to return. These attacks, which took place between 25 October 1944 and 31 January 1945, sank 22 Allied ships and damaged over a hundred others. The island of Okinawa was dangerously close to Japan, and an obvious stepping-stone for the Allies who were now making for the mainland. They had encountered bitter resistance at other main Japanese-held bases, particularly Guadalcanal, Saipan and Iwo Jima, and they knew that they could expect no less at Okinawa. The losses on both sides had already been enormous. At Guadalcanal (January–February 1943), the Japanese lost some 14 000 killed and wounded, with another 9 000 dead from starvation and disease while only 1 000 were captured; a total of about 24 000–25 000 men. The Americans lost only about a quarter of this number. At the battle of Iwo Jima (February–March 1945), the next important phase after the reconquest of the Philippines, the Japanese under the command of Major General Kuribayashi, were determined to hold the tiny (8 square mile) island until the last man. They had about 22 000 naval and army personnel who were entrenched in concealed gun emplacements, pillboxes and caves from which they could only be ferreted out by the close-up use of small arms and flame-throwers. The American force comprised three Marine divisions and attacked the island from the south. They had to fight their way ashore, suffering some

2 500 casualties, yet successfully cut off the northern sector of the island. It then took the best part of a month to end all *organized* resistance. Total American casualties were 25 000 including 7 000 killed. Most significantly only 212 of the numerous Japanese force surrendered, all the others were either killed or – in some cases – killed themselves.

The battle of Okinawa was the largest amphibious operation ever attempted in the Pacific War, and involved 180 000 troops and marines. These were backed by the US Fifth Fleet supported by a British carrier force. The Japanese forces designated the Thirty-second Army are believed to have numbered 130 000 under the command of Lieutenant General Mitsuru Ushijima. The Allied naval forces were attacked ferociously by the kamikazi, but despite this the naval bombardment was intensified and the first landings took place on 1 April. The Americans struck the island from two directions, but met with very determined resistance. It is estimated that about 340 kamikazi planes were used to try to repulse the American landings, and on 7 April two US destroyers were sunk in addition to 28 other vessels. Counter-attacks by the Americans accounted for the irreplaceable loss of the Japanese carrier *Yamato* on which many of the crew opted to go down with the ship rather than stand a chance of being rescued by their enemies. Altogether some 400 Japanese planes were shot down, and more than 4 000 Japanese sailors lost their lives.

There were more determined attacks by the kamikazi especially on 6–7 April and 12–13 April bringing the total number of sorties up to about 2 000 and the number of conventional sorties (torpedo bombers and dive-bombers) to about 5 000, although US statistics put the totals rather higher than these. The number of aircraft lost is most uncertain but the minimum figure is about 4 000. This compares with claimed American losses of 763 and British losses as 98. A breakdown of figures, which vary in the US, British and Japanese official histories, shows that the kamikazi attacks, perhaps by their very nature, were more effective than those conducted by conventional warplanes.

By 19 April the marines had made good progress, and there remained about a third of the island left in Japanese hands. In this southern section the Japanese proved extremely difficult to dislodge. One line of defence was penetrated on 24 April, but then on 3–4 May the Japanese launched a fanatical, last-ditch assault but this too was repulsed by the Americans who then commenced an enveloping operation against the remaining Japanese defences. Still the Japanese held on, and resistance did not finally cease until 22 June. American losses are estimated at 13 000 dead and about 37 000 wounded. The incredible resilience of the Japanese cost them over 130 000 dead and an untold number of wounded – estimates that leave room for very few able-bodied survivors. True to the code, one of the dead was the commanding officer who committed hara-kiri (Parkinson: 1979).

At the end of the war the Japanese still had over 10 000 aircraft left, over half of them ready for suicide missions. It was intended that these were to be used once the invasion of the Japanese mainland began. Had events turned out this way, they could certainly have inflicted serious – though not decisive – losses on the Allies. It is not surprising, therefore, that one US authority described the kamikazi as 'macabre, ruthless [and] supremely effective under the circumstances' (quoted by Pitt: 1979, p. 2554).

It hardly needs to be reiterated that there is nothing either new or unusual about the 'good death'. People have been meeting death in battle with courage and resignation from time immemorial. It is said that Spartan mothers used to say of their dead warrior sons, 'Bring his body back on his shield or don't bring it back at all'. In other words, if a son had thrown down his weapons and run away from the battle in fear, then no one would any longer want to know him – not even his family. One thinks of the famous stand of the 300 Spartans against the Persian hordes at the battle of Thermopylai in 480 BC. Admittedly they were not alone, but they were the elite of a force that included some hundreds of their perioikoi (literally 'the living around ones', i.e. non-Spartans who came under the jurisdiction of their Spartan overlords). Leonidas the Spartan leader and his army held out for two days against overwhelming numbers until they were outflanked, and then died to the last man. The contemporary poet Simonides celebrated the event in a famous couplet: 'Go now, and tell the Spartans, passer-by, that here obedient to their laws we lie.'

History records innumerable instances like this. Either where men have held out to the very last, most notably in the various successful sieges that have taken place in the past, or on occasions when people have withstood unsuccessful sieges as at Leningrad (1941–44), or where men have been ordered into battle in conditions where their chances of survival were little better than minimal as in the Dardanelles and Gallipoli (1915–16).

But these situations, regardless of the often reckless courage that was displayed, are still significantly different from 'special attack' operations. Valour (or foolishness) of the kamikazi and similar suicide units – however one wants to regard them – was of quite a different order. Here, in effect, we have men volunteering and training for their own deaths for largely ideological reasons. True, some may have enjoyed high status as members of 'special attack' units, but in most cases it was an enjoyment of disturbing brevity. As one commentator has observed, 'it is all too easy to [see these] suicide pilots as bloodcrazed, nationalistic fanatics ... going joyfully and unthinkingly to their spectacular ends ... drugged, drunk or numbed by pre-mission sex orgies' (O'Neill: 1984, p. 143). Perhaps, in general, this commentator is right. Like others, when they were told to go out and die – they obeyed. But unlike others, they were not just taking a chance. In their case, there was no chance. Theirs was the supreme example of the 'warrior death'.

Summary

In the foregoing discussion we have considered what generates militarism and military regimes. We have also looked at some of the theories – none of them wholly adequate – which are advanced to try to account for these regimes. In what is therefore a kind of afterword, it might be useful to analyse briefly some of the main characteristics of such regimes.

We need also to ask whether anything has really changed since early homonids branched off from their primordial ancestors some 5 million years ago. In militarism we see the 'civilized' version of group solidarity based on aggression against other communities. The main difference, it would seem, between modern man and the homonids is that aggression has been institutionalized. Social cooperation is now undertaken in order to achieve higher levels of organized violence. Will we ever really free ourselves from our biological natures? And if not, can we develop those necessary institutions which will help us to mitigate the effects of our baser instincts? We have seen that in earlier less developed societies, where martial criteria were critically important, status was largely achieved by those with warrior prowess. There were few other bases on which status could be achieved. Today, status is 'recognized' according to a number of criteria, economic, political and so forth. Indeed, with the cult of the celebrity, we even tend to accord status where it hardly belongs. It is more a matter of attribution than real achievement. So much for social values.

In modern society, the military rarely meets with unswerving social approbation – except, of course, when it is needed. This is also very much the case whether it is a trifling and largely ineffective force which may be regarded as something of a joke, or whether it is the powerful, all-pervasive force of the military regime. Unlike complex pre-industrial systems, modern societies are in a state of dynamic equilibrium. No matter how much practices and institutions differentiate to meet new conditions, a process of self-correcting homeostasis operates to maintain the appropriate equilibrium. But this is only over the long term. Societies are often *out* of balance, say, during periods of revolution and rapid social change. This is where the sociological dichotomy between revolutionary and evolutionary models of change breaks down. Taken over a long enough time span, there is only evolutionary change. Revolutions are mere ripples on the surface of time.

The military, in its various guises, is part of the homeostatic process. It is a ubiquitous feature of virtually all known societies. Indeed, in many instances it has been the military which has kept a society in being. Numerous societies owe their very survival to the existence of the military, not least British society. But this is not militarism, as such. This – as we have seen – connotes very much more than the 'military way' to which most societies have resorted *in extremis*. Militarism is different. The characteristics of the ideal-type militaristic society when taken separately are by no means unique, but taken *together* they add up to a particular kind of military culture.

These societies involve:

1. *The inculcation of loyalty*: whether it is to a nation, a regiment, a tribe, a clan, a commander or whatever, the instilling of a keen sense of loyalty is a key feature of the militaristic system. This is what makes possible the seemingly incomprehensible willingness for self-sacrifice when human rationality calls for self-preservation. It was only when Alexander the Great – a military but otherwise questionable genius – had taken his troops halfway across Asia thousands of miles from their homeland that the troops called a halt and said that enough was enough. Until that time they had followed him, for the most part unquestioningly, and engaged in a number of campaigns, often against considerable odds. A goodly proportion of them had not seen their home and families for several years, but they were prepared to go on under Alexander's leadership buoyed up by his promises of rich rewards if they went just a little further. At least, Alexander with all his faults, kept up with the men and shared their disappointments and privations (pre-eminently in the long retreat *back* to base in Babylonia). No one doubted Alexander's bravery or ability. But what would have been next – Carthage, Sicily, Italy? For Alexander it was wherever there were rich pickings. He had an insatiable lust for conquest.

   A sense of loyalty is a potent force, and certainly helps to anaesthetize men against the dangers of battle, but even for seasoned campaigners there can come a time when they begin to question the purpose of it all. It is then that loyalties can alter, and the focus of loyalty changes. This happened in the Russian Revolution, with the military joining the revolutionaries, and more recently in the 1977 Revolution when the Iranian army switched sides and deserted the Shah and went over to the people and the mullahs. It was loyalty just the same, but with a new ideological alignment.

2. *A preoccupation with military display*: this, it will be recalled is Alfred Vagts's point, that militarism is all about uniforms, rank, parades, saluting the colours and so forth (Vagts: 1959). There is

no doubt that this is one outward expression of militarism. This is a necessary adjunct of the loyalty theme. Though nothing *by itself*, military ostentation is a fillip to morale. Soldiers are encouraged to take a pride in the regiment in the same way that medieval knights were expected to honour their heraldic symbols. It is probably a mistake at the present time that British War Department policy has undermined this aspect of military organization. Regimental affiliations are gradually going and all the old historical associations and battle honours are being lost. Only a few Special Force groups such as the SAS and the Parachute Regiment are being allowed to retain their acknowledged identity. This erosion of tradition by government ministers who themselves have never been part of the military will do nothing to encourage the esprit that was once considered critical to the warrior mentality.

3. *Ideological motivation*: soldiers must fight for *something*. In actual battle conditions this might well be simply the attempt to survive, but usually their very presence on the battlefield means that they see some purpose in what they are doing. It is true that soldiers can get locked into a wartime situation where, having been conscripted, they are not really sure what they are doing there. One senses that this was the case for many during the First World War. As the war dragged on, many a denizen of the trenches must have wondered what it was really all about, and whether such carnage was really necessary. A common British army refrain sums it up: 'We're here because we're here because we're here because we're here'. In other words, there is no really satisfactory reason, it is a question of being 'here', and having to make the best of it. It is a PBI (poor bloody infantry) ideology – the predominant sentiment is to get it over with and go home as soon as possible.

But in the militaristic system things are rather different. There are forms of direct and indirect indoctrination, and this constitutes a kind of conditioning. The militaristic rationale may emphasize the superiority of the system over other systems. The focus of aggression, often a neighbouring state, may not only be regarded as ripe for conquest, but 'deserving' to be taken over. This was certainly the Nazi mentality. Other European states, especially Slavic states, were seen as degenerate, bastardized people of no pure ethnic stock who were fit for nothing except as slaves in the service of the Greater German Reich. There was nothing really new in this. In fifth century Greece, the political leader, Perikles, held similar views about the superiority of the Athenians and their justification in seeking an empire. And various colonial powers have been like-minded in relation to the indigenes of their conquered states. It is just that the Nazis took conquest to its 'logical' conclusion. Many colonial powers did, at least, embark upon educational schemes which might one day bring the conquered up to European standards. But in the early 1940s, the Germans had no such intentions. As Hitler once cynically put it, the Slavs (namely Russians and Poles) were to have just enough education to enable them to read the road signs so as not to get themselves run over. Those that were allowed to live were to be a leaderless labour force, uneducated, unenfranchised and unrepresented. Indeed, in 1940, Himmler, the Reichsführer SS, reckoned that within ten years the rump Polish state known during the occupation as the Government-General, would consist of a mere remnant of substandard beings (Carlton: 1992, p. 154). The irony was that before the war ended, the Reich was so desperate for manpower that the SS were recruiting from many of the occupied territories (mainly in Western Europe) and the Wehrmacht actually raised a contingent of Ukrainian volunteers under General Vlaslov, a Russian defector. Perhaps, after all, when the need is urgent enough, the influence of ideology will sometimes break down under the force of necessity.

The potency of ideology can be clearly seen in the fanaticism with which devotees will pursue their interests, especially in conflict situations as is particularly evidenced by the many fundamentalist Muslim groups operating today. Belief advances the cause, and if this were not enough, Islam also holds out the promise of post-mortal rewards. The other great bonus of ideology is not only that it induces compliance, it is also remarkably inexpensive. Indeed, if rightly formulated and applied, it goes along with 'bread and circuses' as an effective means of keeping the masses in order and in generating the necessary fervour for the pursuit of regime-inspired ends.

4. *Clarity of goal orientations*: no matter how effective the ideologically inspired military regime happens to be, it also requires a hard-headed leadership with clear ideas as to how the system is going to be organized and what are to be its objectives. The autocracy or oligarchy, or whatever, has got to decide how the economy has to be systematized so as to produce the necessary surplus to provide the wherewithal for an army. After all, all the time that people were having to grub for a living – which has been for most of history – there could not be trained, professional armies suitably supplied from central arsenals. Ancient armies were for the most part citizen armies composed of men who had to find their own weapons and accoutrements. They could only be sustained for

short campaigning seasons unless they lived off the land by pillaging enemy property and supplies, and thus often inducing mass starvation. The Israelite prophets, it will be recalled, talked of the predatory Assyrians as 'locusts' who left nothing standing in their wake, and left the bulk of the people to fend for themselves as best they could. War could be terrible for soldiers and people alike.

Ideology is sometimes cynically harnessed by ambitious leaders not only as a means of inducing control, but also as a way of advancing their own careers. We need only ask ourselves how many successful conquerors have ever been content with modest gains. Usually their own inordinate acquisitiveness drives them on until more and more territory brings them more and more bad friends. Indefinite expansion and the realization of ever more goals so often results in increasingly marginal returns. This was the experience of Napoleon and the Grand Army which after an unbroken succession of victories from which it was felt they would never look back, took on Russia in 1812 and thereafter did nothing else but look back. The ambitions of one of the greatest figures in military history, Gustavus Adolfus, king of Sweden, met a similar fate. He was an astute tactitian and organizer and had significant successes against the Poles (1628) and the Germans (1631). But eventually, this 'Lion of the North' was killed in one of the interminable battles of the Thirty Years War when only 38 years of age (1632). To have clearly defined goals is all very well as long as one's grasp is consistent with one's reach.

5. *Expendability of personnel*: expansionist military systems have to be prepared to lose men. Indeed, such losses may well be regarded as a secondary consideration providing the system's goals can be realized. For exemplification of the expendability theme we have only to look once again at the Japanese situation at Okinawa during the Pacific War (1941–45). The officer in command of the Japanese forces there, General Ushijima – incomprehensibly – chose not to defend the beaches, and instead withdrew the bulk of his troops to the southernmost part of the island. This meant that they occupied a mere 10 miles of an island 60 miles long. By letting the Americans land virtually unhindered, before dark on the first day some 50 000 US troops were already firmly ashore and preparing their advance into the interior. Admittedly, there was a considerable bombardment of the beachhead by the US Navy before the Americans disembarked. They must have thought that this had done the trick. They were surprised at how easy it all was as they took over two of Okinawa's airfields at no cost whatsoever. Their

engineers set to work, and within six days these airfields were once again operational and being used by 200 US fighter planes.

From the Japanese point of view this seems like a genuine tactical error. Ushijima had several hundred guns with which he could have caused havoc among the invading troops before they were barely ashore. There were good defensive positions for his men, and – in retrospect – it would appear that he could have sacrificed a battalion or so in order to take out many more of the enemy.

This hardly sounds like the action of a ruthless, determined adversary, but this is possibly to judge on initial impressions. Ushijima, it is now believed, fully realized that he could not win, and had therefore prepared himself to fight a 'last redoubt' type of battle. He had prepared a truly formidable defensive system of pillboxes and underground tunnels, and was bent on inflicting the highest number of casualties possible, but in doing so it would mean sacrificing his whole army.

For several weeks the strategy worked. In just a month, the Americans gained only 133 yards at the cost of 20 000 casualties. But by the end of May 1945, the Japanese had lost about 68 000 killed, and by the end of hostilities in June thousands more had died with only a small percentage of their total forces choosing to surrender. Many committed suicide as did also General Ushijima and his Chief-of-Staff, Colonel Cho, both in the time-honoured seppuku fashion by baring their abdomens to the ceremonial knife just as the Americans were approaching the cave in which both had just toasted their victorious defeat. Appositely the American leader, General Buckner, had been killed by shellfire just two days before the Japanese capitulation.

Expendability has never been much of a problem for militarists. Was it not Napoleon, when surveying the body-strewn landscape after the battle of Borodino, who said that 'one night in Paris will make up for this'? Lives have been more liberally squandered especially in modern wars, often for no particular purpose – and certainly not for very much gain. The First World War is a classic example, and we find similar instances in the Second World War such as the waste of the entire sixth army at Stalingrad in 1943 (all told about 300 000 men) mainly because Hitler refused to sanction a retreat. He gave similar instructions to the Afrika Korps in North Africa at about the same time, but Rommel – unlike Field Marshal Von Paulus in Russia – ignored the Führer's order and preferred to try to save his men. Even in current war situations, lives are often of secondary importance. In the critical battles in Cambodia in the

1970s and in Burma in the 1990s, life was so cheap that the antagonists have thought nothing of enlisting youths of 13 and 14 to fight for the cause. Often they are hastily trained, and consequently stand little chance against more experienced opponents, although they can often be just as brutal as battle-hardened veterans.

6. *The capacity to act as potential or actual governments*: all too often the military *is* the government, the rationale being that unless the military are in charge there will be no stability, and the country will degenerate into chaos. This is, of course, sometimes an excuse for authoritarianism, but in other cases it is probably an accurate assessment of the situation. In this way the military becomes the ultimate agent of social control. It is not a case of rule without law; military regimes make their own laws. When in power, they *are* the law.

Nowhere is this better illustrated than in the mixed post-colonial fortunes of Africa. In so many African states where hope was high that independence would result in the adoption of democratic forms and developed economies, the situation is hardly better than in the days of the colonial powers. In some states there are grounds for optimism, but even here – as, indeed, in current South Africa – few are actually agog with expectation. A number of states have suffered or are still suffering from all manner of internal problems. Some of these have been exacerbated by external pressures and ecological difficulties, but much has been the result of sheer bad management, if not actual corruption. Uganda is the classic example of a country impoverished by the repressive military regime of Idi Amin which accounted for untold lives, and which is now trying desperately to recover despite the fact that its mobilized resources are minimal and that the HIV/AIDS epidemic is ravaging the population (estimates are that about one in 12 are affected). Similarly, Kenya is beset by corruption and ethnic unrest, and Tanzania, although 'quiet' and rarely in the news, still has its own share of poverty after all these years of 'liberation'.

Civil war has played a key role in the fortunes of many states. Zimbabwe, having suffered the dynamics of a civil conflict, is merely a pseudo-socialist state under a virtual dictator. It once thrived as a highly questionable tobacco economy, but is now (2001) regarded as so corrupt that it is on the brink of economic collapse. Nigeria, a potentially wealthy country, has long promised democratic reforms, but has been ruled by a succession of military regimes, each one no better than its predecessor. Ghana, where

Nkrumah's extravagance, state socialism and anti-colonial posturing set the pattern for future rulers (see *The Times*, 8 January 1999) and Eritrea have not been that much better. Sierra Leone is currently embroiled in yet another civil war while other conflicts elsewhere are still rumbling on. War, for some reason or another – often, though not always, combined with some form of military dictatorship – has vitiated the fortunes of the Congo (misleadingly referred to as the 'Democratic Republic of Congo'), Angola, Rwanda, Burundi, Ethiopia and particularly the Sudan. All have been left in turmoil, and the often pathetic GNP of these states has been fractionalized by the need to purchase arms from the West.

What we see here is a sorry – indeed, tragic – tale of lost opportunity. A combination of misrule and mismanagement linked all too often with war and genocide have denied so many people the prosperity they might have had. This is not to minimize the deficiencies and indifference of some of the previous colonial rulers, particularly the Belgians and the Portuguese who were ruthlessly exploitative in feeding back the profits from their mining operations into their own pockets rather than developing native industries and building up resources. But that said, intertribal warfare and a whole series of incompetent and autocratic rulers have conspired to make progress well-nigh impossible.

This is not to suggest that such problems are peculiar to Africa. The sad fact is that they have been – and still are – found throughout the world, certainly in parts of Asia and in Europe. The argument here is not that they are characteristic of certain kinds of people, but that they are characteristic of just about *all* people given the wrong circumstances. Egocentricity and the capacity for aggression are innate; circumstances merely supply the appropriate social context. Thus the need for social control for which the military – *not* militarism – may always have a necessary role.

Bibliography

Alcock, N. (1972), *The War Disease*, Oakville, Ontario, CPRI Press.
Allmand, C. (1988), *The Hundred Years War*, Cambridge, CUP.
Andreski, S. (1968), *Military Organisation and Society*, London, RKP.
Angell, W. (1910), *The Great Illusion: A Study of the Relation of Military Power to National Advantage*, New York, Putnam.
Ardrey, R. (1963), *African Genesis*, London, Collins.
Ardrey, R. (1967), *The Territorial Imperative*, London, Collins.
Aron, R. (1965), 'Conflict and War from the Viewpoint of Historical Sociology', in E. McNeil (ed.), *The Nature of Human Conflict*, Englewood Cliffs, NJ, Prentice-Hall.
Auguet, R. (1972), *Cruelty and Civilisation: The Roman Games*, London, Allen & Unwin.
Banse, E. (1934), *Germany Prepares for War: a Nazi Theory of 'National Defense'*, trans. A. Harris, New York, Harcourt, Brace and Co.
Barber, N. (1972), *Lords of the Golden Horn*, London, Macmillan.
Barnett, C. (1960), *The Desert Generals*, London, W. Kimber.
Barnett, C. (ed.) (1990), *Hitler's Generals*, London, Weidenfeld & Nicolson.
Baron, R. and Byrne, D. (1987), *Social Psychology: Understanding Human Interaction*, 5th edn, London, Allyn & Bacon.
Basham, A. (1971), *The Wonder that was India*, London, Fontana.
Battuta, I. (1927), *Travels of Ibn Battuta in Asia and Africa*, trans. H.A.R. Gibb, London, RKP.
Becker, P. (1979), *Path of Blood*, Harmondsworth, Penguin.
Beevor, A. (1998), *Stalingrad*, London, Viking.
Berkowitz, L. (1962), *Aggression: A Socio-psychological Analysis*, New York, McGraw-Hill.
Best, G. (1980), *Humanity in Warfare*, London, Weidenfeld & Nicolson.
Bethell, N. (1976), *The War that Hitler Won*, London, Futura.
Bidney, D. (1967), *Theoretical Anthropology*, New York, Schocken Books.
Birnbaum, N. (1962), *The Sociological Study of Ideology, 1940–1960*, Oxford, Blackwell.
Boak, A. and Sinnigen, W. (1965), *A History of Rome to AD 565*, 5th edn, New York, Macmillan.
Bosworth, A. (1988), *Conquest and Empire*, Cambridge, CUP.
Bowle, J. (1980), *A History of Europe*, London, Heinemann.

Bramson, L. and Goethals, G. (eds) (1968), *War*, New York, Basic Books.
Braybrooke, D. (ed.) (1965), *Philosophical Problems of the Social Sciences*, New York, Macmillan.
Brinton, D. (1901), *Races and Peoples*, Philadelphia, McKay & Co.
Brodie, B. (1973), *War and Politics*, London, Macmillan.
Brondsted, J. (1965), *The Vikings*, Harmondsworth, Penguin.
Brooke, L. (1971), *The Saxon and Norman Kings*, 6th edn, London, Fontana.
Burland, A. (1976), *Peoples of the Sun*, London, Weidenfeld & Nicolson.
Burn, A. (1973), *Alexander the Great and the Middle East*, rev. edn, Harmondsworth, Penguin.
Caesar, J. (1951), *The Conquest of Gaul*, Harmondsworth, Penguin.
Carlton, E. (1977), *Ideology and Social Order*, London, RKP.
Carlton, E. (1990), *War and Ideology*, London, Routledge.
Carlton, E. (1992), *Occupation: The Policies and Practices of Military Conquerors*, London, Routledge.
Carlton, E. (1994), *Massacres: An Historical Perspective*, Aldershot, Scholar Press.
Carlton, E. (1995), *Faces of Despotism*, Aldershot, Scholar Press.
Carlton, E. (1998), *Treason: Meanings and Motives*, Aldershot, Ashgate.
Carver, Lord (1990), 'Manstein', in C. Barnett (ed.), *Hitler's Generals*, London, Weidenfeld & Nicolson.
Cary, M. (1972), *A History of the Greek World, 323–146 BC*, London, Methuen.
Chadwick, N. (1970), *The Celts*, Harmondsworth, Penguin.
Clausewitz, K. von (1950), *On War*, Washington, Infantry Journal Press.
Coe, M. (1966), *The Maya*, Harmondsworth, Penguin.
Collier, R. (1972), *Duce: The Rise and Fall of Mussolini*, London, Fontana.
Costigan, G. (1978), 'Einstein and Freud on War' in L. Farrar (ed.), *War: A Historical, Political and Social Study*, Santa Barbara, CA, ABC-CLIO.
Crankshaw, E. (1995), *The Fall of the House of Hapsburg*, London, Macmillan.
Crawford, M. (1978), *The Roman Republic*, London, Fontana.
Davies, N. (1981), *Human Sacrifice*, New York, W. Morrow.
Davies, N. (1983), *The Ancient Kingdoms of Mexico*, Harmondsworth, Penguin.
Downing, D. (1978), *The Devil's Virtuosos: German Generals at War, 1940–45*, London, NEL.

Dyer, G. (1985), *War*, London, Bodley Head.
Earle, P. (1975), *Henry V*, London, Sphere Books.
Emery, W. (1972), *Archaic Egypt*, Harmondsworth, Penguin.
Fagan, B. (1984), *The Aztecs*, Oxford, Freeman.
Fagan, B. (1998), *Clash of Cultures*, 2nd edn, London, Sage.
Farrar, M. (1978), 'World War 2 as Total War', in L. Farrar (ed.), *War, a Historical, Political and Social Study*, Santa Barbara, CA, ABD-CLIO.
Farrell, B. (1981), *The Standing of PsychoAnalysis*, Oxford, OUP.
Fellner, F. (1995), 'Austria-Hungary', in K. Wilson (ed.), *Decisions for War 1914*, London, UCL.
Ferguson, R.B. and Whitehead, N. (eds) (1992), *War in the Tribal Zone*, New Mexico, School of American Research Press.
Fine, J. (1983), *The Ancient Greeks: A Critical History*, Cambridge, MA, Belknap Press.
Finer, S. (1962), *Man on Horseback: The Role of the Military in Politics*, London, Pall Mall.
Firth, E. (ed.) (1960), *Man and Culture*, London, RKP.
Fotion, N. and Elfstrom, G. (1986), *Military Ethics*, London, RKP.
Freedman, L. (1994), *War*, Oxford, OUP.
Gallenkamp, C. (1981), *Maya: The Riddle and Discovery of a Lost Civilisation*, 2nd edn, Harmondsworth, Penguin.
Gallie, W. (1991), *Understanding War*, London, Routledge.
Gibb, H. (1969), *Mohammedanism*, Oxford, OUP.
Giddens, A. (1990), *Sociology*, Cambridge, Polity Press.
Gorer, G. (1938), *Himalayan Village*, London, Michael Joseph.
Grant, M. (1982), *From Alexander to Cleopatra*, London, Weidenfeld & Nicolson.
Grant, M. (1987), *The Rise of the Greeks*, London, Weidenfeld & Nicolson.
Gray, G. (1967), *The Warriors: Reflections on Men in Battle*, New York, Harper & Row.
Green, P. (1982), *Alexander the Great*, London, Weidenfeld & Nicolson.
Green, P. (1991), *Alexander of Macedon*, Berkeley, CA, University of California.
Hackett, J. (1983), *The Profession of Arms*, London, Sidgwick & Jackson.
Hammond, N. (1991), *The Miracle that Was Macedon*, London, Sidgwick & Jackson.
Hardach, G. (1977), *The First World War, 1914–1918*, London, Allen Lane.
Harvey, J. (1972), *The Plantagenets*, London, Fontana.

Herwig, H. (1997), *The First War World, Germany and Austria-Hungary, 1914–1918*, London, Arnold.
Hibbert, C. (1965), *Benito Mussolini: The Rise and Fall of Il Duce*, Harmondsworth, Penguin.
Hibbert, C. (1982), *Africa Explored*, London, Allen Lane.
Hiro, D. (1988), *Islamic Fundamentalism*, London, Paladin.
Hitti, P. (1970), *History of the Arabs*, 10th edn, London, Macmillan.
Hohne, H. (1972), *The Order of the Death's Head*, London, Pan Books.
Holmes, G. (1974), *The Later Middle Ages, 1272–1485*, London, Cardinal Books.
Hopkins, K. (1985), *Death and Renewal*, Cambridge, CUP.
Howard, M. (1983), *The Causes of War*, London, Unwin.
Hoyt, E. (1987), *Japan's War*, London, Hutchinson.
Hultkrantz, A. (1980), *The Religions of the American Indians*, Berkeley, CA, University of California Press.
Humble, R. (1976), *Hitler's Generals*, London, Panther Books.
Hyland, G. and Gill, A. (1998), *The Last Talons of the Eagle*, London, Headline Books.
James, E.O. (1962), *Sacrifice and Sacrament*, London, Thames & Hudson.
Janowitz, M. (1960), *The Professional Soldier: A Social and Political Portrait*, Glencoe, NY, Free Press.
Janowitz, M. (1967), *The New Military*, New York, John Wiley.
Jary, D. and Jary, J. (1991), *Dictionary of Sociology*, London, HarperCollins.
Jeffrey, L. (1976), *Archaic Greece: The City States: c700–500 BC*, London, Ernest Benn.
Johnson, H. (1965), *Sociology: A Systematic Introduction*, London, RKP.
Joll, J. (1984), *The Origins of the First World War*, New York, Longman.
Jones, G. (1968), *A History of the Vikings*, Oxford, OUP.
Keegan, J. (1993), *A History of Warfare*, London, Hutchinson.
Keegan, J. (1998), *The Reith Lectures BBC April 14–May 6 1998*, London, Hutchinson.
LaPiere, R. (1954), *A Theory of Social Control*, New York, McGraw-Hill.
Large, D.C. (1990), *Between Two Fires*, New York, Norton.
Levy, R. (1971), *The Social Structure of Islam*, 2nd edn, Cambridge, CUP.
Lewis, B. (1958), *The Arabs in History*, London, Arrow Books.
Liddell Hart, B. (1942), *The Ways to Win Wars*, London, Faber.

Lider, J. (1977), *On the Nature of War*, Farnborough, Hants, Saxon House.
Linklater, E. (1966), *The Conquest of England*, London, Hodder & Stoughton.
Lloyd, P. (1972), 'The Political Structure of African Kingdoms', in M. Banton (ed.), *Political Systems and the Distribution of Power*, London, Tavistock,
Lorenz, K. (1966), *On Aggression*, New York, Harcourt, Brace & World.
MacDonald, N. (1975), 'The Biological Factor in the Etiology of War: A Medieval View', in M. Nettleship (ed.), *War, Its Causes and Correlates*, The Hague and Paris, Mouton.
Mack Smith, D. (1979), *Mussolini's Roman Empire*, Harmondsworth, Penguin.
Mack Smith, D. (1994), *Mussolini*, London, Phoenix Books.
Malinowski, B. (1922), *Argonauts of the Western Pacific*, London, RKP.
Malinowski, B. (1926), *Crime and Custom in Savage Society*, London, RKP.
McCrystal, C. (1993), 'The World at War', *Independent on Sunday*, 14 March.
McKisack, M. (1959), *The Fourteenth Century, 1307–99*, Oxford, OUP.
McLynn, F. (1992), *Hearts of Darkness*, London, Hutchinson.
McNeil, E. (ed.) (1965), *The Nature of Human Conflict*, Englewood Cliffs, NJ, Prentice-Hall.
McNeil, W. (1983), *The Pursuit of Power*, Oxford, Blackwell.
Miller, S. (ed.) (1985), *Military Strategy and the Origins of the First World War*, Princeton, NJ, Princeton University Press.
Moctezuma, E.M. (1988), *The Great Temple of the Aztecs*, London, Thames & Hudson.
Momigliano, A. (1961), *Claudius*, Cambridge, CUP.
Montgomery, B. (1972), *A Concise History of Warfare*, London, Collins.
Moore, D. and Anderson, A. (1965), 'Puzzles, Games and Social Interaction', in D. Braybrooke (ed.), *Philosophical Problems of the Social Sciences*, New York, Macmillan.
Moran, Lord (1945), *The Anatomy of Courage*, London, Constable.
Morris, D. (1967), *The Washing of the Spears*, London, Sphere Books.
Morris, D. (1971), *Imperial Animal*, New York, Holt, Rinehart & Winston.
Mortimer, E. (1982), *Faith and Power: The Politics of Islam*, London, Faber & Faber.

Morton, F. (1991), *Thunder at Twilight: Vienna 1913–14*, London, P. Owen.
Mosca, G. (1939), *The Ruling Class*, London, McGraw-Hill.
Myers, A. (1969), *England in the Late Middle Ages*, 2nd edn, Harmondsworth, Penguin.
Needham, J. (1975), *The Development of Iron and Steel Technology in China*, Cambridge, CUP.
Nettleship, M., Givens, R.D. and Nettleship, A. (eds) (1975), *War, its Causes and Correlates*, The Hague and Paris, Mouton.
Newark, T. (1986), *Celtic Warriors*, London, Blandford Press.
Nilsson, M. (1962), *Imperial Rome*, New York, Schocken Books.
O'Neill, R. (1984), *Suicide Squad*, New York, Ballantine Books.
Oakeshott, M. (ed.) (1957), *Leviathan (1651) by Thomas Hobbes*, Oxford, Blackwell.
Ogilvie, R. (1976), *Early Rome and the Etruscans*, Glasgow, Fontana.
Oliver, R. (ed.) (1968), *The Dawn of African History*, Oxford, OUP.
Oliver, R. and Oliver, C. (1965), *Africa in the Days of Exploration*, Englewood Cliffs, NJ, Prentice-Hall.
Ottenberg, S. (1978), 'Anthropological Interpretations of War', in L. Farrar (ed.), *War, a Historical, Political and Social Study*, Santa Barbara, CA, ABD-CLIO.
Pallotino, M. (1991), *A History of Earliest Italy*, London, Routledge.
Parkinson, R. (1979), *Encyclopaedia Of Modern War*, London, Paladin.
Parsons, T. (1966), *Societies: Evolutionary and Comparative Perspectives*, Englewood Cliffs, NJ, Prentice-Hall.
Payne, R. (1964), *The Roman Triumph*, London, Pan Books.
Peers, D. (ed.) (1997), *Warfare and Empires*, Aldershot, Ashgate.
Pine, L. (1966), *They Came with the Conqueror*, London, Evans.
Pitt, B. (ed.) (1979), *The History of the Second World War*, vol. 6, Paulton, Som., Purnell.
Rachman, S. (1990), *Fear and Courage*, 2nd edn, New York, Freeman.
Roberts, B. (1977), *The Zulu Kings*, London, Sphere Books.
Ross, A. (1970), *Everyday Life of the Pagan Celts*, London, Batsford.
Rousseau, J.J. (1950), *The Social Contract and Discourses*, Everyman's Library Edition, New York, Dutton & Co.
Ruthven, M. (1984), *Islam in the World*, Harmondsworth, Penguin.
Salmon, E. (1972), *A History of the Roman World, 30 BC to AD 138*, London, Methuen.
Schapera, I. (1956), *Government and Politics in Tribal Societies*, London, Watts.

Schele, L. and Freidel, D. (1990), *A Forest of Kings*, New York, W. Morrow.
Scullard, H. (1963), *From the Gracchi to Nero*, London, Methuen.
Service, E. (1978), *Profiles in Ethnology*, 3rd edn, New York, Harper & Row.
Sharer, R. (1994), *The Ancient Maya*, 5th edn, Stanford, CA, Stanford University Press.
Shirer, W. (1964), *The Rise and Fall of the Third Reich*, London, Pan Books.
Smith, D. and Smith, R. (1983), *The Economics of Militarism*, London, Pluto Press.
Smith, R. (1969), *The Kingdoms of the Yoruba*, London, Methuen.
Snyder, L. (1998), *Encyclopaedia of the Third Reich*, Ware, Herts, Wordsworth.
Southern, R.W. (1959), *The Making of the Middle Ages*, London, Arrow Books.
Stoessinger, J. (1993), *Why Nations go to War*, 6th edn, London, Macmillan.
Stone, N. (1976), *The Eastern Front, 1914–1917*, New York, Scribners.
Stone, N. (1983), *Europe Transformed, 1878–1919*, London, Fontana.
Sumner, W. (1968), 'War', in I. Bramson and G. Goethals (eds), *War*, rev. edn, New York, Basic Books.
Thaper, R. (1976), *A History of India*, vol. 1, Harmondsworth, Penguin.
Thompson, E.P. and Smith, D. (eds) (1980), *Protest and Survive*, Harmondsworth, Penguin.
Thompson, J.E. (1966), *The Rise and Fall of Maya Civilisation*, 2nd edn, Norman, OK, University of Oklahoma Press.
Thucydides (1972), *The Peloponnesian War*, trans. R. Warner, Harmondsworth, Penguin.
Tilly, C. (1975), *The Formation of the National States in Europe*, Princeton, NJ, Princeton University Press.
Tinberger, N. (1968), 'On War and Peace in Animals and Man: An Ethologist Approach to the Biology of Aggression', *Science*, 160, 28 June.
Toynbee, A. (1957), *A Study of History*, abridged D. Somervell, Oxford, OUP.
Tucker, R. (1960), *The Just War*, Baltimore, MD, Johns Hopkins University Press.
Turner, L. (1970), *Origins of the First World War*, London, Arnold.
Vagts, A. (1959), *A History of Militarism*, rev. edn, New York, Free Press.

Walbank, F.W. (1981), *The Hellenistic World*, London, Fontana.

Walton, D. (1986), *Courage: A Philosophical Investigation*, Berkeley, CA, University of California Press.

Waltz, K. (1959), *Man, the State and War*, New York, Columbia University Press.

Walzer, M. (1980), *Just and Unjust Wars*, Harmondsworth, Penguin.

Weber, M. (1964), *Theory of Social and Economic Organisation*, London, Free Press.

Wilson, D. (1970), *The Vikings and their Origins*, London, Thames & Hudson.

Wilson, T. (1986), *The Myriad Faces of War*, Cambridge, Polity Press.

Windrow, M. and Mason, I. (1997), *Dictionary of Military Biography*, Ware, Herts, Wordsworth.

Wittfogel, K. (1957), *Oriental Despotism*, New Haven, CT, Yale University Press.

Wolff, L. (1958), *In Flanders Fields*, London, Longmans Green.

Wolpert, S. (1989), *A New History of India*, 3rd edn, Oxford, OUP.

Wright, G. (1968), *The Ordeal of Total War 1939–45*, New York, Harper & Row.

Wright, Q. (1942), *A Study of War*, Chicago, University of Chicago Press.

Index

Aachen 98
Abbasid dynasty 159ff.
Abraham 151–2
Afghanistan 156, 158, 164
Africa 16, 36ff., 42ff., 198ff.
Afrika Korps 132, 198
Aggression 8ff., 16ff., 26ff., 37ff., 48ff., 55ff., 62ff., 74ff., 81, 97ff., 123ff., 170ff., 193, 195
Agincourt 77
Ahuizotl 152
Alamein 19
Albania 110, 132
Alcock, N. 22
Alexander (the Great) 52, 55, 56, 57, 60, 64, 81, 89, 107, 158, 166, 194
Alfred the Great 99
Allmand, C. 77
Ambury, D. 182
Ammianus Marcellinus 83
Andreski, Stanislav 11, 35, 79–80
Angell, W. 95
Anglo-Saxons 105
Angola 43, 200
Antiochus 89
Antwerp 98
Apollo 88
Aquitaine 68, 72, 73, 74, 76, 103
Arabia/Arab(s) 5, 34, 98, 156–7ff.
Arapesh (New Guinea) 41
Archelaus 28
Ardennes 129, 182
Ardrey, R. 22, 79, 81
Ares 5
Argentina 12, 19
Aristion 28
Armenia 27, 34
Aron, R. 95
Ashanti 36, 46
Ashoka 54ff.
Asia Minor 26ff., 61, 89, 91
Assyia/Assyrians 7, 12, 55, 91, 157, 197
Athelstan 100
Athena 146

Athens 3, 28, 38, 55, 57, 58ff., 65, 66, 88, 90, 92, 107, 132, 195
Atrocities 22ff., 37ff., 59, 74, 77, 80, 81, 89, 97, 127, 133ff., 157ff., 164, 167, 175
Attalus 82
Auguet, R. 34
Augustine 23
Augustus 29, 30
Austria/Austria-Hungary 108ff., 132, 168, 171, 173ff.
Axis 123, 125ff.
Aztecs 84, 96, 142, 143, 147, 148, 152, 181

Babi Yar 136–7
Babylonians 157, 194
Bach-Zelewski, E. von 135
Baganda (of Uganda) 42
Bagdolio, P. 177
Baghdad 157ff.
Balkans 16, 20, 58, 110ff., 130, 132, 137, 158
Baltic States 134
Bangladesh 151
Bannockburn 69
Banse, E. 131
Bantu 13
Barber, N. 18
Barbosa, D. 43
Barnett, C. 179
Baron and Byrne 167
Basuto 46
Battell, A. 43
Bavaria 98
Becker, P. 39, 81
Beevor, A. 137
Belgium 17, 112, 125, 128, 137, 200
Berkowitz, L. 25
Best, G. 124
Bethell, N. 18, 128
Bible 2, 163
Bidney, D. 38
Bithynia 27
Black Death 72, 73
Black Prince 71, 73

Black Sea 26ff., 90, 110
Blaskowitz, General 133
Boak and Sinnigan 86
Bock, General von 128, 132
Bordeaux 98
Borneo 151
Bornu-Kanem 44
Boroughbridge 69, 70
Boudicca 84
Bowle, J. 97, 98
Brahmins 53–4, 153
Bramson and Goethals 36
Brauchitsch, General von 128, 133
Brennus 88, 89
Brinton, D. 166
Britain/British 5, 15, 18–19, 30, 67, 80, 81, 95, 108, 109, 110, 112, 116, 121, 123, 125ff., 169, 170, 171ff., 183, 190, 194, 195
Brooke, C. 104
Bruce, R. 69
Buddhism 54, 184
Bulgaria/Bulgars 110, 119, 132
Burma 151, 199
Burn, A.R. 61
Burundi 200
Bushido 185
Bushman (Kalahari) 41, 46
Byzantium 65, 98, 158, 159

Cadiz 103
Caesar, Julius 9, 30, 83–4, 87
Calais 72, 73, 74, 76, 78
Caligula 29, 30
Caliphates 157ff.
Cambodia 198
Cappodocia 27
Carlton, E. 9, 25, 41, 49, 52, 74, 96, 123, 139, 155, 196
Carthage (Phoenicians) 13, 26, 30, 87, 91, 107, 152, 158, 194
Cartimandua 84
Carver, Sir M. 19
Cary, M. 89
Caste system 53ff.
Chadwick, N. 83, 84
Chaironia 60
Chandragupta 52–3, 54
Charlemagne 97, 99, 160
Charles IV 69

Charles VI 74–5, 77
Charles VII 78
Charles the Bad 73
Chile 3, 8
Ch'in Huang-Ti 54
China 3, 18–19, 20, 54, 63, 65, 152, 183
Churchill, W. 125, 130, 166
Cicero 30
Claudius 29ff.
Clausewitz, General von 10
Clive, R. 16
Cnut 102
Cobden, R. 10, 65
Collier, R. 171
Colonization 16, 80, 89ff., 195–6, 200
Communism 182
Confucianism 184
Congo 200
Constantinople 18; *see also* Byzantium
Cook, Captain 40
Cooley, C. 37
Corcyra (Corfu) 90
Corinth 60, 90, 91
Costigan, G. 24
Crankshaw, E. 114
Crawford, M. 86
Crécy 72, 73
Crete 132
Crusades 20, 96, 139, 164
Cuba 95
Cyrene 92
Czechs/Czech Crisis (1938) 67, 110, 126

Dacia (Romania) 33ff.
Dahomey 36, 45, 148
Dalai Lama 109
Damosthenes 59–60
Dani 142
Danzig 126
Decibalus 33ff.
Delos 28
Delphi 28, 59, 81, 88
Denmark/Danes 99ff., 129, 137
Didyma 89
Dionysios 87
Domitian 32–3, 34
Downing, D. 136, 138

Druids 84
Dunkirk 129
Durkheim, E. 37
Dyer, G. 21, 49

Earle, P. 77
East Africa (Italian) 169
Ecuador 39
Edward I 68
Edward II 68–9, 71
Edward III 70ff.
Edward the Confessor 102, 104
Egypt 54, 65, 92, 148, 151, 153, 157, 159, 162, 164
Einsatzgruppen, *see* SS/SD
Einstein, A. 23–4
Eisenhower, D. 11, 65
Emery, W. 151
Engels, F. 10
England 68ff., 84, 96, 98ff., 164
Eric Bloodaxe 100
Eric the Red 98
Eritrea 200
Ethelred 101, 102
Ethiopia 3, 110, 170–71, 200
Etruscans 13, 30, 85, 91, 107
Europe, medieval 14, 67ff.
Expansionism, *see* Aggression

Fagan, B. 96, 152
Falklands 19
Farrar, M. 126
Farrell, B. 181
Fascists 168ff.
Fellner, F. 112, 113
Feminism 9
Ferdinand, Archduke 111
Feudal system 67ff.
Fine, J. 92
Finer, Samuel 12
Finland 16
First World War 5, 13, 23, 38, 63, 66, 109, 110ff., 126, 129, 166, 168, 169, 170, 172, 177, 179, 181, 195
Flanders 72
Fotion and Elfstrom 123
France 5, 67ff., 96, 102, 103, 109, 112, 121, 125ff., 137, 158, 169, 172ff.

Franco 170
Franco-Prussian War 8
Frank, Hans 127
Franks 97, 99, 158
Franz Joseph, Emperor 111ff.
Frederick the Great 109
Freud 2, 23–4, 35, 180–81
Fronto 34

Gaha 46
Galatia 27
Gallipoli 191
Games theory 139–40
Gaul (Celts) 9, 13, 82ff.
Gaveston, Piers 69
Gaza 81
Geneva Convention 10, 124
Genghis Khan 20
Genocide, *see* Atrocities
Germany/German 14, 15, 16, 24, 67, 87, 95, 108ff., 124ff., 170, 172ff., 183–4, 188, 195–6, 197
Ghana 43–4, 199
Gibb, H. 163
Giddens, A. 49, 65, 79
Gladiatorial displays 34
Goebbels, J. 124
Goering, H. 136, 184
Gorer, G. 41
Graves, R. 29
Gray, G. 181
Graziani, R. 175
Greece/Greeks 3, 5, 11, 14, 21, 26ff., 38, 52, 55ff., 71, 81, 82, 83, 87ff., 95, 96, 107, 110, 119, 132, 143, 152, 153, 157, 179, 195
Green, P. 61
Greenland 98
Guadalcanal 189
Guatemala 143
Guderian, H. 137
Gulf War 5, 123
Gustavus Adolfus 197

Habsburgs 112ff.
Hackett, Sir J. 20–21
Haile Selassie 171–2, 174
Halder, General von 128
Hammond, N. 56, 61

Hara-kiri (seppuku) 185
Harald Hardrada 102–3, 105
Hardach, G. 119
Hardy, T. 180
Harold 102–3, 104ff.
Harold Fairhair 100
Harun-al-Rashid 159ff.
Harvey, R. 68, 74
Hathor 146
Hausa-Fulani 44
Hebrews, *see* Jews
Hebrides 98
Hegel, F. 10
Henry I of France 124
Henry II 68
Henry IV 76
Henry V 76
Henry VI 77
Herod Agrippa 31
Herwig, H. 111, 114, 118, 121
Hesiod 90
Heydrich, R. 135
Hibbert, C. 36, 44
Himmler, H. 135, 184, 196
Hindenburg, P. von 115, 116, 118, 119
Hinduism 54, 153, 184
Hiro, D. 162
Hiroshima 24, 187
Hitler 9, 20, 37, 64, 123, 124, 125ff., 166, 168, 170–71, 172ff., 184, 188, 196, 198
Hitti, P. 160
HIV/AIDS 199
Hobbes, T. 62
Hohne, H. 134, 135
Holmes, G. 71
Holtzendorf, Baron 113, 115, 116, 117ff.
Homosexuality 56, 60, 69, 102
Hong Kong 19
Hopkins, K. 31
Howard, M. 13, 14, 15, 19
Hoyt, E. 16, 186
Hultkrantz, A. 146
Humble, R. 128, 136
Hundred Years War 67ff.
Hungary 98, 110, 132
Hussein, Saddam 5, 15
Hyland and Gill 184

Ibn Battuta 44
Iceland 98
Ideology 4–5, 18, 20, 30–31, 63, 64, 72, 78, 81–2, 84, 96, 98, 101, 139ff., 150ff., 153ff., 182ff., 195
Idi Amin 199
Illyrians 57, 58
Imperialism 16ff.
Incas 147
India 16, 52ff., 80, 153, 158, 162, 164
Indonesia 3
Indus Valley 152
Iran 15, 156, 194
Iraq 5, 15, 19, 157ff.
Ireland 70, 75, 84, 96, 98, 100
Iroquois 63
Isaac 15
Isabella, Queen 69–70
Islam, *see* Muslims
Isocrates 59
Israel 3, 5
Italy 13, 14, 16, 30, 85ff., 91, 98, 106, 108, 109, 110, 117, 121, 132, 168ff., 183, 194
Iwo Jima 189–90

Jackson, R. 137–8
Jagas 43
Jains 54
James, E. 151
Janowitz, M. 13, 139–40
Japan 14, 15–16, 25, 132, 133, 172, 177, 179, 183ff., 197–8
Jary and Jary 94
Jason 90
Jews (Hebrews/Israelis) 25, 31, 34, 38, 127, 133ff., 151–2, 153, 156–7, 158, 163, 164, 182
Jihad (holy war) 157ff.
Jivaro 39ff.
Joan of Arc 77–8
Johnson, H. 68
Joll, J. 121
Joseph Ferdinand, Archduke 118
Joyce, J. 113
Judea 31
Jugurtha 26

Kaiser 111ff.

INDEX

Kamikazi 183ff.
Katyn Forest massacre 127
Keegan, J. 5–6
Keitel, W., Field Marshal 137
Kenya 199
Khonds 151
Kiev 136–7
Kluge, General von 128
Korea/Koreans 182–3
Kublai Khan 185
Kukawa 44
Kulkulcan (Quetzalcoatl) 146
Kurds 3
Kuribayashi, General 189–90

Lancaster, Earl of 69
Landa, Diego de 143, 144
Lanfranc 104
LaPiere, R. 80
Large, D. 169, 178
Lascaux (and Carnac) 150
Latin America 12, 25, 142ff., 150, 173
Laval, E. 172
League of Nations 171ff.
Leeb, General von 128, 132
Legitimation 4–5, 108–9
Leningrad 191
Leonidas 191
Lepchas (Sikkim) 41
Levy, R. 159
Lewis, B. 156
Libya 169
Liddell-Hart, B. 19
Lider, J. 35, 48
Limoges 74
Linklater, E. 103
Lisbon 103
Livy 85
Lloyd, P. 42
Lorenz, K. 22
Louis XIV 21
Ludendorff, E. von 115, 116, 118
Luftwaffe 126, 127, 132, 136, 137, 184

MacDonald, N. 23
Macedonia 55ff., 88, 110
Mack Smith, D. 175, 178
Macroparasitism 17–18

Maeve 84
Magadha 52
Malinowski, B. 35, 38ff.
Manchuria 179
Manhattan Project 24
Manicheans 162
Manius Aquilius 27
Manstein, E. von 19
Manstein, General von 129
Margaret of Anjou 78
Marius 26
Marseilles (Masilia) 91
Marx (Marxism) 2, 9, 10, 18, 66, 94
Massacre, see Atrocities
Matabele 11, 39, 46, 80
Mauryan dynasty 52–3, 54
Maya 143ff., 151
McCrystal, C. 5
McLynn, F. 36
McNeil, W. 17–18
Mead, M. 35
Megara 60
Megasthenes 52–3
Mehmed 11, 18
Messalina 31
Messenia 92
Methone 58
Mexico 142ff.
Mfecane 36
Militarism
  and colonialism 16ff.
  and culture 35ff.
  and ethics 123ff.
  and 'human nature' 22ff.
  and ideology 18, 20
  and morale 19
  and motivation 48ff.
  and political necessity 107ff.
  and ritual compulsion 139ff.
  and social control 1ff.
  and status 62ff.
  and the economic factor 94ff.
  and the professionals 8ff.
  and the territorial imperative 79ff.
  and the 'warrior death' 180ff.
  as a religious imperative 153ff.
  as a test of manhood 166ff.
Milošović, Slobodan 5
Mithridates 26ff.
Momigliano, A. 31

Mongols 7, 11, 20, 55, 79, 96, 98, 185
Monomotapa 43
Montgomery, B. 19–20
Moran, Lord 180, 183
More and Anderson 140
Morris, D. 39
Morris, Desmond 22
Mortimer, R. 70
Morton, F. 113
Mosca, G. 37–8
Moshesh 46
Muhammad 157, 163ff.
Muslims 18, 20, 43–4, 46, 103, 139, 153ff., 181, 196
Mussolini 9, 131, 132, 168ff.
Mussolini, Vitorio 178
Myers, A. 75
Mzilikazi 46, 80

Nagasaki 24, 187
Napoleon 19, 113, 197, 198
Nazis 5, 24, 66, 67, 108, 125ff., 141, 170, 182, 195–6
Needham, J. 63
Nerva 32
Netherlands 17, 99, 125, 128, 137
Nevilles 72
Newark, T. 88
Nicomedes 27
Niebuhr, R. 23
Nigeria 12, 199
Normandy 76ff., 99ff.
Northumbria 99, 100
Norway 98, 100, 129
Numidia 26
Nupe 4
Nuremberg 125, 137

Oakeshott, M. 62
Ochus 61
O'Connor, R. 179
Okinawa 189–91, 197–8
Oliver and Oliver 43
Oliver, L. 77
Olmecs 142, 146
Olympia 28
Olynthus 58
O'Neill, R. 185, 192
Operation Barbarossa 130ff.

Operation Marita 132
Ottomans 18, 94, 96, 160

Palestine/Palestinian 157, 164, 182
Pallotino 13
Paphlagonia 27
Paris 103
Parkinson, R. 191
Parsons, Talcott 4, 81
Parthia 27, 34
Patna 52
Pausanius 88
Pawnee 151
Peasants' Revolt 75
Pedro the Cruel 73
Peers 16
Peloponnesian War 3, 65
Percies 72
Perikles 195
Peron(istas) 12
Persia (Iran) 3, 16, 53, 59, 60, 61, 64, 65, 81, 88, 157, 162ff., 191
Peru 39
Philip 11, 55ff.
Philippines 151, 189
Phocians 59
Pine, L. 106
Pisa 98
Pitt, B. 186, 191
Plutarch 52
Poitiers 73
Poland 14, 18, 37, 116–17, 125ff., 133, 135, 182, 196, 197
Polybius 84
Polynesia 25, 40ff.
Pompeius (Pompey) 26
Pontus 26–7, 29
Portugal 17, 200
Posidonius 83
Postmodernism 9–10
Praetorian Guard 29, 32
Prostitution 120
Prussia 8, 109, 121
Psychological theory 48ff., 79, 140, 154, 166–7, 180–81
Punic Wars 26ff.
Punjab 52
Pydna 58
Pythian Games 59

Rachman, S. 183
Racism (anti-racism) 9, 24, 66, 108, 133ff., 159
RAF 126, 188
Ragnald 100
Reitsch, H. 184, 188
Religion, see Ideology
Rhodes 27
Richard I (Coeur de Lion) 164
Richard II 74ff.
Roberts, B. 39
Rolf (Rollo) 103
Roman Catholic Church 75, 97, 99, 101, 104, 106, 170, 178
Romanians 110, 112, 119, 132
Rome/Roman 9, 13, 16, 18, 26ff., 55, 64, 80, 82ff., 91, 96, 98, 107, 124, 143, 151, 152, 155, 157
Rommel, E., General 132, 198
Roosevelt, T. 24
Rosenberg, A. 112
Ross, A. 86
Rouen 98, 99
Rousseau, J. 2, 65
Runstedt, General von 128, 129, 132, 137
Ruskin, J. 10
Russell, B. 119
Russia 14, 37, 64, 66, 96, 98, 108, 110–11ff., 124, 125ff., 179, 194, 196, 197
Rwanda 200

Sacred War 59
Sacrifice 142ff., 150ff., 182ff., 198
Saipan 185, 189
Saladin 164–5
Samurai 185
Santayana, G. 185
Sardinia 91
Schapera, I. 46
Schele and Freidel 148
Schweitzer, A. 150
Scotland/Scots 68, 69, 70, 72, 76, 100
Scullard, H. 30
Scythia 58–9
Second World War 5, 9, 12, 14, 15, 25, 38, 65, 95, 109, 116, 123, 124ff., 182ff.

Seleucus 53
Serbia 5
Serbs 110ff.
Service, E. 40, 42
Sestus 58
Shaka 1, 26, 46, 80
Sharar, R. 149
Shintoism 184
Sicily 91, 94, 96, 98, 106, 194
Sierra Leone 200
Simonides 191
Skorzeny, O. 188
Slavery 25, 37ff., 58, 64, 84, 97, 143–4, 158, 161–2, 172, 174
Slavs 25, 37, 127, 133ff., 195–6
Smith and Smith 15
Smith, R. 45–6
Snyder, L. 138
Sobhuza 46
Social anthropology 35ff.
Social control 1ff., 144, 199, 200
Social Darwinism 10, 11, 37, 112
Social War 26
Sociology 62ff., 78, 79, 154ff., 166
Solon 90
Somme 63
Sorge, R. 133
Soshangana 46
South Africa 13
Soviets 14, 16, 108, 115, 125ff.
Spain/Spanish 18, 32, 73, 83, 98, 109, 143ff., 152, 158, 162, 169, 170, 182
Spanish 'flu' 121
Spartans 9, 21, 37, 38, 61, 65, 87–8, 92, 107, 145, 191
Spencer, H. 11, 112
Spinoza 23
SS/SD 127, 133ff., 182, 196
Staffenberg, Claus von 137
Stalin 9, 20, 129, 130
Stalingrad 136, 198
Stoessinger, J. 18, 19, 131, 136
Strabo 83, 84, 92
Sudan 200
Suetonius 30, 31
Suicide missions 183ff.
Suleiman (the Magnificent) 18
Sulla 26, 28–9
Sumner, W. 166

Swazi 46
Swedes 102, 123, 197
Switzerland 123
Syracuse 66, 87, 91
Syria 54, 157, 162, 164

Tacitus 30–31
Tahiti, *see* Polynesia
Tamerlane (Timur) 96
Tanzania 199
Tartars 11, 20, 79, 96
Thebes 57, 59, 60, 88, 107
Thera 92–3
Thessalonians 59, 60
Thompson, E. and Smith 66
Thorkell 101
Thrace 58, 88, 89, 92
Thucydides 65, 66
Tiberius 29, 31
Tigranes 27
Tilly, C. 63
Tinberger, N. 23
Titus 34
Tokyo 187
Toltecs 142–3, 145, 147, 148
Tostig 102–3
Toynbee, A. 35, 55
Trajan 32ff.
Tripartite Pact 14
Trobriand Islands 38, 40
Tsonga 46
Tunisia 162, 171
Turkey/Turks 18, 110, 158–9, 162; *see also* Ottomans
Tyre 81

Uganda 199
Ukraine 134, 135, 196
Umayyad dynasty 160
Ur (of the Chaldees) 152
US Air Force 183–4
USA/America 14, 15–16, 24, 38, 65, 95, 98, 116, 121, 123, 125, 129–30, 169, 173, 174, 182, 183, 185ff. 197–8
Ushijima, General 190, 197–8
Utilitarianism 124

Vagts, A. 7, 8ff., 123, 194
Values 4
Vansittart, R. 173
Vecchi, C. de 175
Vercingetorix 87
Verdun 119
Vienna 112ff.
Vikings/Norsemen/Normans 82, 94, 96ff., 181
Visigoths/Goths/Huns 96, 158
Vladimir of Kiev 98
Vlasov, General 196

Walbank, F. 89
Wales/Welsh 68, 69, 71, 76, 102
Walton, D. 182
Waltz, K. 23
Waltzer, M. 124
War 3, 5, 6, 7ff., 19ff., 25ff., 35ff., 54ff., 67ff., 79ff., 83ff., 94ff., 123ff., 142ff., 157ff., 182ff., 198ff.
Warwick, Earl of 69
Weber, Max 4, 108–9
Wehrmacht 126ff., 182, 196
William I 103ff.
Wilson, D. 99, 100
Wilson, T. 63
Wilson, Woodrow 111
Windrow and Mason 74
Wittfogel, K. 64
Wolff, L. 13
Wolpert, S. 53, 54
Wright, Q. 35

Xenophon 88

Yahgan (of Tierra del Fuego) 41–2
Yavani 53
York 99, 100
Yoruba (Nigeria) 44ff.
Yucatan 143ff.
Yugoslavia 28, 132

Zimbabwe 46, 199
Zoroastrians 162
Zulus 7, 11, 16, 36, 39, 46, 80–81

For Product Safety Concerns and Information please contact our EU
representative GPSR@taylorandfrancis.com
Taylor & Francis Verlag GmbH, Kaufingerstraße 24, 80331 München, Germany

www.ingramcontent.com/pod-product-compliance
Lightning Source LLC
Chambersburg PA
CBHW052110300426
44116CB00010B/1615